THE WAR WITH MEXICO REVIEWED.

THE

WAR WITH MEXICO

REVIEWED.

BY

ABIEL ABBOT LIVERMORE.

SEVENTH THOUSAND.

BOSTON:
PUBLISHED BY THE AMERICAN PEACE SOCIETY.
1850.

PRINTED BY
ABNER FORBES, 37 CORNHILL.

NOTE.

The Committe of Award, consisting of the Hon. SIMON GREENLEAF, LL. D., the Rev. WILLIAM JENKS, D. D., and the Rev. BARON STOW, D. D., adjudged to the following work the Premium of FIVE HUNDRED DOLLARS offered by the American Peace Society for "the best Review of the Mexican War on the principles of Christianity, and an enlightened statesmanship."

GEORGE C. BECKWITH,

Cor. Sec. Am. Peace Society.

1*

PREFACE.

The delay in publishing this Review demands a word of apology or explanation. The author was absent in the West Indies for the benefit of his health when the award was made by the judges, and he did not return home until June. Since that date the leisure which could be snatched from numerous professional duties has been devoted to a careful revision of the work, and the incorporating of some new materials, procured at the seat of government by personal research and the kindness of friends. For a session of Congress has intervened since the essay was written, which has confirmed and developed some important points. Hence the attempt is made to bring its conclusions down to the present time.

The conflict with Mexico was short, and, measured on the scale of European warfare, comparatively insignificant, but in its lessons it is instructive, and in its effects on a forming national character powerful. To draw good out of its evils, is the aim of the American Peace Society, and of the work which now goes forth under its auspices. War, the great social wrong, like idolatry, the great spiritual injury, must fall in due time before the progress of the Gospel. To doubt this result, seems to presume that the Prince of Peace has come in vain, and that finite creatures can eventualy frustrate the plan of the Infinite Creator. Meanwhile, for the justification of the humble labors of any individual or society in so stupendous a regeneration, it is enough to say, that God works by means and by men. When was the lowest whisper of prayer unheeded, or the faintest effort unblessed, that ran parallel with his benevolent purposes and his eternal laws ?

The highest ambition of the writer will be amply satisfied, if these pages shall contribute to swell in a small degree the rising tide of public opinion in favor of Peace, and awaken a deeper abhorrence for the bloody and needless arbitration of the sword.

A. A. LIVERMORE.

KEENE, N. H., *September* 11, 1849.

CONTENTS.

CHAPTER XVII.

CHAPTER XVIII.

CHAPTER XIX.

CHAPTER XX.

CHAPTER XXI.

CHAPTER XXII.

CHAPTER XXIII.

CHAPTER XXIV.

CHAPTER XXV.

CHAPTER XXVI.

THE WAR WITH MEXICO REVIEWED.

CHAPTER I.

INTRODUCTION.

"The principles of true politics are merely those of morality enlarged." — BURKE.

HISTORY has assumed, under the light of the Gospel, a new value. It is no longer regarded as owing its chief interest to its royal genealogies, or its bloody record of battles. It is beginning to be understood, that the Providence of God is manifested through the rise and fall of nations. The actors in the scenes of the past have been the agents of a higher power than they themselves recognized. "The hoary registers of time" are the map of the grand march of humanity. To draw the moral of history, therefore, becomes of equal importance to the office of narrating its events. If it be "philosophy teaching by example," it becomes a question of the first importance to learn what the examples teach; what warning of evil, what encouragement to hope; what lessons for rulers, or for the people. And since the light has shone down out of Heaven upon the dark confusion of human affairs, we can discern a meaning in the most perplexing passages, and trace a guiding clew through labyrinths more intricate than that of Crete.

In harmony with the comprehensive use, thus briefly indicated, of civil and political history, the American Peace Society wished to subject the late war between the United States and Mexico to the crucible of a philosophical and Christian analysis. The friends of peace have often drawn their arguments and illustrations in vindication of their holy cause from Herodotus and Thucydides, or Hume and Robertson; but unhappily they have now been provided with a fearful strife nearer home, whose fields of blood are hardly yet dry, and whose wounds are still ghastly, from which they may teach the evils of international war. And now the thunder of artillery and the shrieks of the wounded having died away, they wish to repeat again in mournful recitative, though it be but with a jarring human tongue, the angel's sweet hymn, "on earth peace, good will toward men."

The language of the schedule, issued by the Society in February, 1847, was as follows: "The Review should be written without reference to political parties, and present such a view of the subject as will commend itself, when the hour of sober and candid reflection shall come, to the good sense of fair-minded men in every party and in all sections of the country. The war, *in its origin, its progress, and the whole sweep of its evils to all concerned,* should be reviewed on the principles of Christianity and of enlightened statesmanship; showing especially *its waste of treasure and human life; — its influence upon the interests of morality and religion, — its inconsistency with the genius of our republican institutions, as well as with the precepts of our religion, and the spirit of the age, — its bearings immediate and remote, on free, popular governments here and through the world; — how its evils might have been avoided with better results to both parties; — and what means may and should be adopted by nations to prevent similar evils in future.* Our sole aim is to promote the cause of permanent peace, by turning this war into effectual warnings against resorts to the sword hereafter."

Here, then, is a distinct purpose, avowed at the outset, to use the Mexican War as an argument for the cause of peace; to "beat its swords into ploughshares, and its spears into pruning hooks," for the culture of humane and Christian sentiments. Without following the above-mentioned order of topics, with rigid accuracy, it will then be the aim, both of our logic and our rhetoric, in this Essay, to draw the moral of this event in the nineteenth century, and to employ it as a powerful instrument, furnished by our opponents themselves, — if peace have any opponents, — to scatter the illusions of military glory, and to reveal the incalculable evils of international war. We have great advantages for the accomplishment of this purpose, in the very recent occurrence of the contest; the voluminous public documents, correspondence, and speeches; the numerous memoirs, sketches, and letters, written by eye and ear-witnesses and actors in the field and the camp; and in able and eloquent essays, for and against the war, which have been laid before the public during its progress. Much of the history of the blood-stained past has been written and sung by the advocates of war, the bards and historians of the world's boisterous childhood, who have showered the richest gifts of their genius upon those fierce heroes, who were ready to

"Wade through slaughter to a throne,
And shut the gates of mercy on mankind."

But the time has now come to examine the subject of war in all its aspects and all its issues; to decompose its glittering fabric of glory into its constituent elements; and while it is "fresh and gory," to arrest the fugitive attention of the public, and confine it to the solemn lessons of Providence and

Revelation. And he, whose pen is moved by pulses from a Christian heart, will not fear to question any customs, usages, or laws pertaining to this relic of barbarism, according to the plain and positive precepts of Christ, and the whole spirit of his religion. Such is the subject, plan and promise of the following pages; the fulfilment must rest with Him, who deigns to be a co-worker with the humblest of his creatures for good.

In the investigation of this war, we would rise, as suggested in the circular of the Society, far above the tempestuous region of partisan politics, and the extravagances of zealous, but injudicious reformers. We would speak, as men bound by the laws of natural justice, and as Christians bowing to the benevolent precepts of Christ, as the ultimate authority in every question of public, not less than of private morals. One of the vices of the times is headlong ultraism; — the ultraism of conservatism, as well as that of radicalism. Impatient of halves, men "go the whole," to use the national phrase. It is not a day of qualification, or moderation. Parties tolerate none in their ranks, that will not ride the pendulum of their peculiar notions to the utmost point of its swing. The very nature and form of social progress, developed in our country, predisposes us to this fierce intolerance. The rush and eagerness of our daily life, the earnest enterprise that is busy all over the land, that plies every tool and machine, spins along the lines of city intercourse, pours forth into forests and prairies, skims every river and lake, and careers over every ocean, in the pursuit of wealth, naturally incline our people to adopt very decided opinions upon every subject. They act under a momentum that easily throws them into extremes. We would guard against this weakness. We would speak "the words of truth and soberness." However severe may be our judgment of the late contest between the United States and Mexico, it shall be a censure within the bounds of reason and religion, and therefore commending itself to whatever there may be of reason and religion in the minds of our readers; and all the more severe because springing not from wholesale and indiscriminate abuse, but from the simple and eternal principles of right. It requires no far-fetched proofs or strained positions; no fanatic appeals or ultra doctrines, to brand the war in question with an adequate seal of infamy. For its own history is its sufficient exposure. Its origin, causes, purposes, and results are truth-telling witnesses against it. To be abhorred and condemned, it needs but to be recorded and reviewed.

CHAPTER II.

CIRCUMSTANCES PREDISPOSING TO THE WAR WITH MEXICO.

> "If that the Heavens do not their visible spirits
> Send quickly down to tame these vile offences,
> 'T will come. * * *
> Humanity must, perforce, prey on itself,
> Like monsters of the deep." — SHAKSPEARE.

No event in history has an independent and solitary existence. All its facts may be said, in one sense, to be the effect of all that precedes, and the cause of all that follows. For history is not so much a chain, as a network. Its transactions do not obey a law of simple succession, but of intricate combination. The working out of the great designs of Providence is furthered by a diversity of agencies, — some in conflict, and others in alliance. We can, therefore, understand historically nothing by itself. To know even one nation truly and thoroughly, we need to know all nations. Viewed according to this judgment, the history of mankind is a unity, and its truest designation is universal.

This general principle holds true, in its application to the important matter under review. To comprehend it aright, we need to have been diligent students of the past as well as the present. It involves, especially, the great questions of European colonization in America, in the sixteenth and seventeenth centuries, under the English, or Protestant, and Continental, or Catholic forms, and their respective issues down to this moment.

In truth, far back even beyond the third and fourth generation, the causes have been in process to predispose us to this Mexican crisis, and, if prudence and wisdom did not govern both the aggrieved and the aggressor, to plunge us in a brute strife. This is no sudden leap. This is no mine sprung without warning. On both sides, the elements have been silently brewing, through many years, for the issues of to-day. As the cannons that have mowed down ranks of living men, and the deadly bombs that have crashed through homes of affection, have in many cases been lying rusty and ancient, the relics of days gone by; so have the causes that set these horrid engines in operation been long accumulating in the arsenal, so to speak, and lying unused, until the fatal imprudence or passion of one or both parties has summoned them into action.

To specify a leading cause, we would advert to what Sir Robert Peel has called, in the British Parliament, "a development of military ambition in the United States;" in one sense, both cause and effect of the war with Mexico. The attentive student of history will be at no loss to trace the origin and growth of this fearful passion. For the time we have existed as a people, we have been no sluggards in the use of the sword. The old French and Indian wars occupied our great grandfathers; the Revolution our grandfathers; the war of 1812 our fathers; and Creek and Cherokee expatriations, and Black Hawk, Patriot, Seminole, and Mormon skirmishes their sons. The martial spirit is always a tiger, and we have given the tiger too much room and freedom. In fact, the Temple of Peace has not remained long shut during our national existence. Though most of our wars have been small ones, that circumstance has not prevented their imbuing a large portion of our citizens with the ambition of arms. It is one of our maxims, that "in time of peace we should prepare for war." The whole population are armed; there is not, probably, a house in the country, unless it belong to a Quaker or a Non-resistant, without its sword, pistol, musket, or rifle. The expenses of our army and navy, even in time of peace, have always exceeded, by many millions, the maximum of the civil list. Hence there is always existing a large profession of men, whose seeming interest it is to have their country engaged in war; for then every expenditure in this direction is enormously increased; active service creates vacancies and accelerates promotions; and the prize money of war is better than the earnings of industry.

But other causes, besides those above noted, have contributed to awaken in "Young America" the aspiration for military renown. General literature, whether in the form of poetry, oratory, or history, and whether imported or domestic, has always thrown the decisive preponderance of its influence into the war scale. Republicans have wished to show that they were equal to the performance of any feat that king or kaiser ever dared, or that minstrel ever sung. It has been openly avowed on the floor of Congress, by the most distinguished men of the country, that the time had arrived for us to do "some great thing," to let the Old World know that we were not the cowards or sluggards they might otherwise suppose us to be. As if it were not well known in every land, from north to south, that the

United States was rising to be a leading power in the earth; as if two wars with the British monarchy, in which we certainly were not worsted, were not sufficient witnesses to our valor, without seeking a quarrel with a rent and distracted nation to show our republican manhood; as if the good opinion of the crumbling, bankrupt, starving, war-taxed, and groaning kingdoms of Europe were to be purchased at the fearful price of one drop of human blood unrighteously shed. In the recent tremendous agitations, that have swept like a resistless tide over that continent, the example of republican America has been loudly and cheeringly quoted; — would that we were more worthy of the title of the banner republic! — but what has been quoted for imitation, for inspiration, for justification, by the masses struggling for their inalienable rights, has not been our wars, our slaveries, our inconsistencies, but our equal rights, our bread enough and to spare, our wise institutions, our world-renowned enterprise and industry, and our unrivalled prosperity.

Again; the pride of race has swollen to still greater insolence the pride of country, always quite active enough for the due observance of the claims of universal brotherhood. The Anglo-Saxons have been apparently persuaded to think themselves the chosen people, the anointed race of the Lord, commissioned to drive out the heathen, and plant their religion and institutions in every Canaan they could subjugate. The idea of a "destiny," connected with this race, has gone far to justify, if not to sanctify, many an act on either side of the Atlantic; for which both England and the United States, if nations can be personified, ought to hang their heads in shame, and weep scalding tears of repentance. When they can produce any Mosaic commission from the Almighty King of kings, to diffuse the gospel of peace at the point of the bayonet, or the benign arts and sciences of a civilized age by the brute force of an earlier period, it will be quite time enough to consider their authority. Meanwhile, the inquiry presses powerfully, are these same destined Anglo-Saxon missionaries so immaculate in their character, so wise in their great national ideas, and so unbendingly true in their realization of them, that they have earned a title or authenticated "a divine right" to conquer and colonize the rest of God's earth? And when on one shore we have taken the guage of Ireland's woes and wrongs, and the oppressions of the factories, collieries, ships, and colonies of England; and, on the other shore, recalled the repudiation of State debts, the slavery of three millions of immortal beings, and the endless wrongs of the natives of the soil, which we so proudly tread, to enumerate no other crimes; — we shall admit, with great reluctance, that either of the gigantic progenies of the Anglo-Saxon race has established by past wisdom, fidelity, or consistency, a presumptive title to be appointed guardian over the decrepid races of the Eastern or Western hemisphere. They may, doubtless, plead the right of might; but that is far from being the might of right. They may use the old appeal, *ultima ratio regum*, the ultimate resort of kings, and alas! we now see, of republics too; but so long as they have no more divine method than that, of civilizing the savage, and Christianizing the heathen, they are held down by an eternal gravitation to the vulgar level of

"Macedonia's madman and the Swede."

True, they possess arts and arms, but there are even more potent agents than these in the progress of humanity. Have we read the history of sixty centuries, and failed to learn even the alphabet of the sublime lessons she would teach, — that truth, love, righteousness, great and heavenly principles only, can worthily and successfully preside over the processes of human improvement? It is still an unsettled question, whether the Crusades, the Norman conquest, or the wars of the old French Revolution, did more evil or good. But there is not the glimmer of a doubt that the mariner's compass, the art of printing, the steamboat, the railroad, and the telegraph, have been ministers of good to mankind. We must be dull scholars in the Christian lore, and the veriest laggards in the work of the present age, if we still cherish the old folly of ambition and vainglory that has demonized the nations of the dead. But not to dwell longer upon considerations that will come up again in another connection, none can be blind to the pride of race as one of the causes that has prompted the hostilities in Mexico.

European emigration, too, has had its effect. Hundreds of thousands, with all their old-world ideas, unbaptized into the spirit of liberty, except it be as license, have been transplanted into the vast regions of the Middle States, the West and South-West. They have been accustomed to the bloody dramas of Europe, and they have supposed that the same must be acted over again in America. Far be it from us to take up any slanderous speech against our emigrant brethren, many of whom have shown themselves capable of understanding the rights and discharging the obligations of freemen, and have added much to the wealth, intelligence, and morality of their adopted country. But it is well known that no inconsiderable part of the American army has consisted of foreigners. They have been warmly commended as showing, by their readiness to enlist, and espouse our quarrels, their enthusiasm in the cause of liberty, and fidelity to their land of refuge. But the lover of peace will see, at the bottom of this fair-seeming, the dangerous element of military habits, acquired during the turbulent scenes of the last fifty years, transferred from the banks of the Rhine, the Elbe, and the Shannon, to those of the Ohio, the Missouri, and the Colorado. The roots of the old war-encumbered civilization, — torn and broken, indeed, but possessing an unyielding tenacity of life, — are set out in the rich soil of the American prairies. Whether they live and bear their bitter fruits, or wither and die, is for the friends of peace, under God, to decide. The great valley of the West may become the hot-bed of war; and nothing but a wide and early dissemination of the pacific principles of the Gospel, by books, tracts, lectures, and conversation, can prevent our late foray into a sister republic from being the prolific seed of sorrows without end.

Indeed, the slow advance in their full power, of the school-house and the church, after the fugitives that have gone into the wilderness, has given time for a rank development of barbaric passions and habits. The tendencies to physical violence, somewhere or upon somebody, it mattered little where or upon whom, have had too little check. The true American ideas have been supplanted by a system of Bedouin morality in the minds of not a few, cast beyond the control of a high-toned public conscience. Powerful as the older and more civilized portions of the Union have been in their enterprize, zeal for freedom, and moral and religious character, wherever their sons have pitched the tents of their wanderings, yet the truth compels us to say, that in some portions of the East, the Centre, the feudal South, and South-West, and the rude West, the good principles of an earlier day have lost their savor, and the way has been opened for precisely such results as have been developed during the last four years, — the Annexation of Texas, a sanguinary and embittered war, and the dismemberment of Mexico. The relations of cause and effect hold true in the moral as surely as in the material world. Nations reap what they sow. We have, in sober fact, been educating ourselves for a considerable time for just such issues as have lately been developed. Our treatment both of the red man and the black man, has habituated us to "feel our power, and forget right." Wars enough have been waged to keep our muskets bright. Our fourth-of-July oratory has inserted in youthful veins the deadly virus of warlike passion. The dauntless enterprize of the emigrants who have battled with the wolf and the savage for their domains, and who have been "famous according as they had lifted up axes upon the thick trees," * has been but too ready, under the promptings of a selfish aggrandizement, to conquer armies as well as forests, and to blow up capitals with as little compunction as steamboats. The West and South have many noble and heroic elements of character; but a true friend of either will not hesitate to bid them respectively beware of War and Slavery, as institutions and customs at variance with free institutions and the Christian religion.

The passion for land, also, is a leading characteristic of the American people. Coming out of the straitened limits of the old countries, where human beings seem to be hydrostatically compressed within the smallest possible limits, they naturally expatiate at large upon the boundless savannahs of an unappropriated soil. A vast, indefinite, but ever-haunting ambition, seizes the new comer. The physical grandeur of scale awakens an aspiring imagination. Territory becomes inwoven to all ideas of personal or national welfare. Almost every man owns his rood or his township of this generous fee-simple of nature; and almost every farmer owns and attempts to till more than is justified by good husbandry. This may prove true nationally, not less than agriculturally. An incessant grasping after more territory has characterized our past policy. The god Terminus is an unknown deity in America. Like the hunger of the pauper boy of fiction, the cry has been, "More, more, give us more." But we must confess that we have actually settled and subdued to the uses of civilization only a minor part of the vast regions we occupy. We have struck the

* Psalm 74: 5.

Pacific Ocean, and, far from being content with the immense slopes of the Rocky Mountains, and the great Valley of the Mississippi on the east, and that of the Columbia on the west, we have chafed against the boundaries of nature and of our neighbors, and, like Jezebel, have coveted their vineyards. The history of the last few years has yielded a melancholy illustration of the eloquent special pleading of the exhorbitant passions, and the self-deceiving justifications of ambition. Prompt excuses have been discovered for this boa-constrictor appetite of swallowing states and provinces, in the glory of free institutions, the blessings of civil and religious liberty, and the extension of our industrial and commercial system. Alas! we have thus discovered opiates to lull our consciences when they were uneasy, and tonics to invigorate our ambition when it was halting. Under the dominion of this lust for territory, however acquired, we have pushed onwards in a hot and unjustifiable invasion, and by a compulsory peace, have extorted from our neighbors more than half a million of square miles of land, reaching from the Atlantic to the Pacific, across the breadth of the North American continent.

CHAPTER III.

THE CHIEF MOTIVE OF THE WAR.

"He finds his fellow guilty of a skin
Not colored like his own; and having power
T' enforce the wrong, for such a worthy cause,
Dooms and devotes him as his lawful prey." — Cowper.

The motives which actuate public men and political parties, are not always openly avowed. There are secrets of state in the administration of republican as well as despotic governments, though not of the same number or extent. The causes which determine the line of national policy, can sometimes only be inferred, though the inference may be raised to a high degree of probability. Important documents, which would no doubt throw great light upon international affairs, are buried in the archives of state, and a seal put upon their publication by the plea, more or less valid, that it would embarrass the public service. We are, therefore, left somewhat in the dark in reasoning upon the events of history, though of a very recent date; and we can hope to reach in our conclusions only a reasonable measure of moral probability, not an irresistible mathematical certainty.

The circumstances enumerated in the last chapter, were predisposing causes of war, but, of themselves, they would not have produced that unhappy result. Hence we look for some more positive and potent element. We are ready to concede something to the pacific settlement of the Oregon question, which turned the war spirit into a new channel;—something to the desire of giving eclat to a new administration;. something to the vast expansion of civil and military patronage produced by war; something to the interested clamor of Mexican claimants and their friends; something to the magic power of Texan scrip; something to a wide-spread suspicion and a quick jealousy of European interference in the affairs of this continent; but we feel confident that we are stating a solemn and incontrovertible truth, when we say that we discern in slavery the main-spring to the war with Mexico. Had the idea of extending the "peculiar" institutions of the South, and the political power resulting therefrom, been entirely excluded from the question, not a shot would ever have been fired.

We desire to make such a record on this point as will stand justified fifty years hence, when the planners and actors in present scenes have passed off the stage. For the purpose of confirming our statements, we shall take the liberty of quoting published and authentic documents, without reference to parties. We shall thus be led directly to the conclusion expressed above.

It is unnecessary here to recount the details of the annexation of Texas to the United States, as our aim is not a history, so much as a review, of an important portion of history, recent and well-known. That event, however, was regarded by Mexico as an act of war in itself, and was, no doubt, one of the prominent causes, notwithstanding all disclaimers, that led to the actual commencement of hostilities; for our armies surely never would have advanced either to the Nueces or to the Rio Grande, had it not been for the ostensible purpose of protecting our newly-acquired domains. But the scheme of Annexation was devised, — as openly declared by some of its staunchest advocates, — to give greater security to the institutions of the South. The clear and direct inference is, that slavery and the war with Mexico have had a cause-and-effect connection. Had slavery not existed in our land, there would have been no annexation; and had there been no annexation, there would have been no strife. Who can dispute these propositions, when he has candidly and truthfully weighed the following declarations of some of the leading politicians of the day? The idea of Southern aggrandizement was early broached and steadily avowed. Let the credible witnesses give their testimony.

Mr. Upshur was a member of the Virginia Convention in 1829, and said in that body: "Nothing is more fluctuating than the value of slaves. A late law of Louisiana reduced their value twenty-five per cent in two hours after its passage was known. If it should be our lot, as I trust it will, to acquire Texas, their price will rise." *

* Debates of that body.

Mr. Doddridge, another member of the same convention, made a similar declaration; "that the acquisition of Texas would greatly enhance the value of the property in question."*

Mr. Gholson said, in the Legislature of Virginia in 1832;† "that the price of slaves fell twenty-five per cent within two hours after the news was received of the non-importation act which was passed by the Legislature of Louisiana. Yet he believed the acquisition of Texas would raise their price fifty per cent at least."

Mr. Calhoun avowed his opinions in the Senate of the United States, as early as May 23, 1836; "there were powerful reasons why Texas should be a part of this Union. The Southern States owning a slave population were deeply interested in preventing that country from having the power to annoy them; and the navigating and manufacturing interests of the North, were equally interested in making it a part of the Union." ‡

Meantime, the Cuban slave-trade had fearfully increased, and fresh commissions were constantly arriving at Havana from Texas, to buy the wretched sons of Africa who had been torn from their native soil, and transported across the ocean by fiends in human shape. President Houston said in his annual Message to the Congress of the Republic of Texas, in 1837; "not unconnected with the naval force of the country is the subject of the African slave-trade. It cannot be disbelieved that *thousands* of Africans have lately been imported to the Island of Cuba, *with a design to transfer a large portion of them into this republic.*" The British commissioners for the suppression of the slave-trade, who resided in Cuba agreeably to the treaty of 1817 with Spain, reported that twenty-seven slave-vessels arrived in Havana in 1833, thirty-three in 1834, fifty in 1836, and in 1835, that

* See note on preceding page.

† Journal of Session, 1832.

‡ 29th Congress, 2d Session, Congressional Globe, pp. 495.

more than fifteen thousand negroes must have been landed! Sir T. F. Buxton stated that in 1837 and 1838, no less than "fifteen thousand negroes had been imported from Africa into Texas." Other accounts rate the number still higher. One Taylor, of Barbadoes, was convicted of sending free negroes to this new market, and selling them. The *Albany Argus* of 1844, mentions the case of one man who sent ten thousand dollars to Cuba for the purchase of human beings. The emigrants from the United States had a palpable motive to expose this infamous traffic, and seek to extinguish it, because it cheapened their own slaves. *

The project of annexation was not suffered to sleep, but from year to year was cherished and developed by its zealous and untiring friends. The great end, too, which it would eventually subserve, was kept distinctly in view.

Mr. Upshur, Secretary of State, wrote to W. S. Murphy, chargé d'affaires of the United States in Texas, in a letter dated Washington, Aug. 8, 1843, as follows; "The establishment, in the very midst of our slave-holding States, of an independent Government, forbidding the existence of slavery, and by a people born for the most part among us, reared up in our habits, and spreading our language, could not fail to produce the most unhappy effects upon both parties. If Texas were in that condition, her territory would afford a ready refuge for the fugitive slaves of Louisiana and Arkansas, and would hold out to them, an encouragement to run away which no municipal regulations of those States could possibly counteract."

* * * * *

"Few calamities could befal this country more to be deplored than the establishment of a predominant British influence, and the abolition of domestic slavery in Texas." †

* Moody's Facts for the People, pp. 69, 70.

† 28th Congress, 1st Session, Senate, 341, pp. 21, 22.

On Sept. 22d, the subject was renewed; he said: — "there is no reason to fear that there will be any difference of opinion among the slave-holding States; and there is a large number in the non-slave-holding States; with views sufficiently liberal to embrace a policy absolutely necessary to the salvation of the south, although, in some respects, objectionable to themselves." *

He wrote to Mr. Murphy, Jan. 16, 1844, "if Texas should not be attached to the United States, she cannot maintain that institution ten years, and probably not half that time." †

Said Mr. Murphy to Mr. Upshur, Sept. 23d; "Saying nothing therefore which can offend even our fanatical brethren of the North; let the United States espouse at once the cause of civil, political and religious liberty (?) in this hemisphere; *this will be found to be the safest issue to go before the world with.*" ‡

* * * * He wrote on Sept. 24th; "The Constitution of Texas § secures to the Master, the perpetual right to his slave, and prohibits the introduction of slaves into Texas from any other quarter than the United States.

"If the United States preserves and secures to Texas the possession of her Constitution, and present form of Government, then we have gained all we can desire, and also all that Texas asks or wishes."

* * * * *

"Take this position on the side of the constitution and the laws, and the civil, political and religious liberties of the

* 28th Congress, 1st Session, Senate, 341, p. 26. † Ibid. p. 46.

‡ Ibid. p. 25.

§ Art 8. Sec. 1. *Laws of Texas.* "The Legislature shall have no power to pass laws for the emancipation of slaves, without the consent of their owners, nor without paying their owners previously to such emancipation, a full equivalent in money for the slaves so emancipated."

people secured thereby, (*saying nothing about abolition*) and all the world will be with you." *

Mr. Upshur writes, Nov. 21, 1843, in a letter to Mr. Murphy, "we regard it, (annexation) as involving the security of the South; and the strength and prosperity of every part of the Union."

It would be easy to quote by chapter and verse, from the official documents of the time, many passages of a similar import. But as Mr. Calhoun has said,† "I may now rightfully and indisputably claim to be the author of that great event," (annexation), let us look at his declarations on this subject.

His language was to Mr. Pakenham, the British Minister, April 18, 1844: "It is with still deeper concern the President regards the avowal of Lord Aberdeen of the desire of Great Britain to see slavery abolished in Texas.‡

And on the 19th, he wrote to Mr. Green, chargé d' affaires to Texas: "It was impossible for the United States to witness with indifference the efforts of Great Britain to abolish slavery there." §

Respecting the Treaty of Annexation, then under negotiation, he wrote to the British Minister, on the 27th, that "It was made necessary in order to preserve domestic institutions, placed under the guaranty of their (United States

* 28th Congress, 1st Session, Senate, 341, pp. 23, 24.

† Printed speech in the Senate, Feb. 24, 1847, p. 3.

‡ 28th Congress, 1st Session, Senate, 341, p. 50.

Mr. Benton well criticised this extreme sensitiveness, in his speech in the Senate on the Treaty of Annexation, May 16, 18 and 20, 1844. Reported in the *National Intelligencer*, May 30, 1844. "Great Britain avows all she intends, and that a wish — to see — slavery abolished in Texas; and she declares all the means which she means to use, and that is, advice where it is acceptable.

"It will be a strange spectacle, in the nineteenth century, to behold the United States at war with Mexico, because Great Britain wishes — *to see* the abolition of slavery in Texas."

§ 28th Congress, 1st Session, Senate, 341, pp. 54, 66.

and Texas) respective constitutions, and deemed essential to their safety and prosperity." *

And in a speech in the Senate, Feb. 24, 1847, he said,—

"Sir, I admit, even at that early period, I saw that the incorporation of Texas into this Union, would be indispensable both to her safety and ours. I saw that it was impossible that she could stand as an independent power between us and Mexico, without becoming the scene of intrigue of foreign Powers, alike destructive of the peace and security of both Texas and ourselves. I saw more: I saw the bearing of the slave question at that early stage, and that it would become an instrument in the hands of a foreign Power, of striking a blow at us; and that two conterminous slave-holding communities could not co-exist without one being wielded to the destruction of the other." †

The *Galveston Gazette*, April, 1844, rejects the idea that any-thing less than slavery over the whole vast region of Texas would be accepted by the Southern States. It says that "It is thrown out, in some of the papers of the United States, that the annexation of Texas is to be a measure effected by a compromise, a condition being that the Territory of Texas is to be divided into three States, in one of which slavery is to be tolerated while it is to be prohibited in the others. This idea, we think, must have originated from

* This panic was afterwards confessed by some of the chief actors in annexation to be a mere *ruse*, got up for the sake of effect, and without any substantial foundation in facts. See Gen. Samuel Houston's Letter to a friend on the subject, published in 1848, and his speech in the Senate, Feb. 19, 1847, Congress. Globe, 29th Congress, 2d Session. p. 459. And yet so strong was the jealousy of foreign interference thus excited, that Mr. Choate used this language in his speech in the Senate on the Treaty of Annexation, May 22, 1844; "Sir, besides the apprehension that England will, by treaty or influence, induce Texas to emancipate her slaves,—besides this, there is not even the pretence of a reason for this war (by the separation of Texas from Mexico) on your friend. *This apprehension is all.*"

† Printed speech, p. 8.

other than official sources; and the measure proposed would, we believe, be far better calculated to defeat than to secure the success of the project of annexation. It might satisfy the North; but it would displease the South in the same proportion, and would, we feel confident, never receive the sanction of the slave States."

Numerous testimonies to the deep interest taken by Southern statesmen in the measure of annexation, as destined to enlarge, not "the area of freedom," but of slavery, may be gathered from the discussions both in and out of Congress, on the Treaty offered to the Senate for confirmation by President Tyler. In his Message of April 22, 1844, he said: "At the same time, the Southern and the South-Western States will find, in the fact of annexation, protection and security to their peace and tranquillity, as well against all domestic as foreign efforts to disturb them."*

Mr. McDuffie took the same view, in his speech in the Senate, May 23, 1844, reported in the *National Intelligencer*, June 8th. Speaking of the African race, he said: "That population in the United States cannot be diminished, but must be increased. Now, if we shall annex Texas, it will operate as a safety-valve to let off the superabundant slave population from among us, and will, at the same time, improve their condition; they will be more happy, and we shall be more secure. But if you pen them up within our present limits, what becomes of the free negroes, and what will be their condition?"

Mr. Archer, of Virginia, asked in the Senate,† June 8, 1844: "Did this result, of keeping open a drain for slave labor in Texas, involve no advantage to the slave holding States? Certainly, the highest advantage. But it was not

* 28th Congress, 1st Session, Senate, 341, p. 6.

† 28th Congress, 1st Session, Appendix to Congressional Globe, May, 1844 p. 696.

present pecuniary advantage, nor did it tend to the extension of slave-holding influence in the government."

Mr. Foster, Senator from Tennessee, was frank and open in his avowal in the same debate: "It cannot be denied, Sir, but that the measure is essentially Southern in its character and purposes, and intended, if its policy is hereafter faithfully executed, to protect the South and the South West, both at home and from abroad, in the more peaceful and secure enjoyment of certain property, guarantied to the inhabitants of that section of the Union, by the solemn sanctions of the Federal Constitution."

The *N. H. Patriot*, May, 1844, avowed, that "Slavery and the defence of slavery, form the controlling considerations urged in favor of the treaty (of annexation), by those who have been engaged in its negotiations."

Mr. Preston, of South Carolina, in a speech at Baltimore, quoted in the *National Intelligencer*, Oct. 31, 1844, says: "Annexation was desired, for the purpose of sustaining and extending the institution of slavery, — a motive by which he could not be governed. The institution of slavery was one which belonged exclusively to us of the South; it was our own domestic affair; we were to take care of it for ourselves, without any extraneous interference; and he would be the first to resist any such interference. But when he attempted to acquire territory, with a view and for the purpose of extending slavery beyond its proper limits, the case was altered; we had changed our position from the defensive to the aggressive. Were we, who boast of our free principles, to raise the black flag and go to war with a sister republic, to extend the institution of slavery?"

The *New York Evening Post*, April, 1844, took a similar view of the subject, in an article on the Treaty: "It is evident, that this presents to the people of the Union a question entirely new, and which they cannot avoid. This issue is not as to the abolition of slavery in the Southern

States, the District, nor the Territories of the Union, but whether this government shall devote its whole energies to the perpetuation of slavery; whether all the sister republics on this continent, which desire to abolish slavery, are to be dragooned by us into the support of this institution."

Mr. Calhoun writes a letter to Mr. Pakenham, April 18, 1844, in which he goes into a labored defence of slavery; seems almost to doubt whether the Free States have done well in abolishing it; declares that Texas is to be annexed, to guard against the danger of its being abolished in the Southern States; and finally declares: "That what is called slavery is in reality a political institution; essential to the peace, safety, and prosperity of those States of the Union in which it exists."*

The diplomatic agents, both American and Mexican, agreed as to the object of annexation, however they might differ as to its means and modes.

S. Bocanegra, Minister of Foreign Relations in Mexico, wrote to Mr. Green, chargé d'affaires to the United States, May 30, 1844:† "But when, in order to sustain that slavery, and avoid its disappearance from Texas and from other points, recourse is had to the arbitrary act of depriving Mexico of an integral part of her possessions, as the only certain and efficacious remedy to prevent what Mr. Green calls 'a dangerous event;' if Mexico should be silent, and lend her deference to the present policy of the Executive of the United States, the reproach and the censure of nations ought to be her reward."

Mr. Green had previously said, on the 23d of the same month, what would justify this Mexican inference:‡ "The undersigned is also instructed to state to the Mexican Gov-

* 28th Congress, 1st Session, Senate, 341, p. 53.

† Ibid. 2d Session, House of Representatives, Ex. Doc. 2, p. 54.

‡ Ibid. p. 52.

ernment, that this step (Treaty of Annexation) was forced upon the Government of the United States in self-defence, in consequence of the policy adopted by Great Britain, in reference to the abolition of slavery in Texas. It was impossible for the United States to witness with indifference the efforts of Great Britain to abolish slavery in that territory. They could not but see that she had the means in her power, in the actual condition of Texas, to accomplish the objects of her policy, unless prevented by the most efficient measures; and that, if accomplished, it would lead to a state of things dangerous in the extreme to *the adjacent States*, and to the Union itself."

The same idea was continued by Mr. Shannon, American Minister to Mexico, in a letter to S. Rejon, the Mexican Secretary, Oct. 14, 1844:* "It (annexation) has been a measure of policy, long cherished and deemed indispensable to their (United States') safety and welfare, and has, accordingly, been an object steadily pursued by all parties, and the acquisition of the territory made the subject of negotiation by almost every administration for the last twenty years. This policy may be traced to the belief, generally entertained, that Texas was embraced in the cession of Louisiana by France, to the United States, in 1803, and was improperly surrendered by the Treaty of Florida, in 1819; connected with the fact, that a *large portion of the territory lies in the Valley of the Mississippi*, and is indispensable *to the defence* of a distant and important frontier. The hazard of a conflict of *policy upon important points*, between the United States and one of the leading European powers, since the recognition of Texas, has rendered the acquisition still more essential to their safety and welfare; and accordingly, has increased in proportion the necessity of acquiring it."

* 28th Congress, 2d Session, House of Representatives, Ex. Doc. 2, p. 47.

The Treaty of Annexation was lost in the Senate, by a vote of 35 to 16; but when, in 1845, the mode of annexation by Joint Resolution of the Senate and the House of Representatives was under debate, avowals equally bold were made of the pro-slavery views of its warmest friends. I quote out of a multitude only a few of the most explicit declarations.

Mr. Holmes, of South Carolina, member of the House of Representatives, inquired, during the discussion: * "Would Southern gentlemen consent to *divide* Texas into two States: one *slaveholding*, and one *not?* — slavery to be admitted into the portion adjacent to the South, while free labor was confined to the portion which bordered on Mexico. Would any Southerner agree to this? Would he cut off his own egress, and fetter the energies of the slave-holding community? If any Southern man assented to such a proposition, he must be either a fool or a knave: a fool, not to perceive its bearing; and a knave, if perceiving it he did not resist it."

Mr. Merrick, of Maryland, said in the Senate: † "The domestic tranquillity of the country is endangered, and if you reject Texas now for reasons such as these, think you that the South will sit down quietly under it? Will the spirit of abolition cease to goad and war upon the sensitive interest of the South? And to what must its assaults inevitably lead? We are now in a minority in both houses of Congress, in point of fact, on this question. Restore the balance of power, and all will be safe. The South does not want power to encroach upon the North; no one dreads or thinks of that. But we need power to defend and protect ourselves. It has grown into a maxim, that the best security for peace is to be prepared for war. The best security for the South is to be able to protect herself. The

* Appendix to the Congressional Globe, 28th Congress, 2d Session, p. 108.

† Ibid. p. 233.

balance of power once restored, abolitionists would then let us alone, and this blighting agitation would die its natural death. For these reasons, sir, I am warranted in saying, that, for the purpose of *preserving domestic tranquillity*, we should admit Texas."

Mr. Ashley, of Arkansas, said in the same debate in the Senate: * "That if Texas should not be admitted, the Southern States must be *depopulated*. It might be true, that the admission of Texas would change the local position of some of our planters; but that was a matter very immaterial, because their relation to the Union and to the government would still continue the same. All the cotton raised by our citizens would be raised within our own country, and by men having the same feelings and interests with ourselves."

Mr. Johnson, of Louisiana, made these remarks: † "The measure was boldly opposed, in and out of Congress, on the ground that it would perpetuate slavery, and add to the strength and power of the Southern States. Such an opposition, proceeding from such sources, for such purposes, had operated powerfully on his mind in favor of annexation."

"The State he had the honor in part to represent was as deeply interested in the slave question as any other in the Union; and could it be supposed that he could listen with indifference to such attacks, made on the rights of property of its citizens, or oppose a measure calculated, in his opinion, to strengthen those rights, and to promote the permanent prosperity and glory of the nation?"

The *Washington Union* of May 23, 1845, quoted with approbation the words of an American, who had lately been in Texas, and who congratulated the editors on the success

* Appendix to the Congressional Globe, 28th Congress, 2d Session, p. 287.

† Ibid. p. 224.

of annexation, "as giving the South so national a guaranty against the folly of the abolitionists."

So far, then, as the Annexation of Texas involved us in difficulties with our neighbors, or was a preliminary to open war, so far is the institution of slavery in our country implicated in the same unhappy results. For that the latter was an actuating motive to effect the former, is explicitly stated in the above plain declarations, which we might multiply indefinitely. We are not now pronouncing upon the fitness or unfitness of such a connection, but we simply state it as a fact, that is substantiated by the best authority. To have omitted this piece of history, in chapters on the antecedent circumstances and causes of the Mexican War, would be, to use the illustration of another, as absurd as "acting the play of Hamlet, with the part of Hamlet omitted."

But the institution in question has not only been accessory to the war through annexation, but it also acted directly to prolong it, in furtherance of its own ulterior purposes. Let us call some trust-worthy witnesses to the stand.

The *Charleston Courier* speaks thus: * "Besides, every battle fought in Mexico, and every dollar spent there, but insures the acquisition of territory, which must widen the field of Southern enterprise and power in the future; and the final result will be to reädjust the whole balance of power in the confederacy, so as to give us control over the operations of the government in all time to come. If the South be true to themselves, the day of our depression is gone, and gone forever."

In a debate in Congress, upon a bill introduced by Mr. Preston King, but not passed, that slavery should be excluded from the territory that might be acquired from Mexico, Mr. Hilliard, of Alabama, said: † "That gentlemen transcended the rules which should govern them here; if

* Moody's Facts, p. 124. † Ibid. p. 126.

they proceeded, they would rouse a feeling at the South that would rend the bonds of this Union, as Sampson burst the withes that bound him. Was this the doctrine that was to be acted on, — that, acquire what territory we might, free labor might be suffered to go there, but the men of the South should not take their slaves with them there? If this thing was to be done, this government would be unequal, and its days would be numbered."

Mr. Dargan, from the same State, also said:* "What would be thought by the volunteers from the South, when it was announced to them that slavery was to be excluded from the territory, their arms had acquired? This question must be settled before we proceed to acquire more territory, for afterwards it will be too late."

* * * * *

"Say to the South, that they are only fighting to make free territory, that it is only for this that the brave men of Carolina, Georgia, and Alabama, are periling their lives, and they will demand the settlement of this question now, preliminary to any further prosecution of the war."

Mr. Sims, of South Carolina, in a speech in the House of Representatives, Jan. 28, 1847: "And I have no doubt, — I express the opinion here, — that every foot of territory we shall permanently occupy south of thirty-six degrees thirty minutes, will be slave territory." In reply to a question by Mr. Burt, whether it would be in consequence of the state of public opinion in the Northern, Western, or Middle States? or whether it was in consequence of the known determination of the Southern people, that their institutions shall be carried into that country, if acquired? Mr. Sims answered: "It is founded on the known determination of the Southern people, that their institutions shall be carried there; it is founded on the laws of God, written on

* Moody's Facts, pp. 126, 127.

the climate and soil of the country; nothing but slave labor can cultivate profitably that region of country. I have no idea that the North or the West will resist to the death. This Union never will be dissolved on that question."

Mr. Roberts, of Mississippi, demanded in the House of Representatives, Feb. 4, 1847:* "And are we to tell a Butler, a Quitman, a Davis, a Yell, a Price, a Pillow, and a host of other Southern gentlemen, officers, and soldiers, who have bravely volunteered, and shed their blood, and dissipated their treasure, who represent millions of slave holders, that, after the territory that may be acquired has been purchased at so fearful a cost, they, or their wives, or their children, or their friends, or relatives, shall not go upon the territory to possess it, people it, and cultivate it, and build upon it, for themselves and their children? No, sir; they will tell us, and I tell you, the South will have her rights, come what may."

Mr. Calhoun † in the Senate maintained, in like manner, the right of slave-holders to carry their slaves, and hold their slaves in the new territories conquered from Mexico:— "The case of our recently-acquired territory from Mexico, is, if possible, more marked. The events connected with the acquisition are too well known to require a long narrative. It was won by arms, and a great sacrifice of men and money. The South, in the contest, performed her full share of military duty, and earned a full share of military honor; has poured out her full share of blood freely, and has and will bear a full share of the expense; has evinced a full share of skill and bravery, and if I were to say even more than her full share of both, I would not go beyond the truth; to be attributed, however, to no superiority in either respect, but to accidental circumstances, which gave both its

* Printed speech, pp. 6, 7.

† Printed speech, p. 12, June 27, 1848.

officers and soldiers more favorable opportunities for their display. All have done their duty nobly, and high courage and gallantry are but common attributes of our people. Would it be right and just to close a territory thus won against the South, and leave it open exclusively to the North? Would it deserve the name of free soil, if one half of the Union should be excluded and the other half should monopolize it, when it was won by the joint expense and joint efforts of all? Is the great law to be reversed, — that which is won by all should be equally enjoyed by all?"

Forcibly and unanswerably was it argued by Mr. Dix of New York in the Senate, Feb. 28, 1849: * "When the war with Mexico was commenced, we were charged with the intention of acquiring territory with a view to carrying slaves into it. The charge was denied. We repelled the imputation as doing injustice to our motives. Yet, in the very first attempt to establish a government for that territory, the right is insisted upon, the purpose is confessed. Whether the Mexican Government was aware of this imputation, I do not know; but in the negotiation with Mr. Trist, the Mexican commissioners wished us to stipulate not to carry slavery into the territory which was proposed to be ceded.†

* * * * *

"These Mexicans, whom we have been accustomed to

* Printed speech, p. 11.

† "13th. The United States shall compromise themselves not to permit slavery in the part of the territory which they may acquire by this treaty." — *Preliminaries of the Mexican Commissioners*, Aug. 24, 1847.

Mr. Trist, in a letter to Mr. Buchanan, Sept. 4th, mentions that this topic came up in discussion; that the commissioners assured him that if it were proposed to the people of the United States to part with a portion of their territory in order that the *Inquisition* should be established in it, the proposal would not awaken greater abhorrence than that awakened in Mexico by the prospect that slavery would be introduced in any territory parted with by her; that he assured them consider half-civilized, vanquished in the field, driven from their capital, compelled to make peace with us almost on our own terms, and forced to cede a portion of their territory, implore us not to carry slavery into it. Sir, I ask how should we stand before the world, liberal and enlightened as we are, proclaiming to mankind the principle of human liberty as one of the inalienable rights of our race, if we were to disregard these entreaties?"

We deem the frank statements of Calhoun, and others, sufficient proof that the South would neither have embarked in nor pursued the Mexican war, had they supposed that the new conquests would become free territories and states. As this is only a review, and not a history of the war, it is sufficient to give a specimen of the large amount of documentary evidence existing upon this subject.

We are obliged, therefore, shocking as the statement is, and blushing for our native land as we do, while we record it, to declare that the paramount cause and motive of the war with Mexico, without doubt or controversy, was territorial aggrandizement, under the dominion of domestic slavery and the internal slave-trade. This cause, first advocated by a few, and afterwards entangling the nation, severed the province of Texas from Mexico, and annexed it to the United States. This cause carried the sword in its devastating career from Palo Alto to Buena Vista, and from Vera Cruz to the city of Mexico. War has, in former times, made slaves of its captives; but it reserved to this advanced period of the world its chief exploit of seeking to

that he did not differ with them probably on slavery, considered in itself, but that they had erroneous impressions of slavery as it existed in the United States, and that he could not accept the new territory on condition that slavery was excluded, not if its value were increased tenfold, "*and, in addition to that, covered a foot thick all over with pure gold.*" The topic was dropped. 30th Congress, 1st Session, Senate, Ex. Doc., 52, pp. 199, 315.

convert the land of freedom, which it had conquered, into the area of slavery, and of spreading over new parallels of latitude the blight of national injustice and eternal wretchedness.

CHAPTER IV.

PRETEXTS FOR WAR.

"I believe that if the question had been put to Congress before the march of the armies and their actual conflict, not ten votes could have been obtained in either house for the war with Mexico under the existing state of things." — WEBSTER.

THE chief motive to this war, however it might be incidentally dropped by incautious lips or pens in the ardor of debate, or in the anonymous newspaper article, was yet too culpable to be openly avowed in the documents of a republican government. More plausible reasons were assigned. The United States were represented as the injured and insulted party. The war was claimed to be a war of self-defence. The vindication of national rights and honor was loudly insisted on, and a spectator might have supposed that our existence as a people was in danger, and that nothing but the most energetic measures could avert the impending ruin. But we find, now the smoke has cleared away, and the excitement is over, and we can view things calmly and considerately, that what were alleged as reasons for the war with Mexico, prove to have been but windy pretences. Many patriotic and good men of all parties in the United States, did not at the time regard them as worthy causes of such fearful consequences. They received the pointed censure of the wisest and best in the freest countries of Europe. They were soon weighed in the balances, and found wanting, by the votes and voices of a majority of the popular branch of the American Legislature. They were divested of most of their plausibility by the progress of the war, the conditions on which peace was made, and the revelations of subsequent political history; and they now stand in the judgment of impartial history convicted, condemned, and sentenced to go to "their own place."

The first, in order of time and importance, of these pretexts for war, was the non-fulfilment by Mexico of her agreement to indemnify the citizens of the United States for wrongs inflicted upon their business and commerce.

The subject is elsewhere considered in other connections in this review, but the following condensed statement by the venerable Albert Gallatin, will afford all the necessary information to make our argument intelligible: —

"It may be proper, in the first place, to observe, that the refusal of doing justice in cases of this kind, or the long delays in providing for them, have not generally produced actual war. Almost always, long-protracted negotiations have been alone resorted to. This has been strikingly the case with the United States. The claims of Great Britain for British debts, secured by the treaty of 1783, were not settled and paid till the year 1803; and it was only subsequently to that year that the claims of the United States, for depredations committed in 1793, were satisfied. The very plain question of slaves carried away by the British forces in 1815, in open violation of the treaty of 1814, was not settled and the indemnity paid till the year 1826. The claims against France, for depredations committed in the years 1806 to 1813, were not settled and paid for till the year 1834. In all these cases peace was preserved by patience and forbearance.

"With respect to the Mexican indemnities, the subject had been laid more than once before Congress, not without suggestions that strong measures should be resorted to. But Congress, in whom alone is invested the power of declaring war, uniformly declined doing it.

"A convention was entered into on the 11th of April, 1839, between the United States and Mexico, by virtue of which a joint commission was appointed for the examination and settlement of those claims. The powers of the commissioners terminated, according to the convention, in February, 1842. The total amount of the American claims presented to the commission, amounted to $ 6,291,605. Of these, $2,026,140 were allowed by the commission; a further sum of $928,628 was allowed by the commissioners of the United States, rejected by the Mexican commissioners, and left undecided by the umpire; and claims amounting to $3,336,837 had not been examined.

"A new convention, dated January 30, 1843, granted to the Mexicans a further delay for the payment of the claims which had been admitted, by virtue of which the interest due to the claimants was made payable on the 30th of April, 1843, and the principal of the awards and the interest accruing thereon, was stipulated to be paid in five years, in twenty equal instalments every three months. The claimants received the interest on the 30th of April, 1843, and the three instalments. The agent of the United States, having, under peculiar circumstances, given a receipt for the instalments due in April and July, 1844, before they had been actually paid by Mexico, the payment has been assumed by the United States and discharged to the claimants.

"A third convention was concluded at Mexico on the 20th of November, 1843, by the plenipotentiaries of the two governments, by which provision was made for ascertaining and paying the claims on which no final decision had been made. In January, 1844, this convention was ratified by the Senate of the United States, with two amendments, which were referred to the Government of Mexico, but respecting which no answer has ever been made. On the 12th of April, 1844, a treaty was concluded by the President with Texas, for the annexation of that republic to the United States. This treaty, though not ratified by the Senate, placed the two countries in a new position, and arrested for a while all negotiations. It was only on the 1st of March, 1845, that Congress passed a joint resolution for the annexation.

"It appears most clearly that the United States are justly entitled to a full indemnity for the injuries done to their citizens; that, before the annexation of Texas, there was every prospect of securing that indemnity; and that those injuries, even if they had been a just cause for war, were in no shape whatever the cause of that in which we are now involved." *

Thus far Mr. Gallatin; from which, and from other general knowledge on the subject, no doubt possessed by our readers, we come to the following conclusions: —

1. That the claims made by us on other nations, though long refused, were not deemed sufficient causes of war.

2. That Congress, the proper war-making power, had repeatedly declined resorting to arms to collect these debts of Mexico.

3. That, on the whole, the conduct of Mexico, considering her disordered condition, would, upon the question of indemnities, compare not unfavorably with that of England and France.

4. That the annexation of Texas was the chief cause of the non-fulfilment of her engagements by Mexico.

5. That the large amount of claims preferred, and the

* Peace with Mexico, p. 2.

much smaller amount allowed by the umpire, leads to the strongest conviction that many of them were fraudulent, an inference fully sustained by an examination of them individually as published in the reports and documents of the time.*

6. That, although these difficulties were assigned as the cause or excuse for war, subsequently, yet at first, both in the documents of the Executive and the legislative branch of the Government, no explicit declaration was made, when war was declared, of the indebtedness of Mexico to the United States as a *bonâ fide* reason for fighting.

The next pretext was the refusal by Mexico, in 1845 – 6, to receive Mr. Slidell as Envoy Extraordinary and Minister Plenipotentiary, to reside in that Republic. The whole history of that affair is recorded in the journals of the day, and the documents of Government, and need not be tediously repeated here. The main facts are these, and they are not disputed by any party. After the passage of the joint resolution for the annexation of Texas, in March, 1845, Almonte, the Mexican Minister at Washington, demanded his passports and returned home. In September, the President of the United States made proposals for restoring a cordial understanding between the two countries. The Mexican Government replied that they felt deeply injured, but would receive a commissioner to "settle the present dispute," referring to the Texas question, provided the naval forces, placed in a menacing attitude in sight of Vera Cruz, were recalled. This was done by the United States. Mr. Slidell, of Louisiana, was appointed Envoy Extraordinary and Minister Plenipotentiary. He arrived in the city of Mexico Dec. 6, 1845, and left the country about the 1st of April, 1846. He was not recognized by the Mexican Government, as was alleged on their part, because he came as a

* 27th Congress, 2nd Session, Executive Documents, No. 21.

resident Minister, and not as a Commissioner.* But a change of the national administration from the hands of the pacific Herrera to those of the warlike Paredes, which occurred in the interim, was a great obstacle to the success of his mission.

By a comparison of dates, however, it will be found that the American Minister was not finally rejected until after the gates of war were thrown open by the order to Gen. Taylor to take his position of offence on the east bank of the Rio Grande.

Mr. Slidell wrote home,† Dec. 27, 1845, that on the 21st of that month he had "received from Pena y Pena his promised reply, conveying the formal and unqualified refusal of the Mexican Government to receive me in the character for which I am commissioned." This letter was not received by the authorities at Washington, until Jan. 23, 1846, and, therefore, could not have been the basis of the order of Jan. 13th, ten days before, ordering Gen. Taylor to invade the disputed territory on the Rio Grande. Mr. Buchanan states explicitly in a letter to Mr. Slidell, of Jan. 28, 1846, that his despatches of the 27th and 29th of December *were received on the 23d instant.* ‡

But Herrera's power was overturned, and Paredes came to the head of affairs on Jan. 3, 1846. Still, there was hope even with the new warlike administration, of negotiating a treaty. On March 1st, Mr. Slidell, at Jalapa, had letters from the city of Mexico, which spoke "*confidently of his reception,*" § and gave information of it to the Department

* 30th Congress, 1st Session, House of Representatives, Executive Documents, No. 60: "The delay has arisen solely from certain difficulties occasioned by the nature of the credentials." See the Letter of Pena y Pena to Mr. Slidell, Dec. 16, 1845. See his letter also to the Mexican Council, Dec. 11, 1845.

† 30th Congress, 1st Session, House of Representatives, Executive Documents, No. 60, p. 32.

‡ Ibid. p. 54. § Ibid. p. 62.

at Washington. Meanwhile, the *Union*, the official organ, had said, on Feb. 10, 1846, that letters had been received to the 14th of January from Mr. Slidell; that he had not then "been received by the Government in his official capacity; *neither had they declined his reception.*"

On March 12th, Mr. Buchanan wrote to Mr. Slidell, "I am directed by the President to instruct you *not to leave that Republic* until you shall have made a formal demand to be received by the new government."*

On the 14th of January, Mr. Slidell had stated that his notes to Mr. Pena y Pena had "not yet been considered;" and he spoke of the new minister of foreign relations as one whom he knew at heart to be "decidedly favorable to an amicable adjustment of all questions pending between the two governments."†

And it was not till March 18th,‡ more than two months after the virtual war-order of Jan. 13th, that the American Envoy Extraordinary and Minister Plenipotentiary wrote home that he had received his decided rejection by the Paredes Government, and that he had demanded his passports. On that very day Gen. Taylor dated his despatch to the War Department,§ at "El Sauce, 119 miles from Corpus Christi," and, of course, thus far into a disputed territory, as much as that on the north-eastern boundary in debate a few years before, between England and the United States, or that portion between 49° and 54° 40′ on the Pacific slope, negotiated in 1845–6.

The warlike movements of the United States are seen by these letters to have been pushed forward independently of the reception or the rejection of Mr. Slidell. If the defeat of his mission was a real cause of war, and not a pretext, an afterthought, used to justify what had been already done,

* 30th Congress, 1st Session, House of Representatives, Executive Documents, No. 60, p. 64.

† Ibid. p. 50.

‡ Ibid. p. 66.

§ Ibid. p. 123.

the course of modesty would at least have dictated that the onset to arms should not be sounded until the Minister had been able to leave the country, and the Executive had time to lay the matter before Congress to decide the question of peace or war.

The Christian mode of proceeding cannot he better stated than in the words of Mr. Gallatin: "Yet, when Mexico refused to receive Mr. Slidell as an Envoy Extraordinary and Minister Plenipotentiary, the United States should have remembered that we had been the aggressors; that we had committed an act acknowledged, as well by the practical law of nations as by common sense and common justice, to be tantamount to a declaration of war; and they should have waited with patience till the feelings excited by our own conduct had subsided."*

The conclusions are, therefore,

1. That the refusal to receive an Envoy is not, according to the law of nations, a just cause of war, until at least every rational appeal has been exhausted.

2. That the movements of the American army that led to the spilling of blood, were ordered without special reference to the mission in Mexico.

3. That, in case the refusal to receive Mr. Slidell were grave cause enough to involve two great nations in war, the question should have been submitted to the decision of the Congress of the United States, then in session, and authorized by the Constitution to decide precisely such questions.

The final and immediate reason assigned at the beginning of the war was, that "Mexico has passed the boundary of the United States, has invaded our territory, and shed American blood upon the American soil." How amply this reason, when closely investigated, bears the character of a pretext, will be shown in detail in chapters seventh and eighth, to which we refer our readers on the question of boundary.

* Peace with Mexico, p. 5.

CHAPTER V.

PREPARATION OF WAR.

"No, Sir; if we would awaken the desire for peace in the bosom of England, — if we would render America invincible in battle, — *we must prepare the heart of the nation* for the defence of its rights and its honor, by honestly telling the people the real state of the facts, and by giving them the reason for the measures we adopt." — MR. ALLEN, *in Senate of the U. S. Dec.* 16, 1845.

IT was reserved to our day to witness the change of the popular maxim, "*in time of peace prepare for war*," into another rule, of even more questionable morality, "in time of peace prepare war." But, from a careful examination of the documents relating to the Annexation of Texas, and its consequences, and of the leading newspapers of the time, and the means used to act upon the public mind before the war broke out, we cannot avoid the conclusion, that a conflict with Mexico was early anticipated, desired, and prepared for, by those who understood but too well how easily the war spirit could be kindled in the heart of the nation. The reasons assigned for the war were but pretences, covering ulterior designs, which it would not do at once to disclose; but which have, in due succession, all come out, and now stand in their naked deformity before the world: Conquest, Dismemberment, Annexation of new territories, the extension of Slavery, the domestic Slave Trade, and the Slave Power. A distinguished statesman, with equal truth and severity, characterized the war as a "war of pretexts." What can prevent it from occupying that position on the pages of candid and impartial history?

To show that we speak not "without book" on this subject, let us investigate some of the means by which the ball was set in motion, and the pretences by which its crushing progress was justified after it began to roll.

From the moment that Texas was virtually annexed, in March, 1845, the clang of arms resounded through the West and South West. We have already seen that politicians of opposite parties declared the identity of annexation and war. But war did not immediately ensue; and, weak and distracted as Mexico was, there was no immediate likelihood of its occurrence. Time might heal the wound. A pacific administration was in power in that republic, and much was to be hoped from a conciliatory policy. Such were the views and feelings, now on record, of many of the friends of annexation, as well as of its determined opponents.

But other counsels prevailed. An endeavor seemed forthwith to be made, to irritate, rather than to tranquillize, our neighbors. The frontiers southward bristled with arms. In 1844, when the Treaty of Annexation was under consideration, assurances had been made to the Texan authorities, by the United States,* that, during the negotiation and settlement of difficulties, Texas should be defended by the naval and military forces of this republic, in case they conceived Mexico had any serious intention of invasion, and the pledges were redeemed.† But, in 1845, the tone began to change from defence to offence. As soon as the Joint Resolutions were accepted by the Texan Legislature, and before the measure of annexation could be perfected, steps were taken on the part of Texas to receive, and on the part of the United States to send troops, ostensibly to ward off

* Mr. Houston's speech in the U. S. Senate, Feb. 19, 1847. Also, his Letter to the *Texas Banner*, July 18, 1847.

† See Pres. Tyler's Message to the Senate, May 15, 1844, with the accompanying Documents, 28th Congress, 1st Session, Senate, 341, pp. 82 and following.

attacks from Mexico. A formidable naval force, of nine war-ships, was placed in the Gulf; a squadron was despatched to the Pacific coast; an expedition, professedly scientific in its aims, but found capable, afterwards, of being converted into a hostile instrument, was equipped for California and Oregon, and applications to enter it were more numerous than could be received.* In a word, all the elements began to muster their tempestuous powers, and brew the hurricane.

At this critical moment, the press, mighty engine for weal or woe, interposed but too often its vast influence, to fire the warlike passions in our countrymen. In the summer of 1845, no less than three long series of essays appeared in the organ of the national administration, relative to our difficulties with Mexico, and characterized by a belligerent tone of thought and feeling. The distant valley of the West was agitated by "rumors of wars." Texas already snuffed the coming storm. Unusual activity reigned in the barracks, forts, and navy yards of the country. The signs of the times were not to be mistaken; and the wonder now is, that, with all the preparations that were made for war, during the year 1845, any body should have been taken by surprise when it came, in 1846. They who had watched the filling of the magazine were not startled, when the spark was applied, to witness its explosion.

The following paragraphs, from various journals of that period, will show the temper of the times; and, when we consider that the newspaper press has an almost boundless power, both in creating and expressing public opinion in the United States, can we hesitate to believe, since effects must have a cause, that such sentences as these, read, copied, caught up by ardent temperaments, repeated from mouth to mouth, did not a little to precipitate the collision of arms?

* The *Washington Union*, June 14, 1845.

The Harrisburg (Pa.) *Union*, April, 1845, has these remarks on "our Foreign relations:" "Mexico, *pronunciamento*-loving Mexico, threatens the United States with all sorts of perils short of actual war, if the President executes a solemn act of Congress, and the expressed will of his constituents. We pity Mexico, torn as she is by domestic factions, whose sole object is to rob its poor and suffering people; but when she talks of war with a friendly nation, which has spared her on former occasions, we cannot help looking at her situation and resources, and recollecting how tempting it is to be invited by aggression to conquer her territory, and free her enslaved population from their petty tyrants.

* * * * *

"The ports of Mexico on the Gulf, Tampico and Vera Cruz, can be closed by our cruisers in a few days' sail. Her harbors on the Pacific are open and defenceless, and an army marching from Texas would be paid in its rout by the silver mines scattered along its path, and the gold, jewels, and silver of the city of Montezuma, would reward its adventurous assailants, while it paid the debt of its conquest. The settlers of Oregon would take permanent possession of the Californias, which would thus be added to our territory on the shores of the South sea.

"Let Mexico therefore beware how far she tempts us by insolent and threatening language."

The Daily Union at Washington, May 10, 1845, has the following: "The Government of the United States has been compelled in consequence of the hostile demonstrations on the part of Mexico, to despatch a powerful squadron to the Gulf, prepared to prevent or resist any warlike movements. The naval force in the Pacific is, of course, apprized of the posture of affairs. Troops have been assembled on our Southern frontier, ready to act as circumstances may demand.

"These proceedings, however, are purely and exclusively defensive. Unless Mexico should commence hostilities, nothing will be attempted on our side."

The Daily Union, May 14, 1845, has an extract from a private letter from New Orleans: "Are we going to have war or not (with Mexico) . . . War is all the talk here, as you may readily conceive. There are many brave fellows among us who are anxious to show their mettle." Continues the *Union* in comment,—"Sound but the trumpet, and there would pour volunteers enough from the valley of the Mississippi alone, to overrun Mexico, and subdue California. There would scarcely be wanting a single regular soldier to form the nucleus of twenty-thousand volunteers."

The *Nashville Union* of May 24th, quoted in the Washington *Union* of May 31, 1845, discourses thus: "Mexico may declare war, but that will not dissolve the bonds of annexation; it may result in *additional annexation;* and that view of the case deserves to be well weighed in Mexico before war is resorted to. In such a war, it will be found that annexation will be sustained by Whigs as well as Democrats."

Correspondent C. in Art. 14th, on Mexico, in the *Union* May 28th, says: "The other nations of the earth, must either exclude her from the rank which she claims among them, or must compel her to observe those laws of the government to which they voluntarily and cheerfully submit. We have seen, that by a timely resort to those measures of *coercion* which the circumstances of the case rendered necessary, France and England have compelled her to redress the wrongs which she had perpetrated, and to obey that law which she had violated. Were this course universally adopted, Mexico herself would grow richer and happier as well as better."

The Union of June 2d, predicts,—"The march of the Anglo Saxon race is onward. They must in the end accomplish their destiny — spreading far and wide the great principle of self-government; and who shall say how far they will prosecute the work?

"We infinitely prefer the friendly settlement of the great question now pending. It will secure the peace and welfare of the Mexican nation. It can now be done, and it should now be accomplished. For who can arrest the torrent that will pour onward to the West? The road to California will be open to us. Who will stay the march of our Western people? Our Northern brethren, also, are looking toward that inviting region, with much more interest than those of the South. They, too, will raise the cry of Westward, ho! However strongly many of them may now oppose annexation, yet, let California be thrown open to their ambition, and the torrent even of their population will roll westwardly to the Pacific."

Some papers lifted up a warning voice against this war-cry. Thus the *Cincinnati Gazette*, in reference to the last article, justly remarks: "We feel, as we fear, the spirit of the article in *The Union*. It bodes no good; it is evil. Ho! Westward! Halls of the Montezumas, and the mines of Mexico, would start into being 20,000 volunteers! Ay, so it would. What then? Why, in this valley, teeming with life, a spirit of aggrandizement, — of mad and maddening excitement, — of a selfish and burning thirst of power, — of military excitement, — of conquest, in its worst and most detestable form, — would rule as a master tyrant, sweeping all before it, and, as sure as it lives, desolating the hope of the virtuous and the free. Let all parties shun this spirit as they would dishonor. Let the country smite it down in its early manhood, ere that manhood be smitten unto death, by its foul and degrading breath."

The *Houston Star*, of May 24, 1845, says: "We are happy to state here, that arrangements have been made to obtain accurate information of the movements of the Mexican forces; and it is believed that our government will be prepared to repel any incursions of Mexican troops into the disputed territory (previously stated to be the territory 'West of the Nueces.'")

The Washington *Union*, of June 11th, advises that "the Texans themselves should collect their own volunteers, and march to repel the Mexicans from their borders. If the troops of Mexico have crossed the Rio Grande, it would be better for Texas to clear her own confines at once, than wait for the movements of our regulars. We hazard nothing in saying that such, too, would be the decided preference of our own government. We had understood, indeed, that such was also the determination of the Texans, if the Mexicans should be found hovering in the country between the Rio Grande and the Nueces. We do not mean to say, that if the Texans should be found wanting to themselves, we should suffer a hostile foot to tread her legitimate soil, as soon as her Congress and her Convention have ratified our propositions."

The *New Orleans Picayune*, of June 7th, says: "We have received intelligence, by this arrival, to the effect, that the Mexicans are really concentrating a large force on the *Rio Grande*, preparatory to war, in case Texas should agree to Annexation. Our informant states, further, that the feeling in the *latter country is thoroughly warlike;* the talk is of nothing else than a brush with Mexico, if she wishes it."

The Union, of June 23d, confesses: "We are for peace, but it must be an honorable peace. We are for war, if the rights and honor of our country demand it. This is our true position."

Otsego, a correspondent in *The Union*, of June 9th, writes: "Ten years ago, our country rang with applause of the heroes of San Jacinto. It was a New Orleans victory, so far as Texas was concerned, and was universally regarded as a successful termination of the brief but glorious contest she had waged for national freedom."

* * * *

"In spite of the active exertions of its opponents, open or disguised, it is hardly a figure of speech to say, that Annexation is a thing of the past. Its substance was obtained in the determination of the Texan people. They are about to supply the *forms*, when this great American question will proceed steadily, and, it is hoped and believed, peacefully, to its fulfilment. Yet, this may not be. Madness is sometimes inflicted upon nations, as upon man; and, if it be true that the Deity, in his inscrutable wisdom, first dements the people whom he would destroy, it may be that the time is not distant, when the banner of freedom will float on her hill tops, and the Plaza of Mexico be the camping ground of an American army."

The *New Orleans Picayune*, of June 24th, says: "We heard nothing of the rumor ourselves, (that the government had ordered all the troops on the Sabine to advance upon the Rio Grande, to repel the menaced irruption of the Mexicans upon the territory of Texas,) but we must say that we had rather see our troops marching towards the Rio Grande, than to any other quarter of the habitable world."

Mr. Shannon, who had just returned from Mexico, where he had been Minister Plenipotentiary, in a letter of July 2d, to Mr. Buchanan, Secretary of State, writes: "While it may be expected that these drafts (the ones that had not yet been honored by the Mexican government, and that included two instalments, amounting to $275,000) *will be paid by Mexico, so soon as her financial abilities* will enable her to do so, without regard to the future relations of the two countries, I do not feel justified in giving you any assurance that the remaining instalments will be paid, until the difficulties existing between the two countries are finally adjusted, or our government shall adopt strong measures, in order to *coerce* Mexico into a compliance with her treaty stipulations."

The Union, of July 18th, quotes from the *Missouri Expositor*, an extract from a letter dated at Taos, New Mexico:

"The glorious spirit of Annexation is spreading, like a prairie-fire up the Rio del Norte, and rattling the dried bones in New Mexico. * * *

"Both Americans and Mexicans are making large purchases of land upon the streams running into the Rio del Norte and Arkansas, and anticipating Annexation. Ex-Governor Armijo is stirring up and concentrating around him the means of ejecting Mexican domination, and will shortly succeed in so doing."

A plan of the war is sketched in a communication to the *Union* of Aug. 16th: "4,000 militia and 2,000 regulars in Texas, 2,000 militia and 1,500 regulars in other parts of U. S. 9,500 regulars, 25,000 volunteers, = 34,500. With these begin the forward march. *Go a-head!* the word, and prudence and watchfulness to guide. Pass the Rio Grande. Leave a military force to maintain the captured places in Mexico, and keep up our line of communication with our base of operations, and with 30,000 men advance direct upon Mexico. Vera Cruz should be taken," etc.

In this same month of August, 1845, Major-Gen. Gaines made a requisition on the Governor of Louisiana, without any orders, it was said, from the Secretary of War, for 2,000 men, and the troops were received and sent on to the frontiers. The military spirit was rampant in the capital of the Mississippi Valley. The War Department of the United States was put in a state of unusual activity; arms were made ready and despatched even on the sacred day of rest; ships of war were refitted, manned, and commissioned, and all was made ready. Gen. Gaines reviewed the troops in New Orleans on Sunday. Gen. Patterson, of Philadelphia, came to Washington to offer his services to the President, to raise 6,000 volunteers. Hon. R. M. Johnson, ex Vice-President of the United States, in a letter to the President, dated Aug. 25th, offered himself and the brave Kentuckians for the cause. Are not all these things faithfully recorded in the chronicles of that period? and are they not significant facts in the history of this war? The movements of Gen. Taylor to Corpus Christi were eagerly copied into all the journals. The Oregon discussion kept up an excitement during the session of Congress, 1845-6, favorable to warlike preparations, and training the people to be familiar with the idea of a resort to arms. The cry had been loud, "All of Oregon or none; now or never; fifty-four forty, or fight;" and all this inflammatory patriotism was easily turned, when the occasion served, into another channel, and the sword drawn against Mexico instead of England. The conflict burst upon the country suddenly, at last, and took many by surprise; but had they watched the course of public affairs more closely, they would have anticipated from such causes as had been diligently set in operation, the very results which followed. The effect on Mexico of these warlike rumors and preparations, is well described in the following article:

The *Union* of Jan. 12, 1846, says, "Extracts from the papers of Matamoras, published in the *Vera Crusano*, speak of incursions of the American troops, of detachments of parties of forty or fifty soldiers, reconnoitering and spying out the land The position and movements of the United States' troops at Corpus Christi, ever since Gen. Taylor has been there, have excited much alarm, fear, and jealousy, in the minds of the Mexicans. They seem to be hourly expecting that the United States' troops are about to march upon Matamoras, to seize upon that place, and thence, perhaps, to march to capture some others of their cities."

The state of feeling, too, in the United States, among great numbers of the people, was, probably, but too correctly represented in the two sentences below, emanating from two great commercial and political cities.

The *New Orleans Picayune* of January, 1846, says, "Be the result of the rebellion (*pronunciamento* of Paredes) what it may, it seems to us that our relations with Mexico should not be longer kept in a state of doubtful peace."

The *New York Courier*, of the same date, said, "We hope that our Government will promptly force our Mexican affairs to a crisis."

With this development of the spirit of conquest in the heart of the American people, with the extended means which had been put in readiness by land and sea to carry on war, and with the press from almost all quarters sounding the watchword of battle, we are astonished not that the crisis of blood came so unexpectedly, but that it was so long delayed.

There were certain causes assigned for the war, as the old question of claims, and the new one of boundaries, the threatened invasion of an American State, and the rejection of our minister at Mexico; but they have already been partially considered. They were, however, better called pretexts, than causes of war. They cloaked the designs of ambition. They were ready stimulants to national pride in the hands of expert moulders of public opinion. But the real circumstances that predisposed our countrymen to war, and the deep main-spring that moved all the chief agents and advocates in the premises, we have already laid open. The steps taken to accelerate the tremendous crisis, to rouse millions of minds to sanguinary sentiments, and pour forth fire and sword upon Mexico, have been indicated in this chapter. In succeeding ones, we propose to "count the cost" of our national pastime in arms, as it respects property, life, and all the elements of human prosperity and happiness.

CHAPTER VI.

THE BEGINNING AND ENDING OF THE WAR ARGUMENTS FOR PEACE.

"We daily make great improvements in *natural*, there is one I wish to see in *moral*, philosophy, — the discovery of a plan that would induce and oblige nations to settle their disputes without first cutting one another's throats. When will human nature be sufficiently improved to see the advantage of this?" — FRANKLIN.

ALTHOUGH serious difficulties existed between the United States and Mexico previously to the advance of Gen. Taylor from the Nueces to the Rio Grande, yet no doubt war might have been averted, had all parties concerned been deeply convinced of the blessings of peace, the guilt and horrors of a conflict, and the necessity of finally resorting to negotiations, because the sword itself could settle nothing. We had been in as great straits before, and had come out of the danger without shedding one drop of human blood. Granted that this was a peculiarly exasperating case of spoliations upon our commerce;* yet had not the United States a long list of grievances of this kind to adjust with several European powers at the close of the wars of Na-

* Yet so late as Aug. 5, 1836, Gen. Jackson said in a letter to Gov. Cannon, of Tennessee, "Should Mexico insult our national flag, invade our territory, or interrupt our citizens in the lawful pursuits which are guarantied to them by treaty, then the Government will promptly repel the insult, and seek reparation for the injury. But it does not appear that offences of this kind have been committed by Mexico."

poleon, and never thought it necessary to make the appeal to brute force? Granted that this was a case of violated sovereignty and trespass upon the rights of American citizens; yet we had pacifically negotiated with England, but a few years before, the difficult affairs growing out of the "Caroline" and the "Patriot War," and the storm-cloud of danger was scattered. Granted that it was a case of deferred payment of acknowledged claims; yet France owed us more and longer than Mexico, and we bore and forbore; and when, after long but peaceful urgency, we obtained the money, our burning sense of justice suddenly congealed, and we have not to this day paid over what we have received to the individual claimants for damages! Granted that it was a most delicate and difficult question of boundary lines; still we had hardly seen the ink dry on "the treaty of Washington," and the negotiations of Oregon, by which our limits were adjusted on the north from the Atlantic to the Pacific. What but the lust of territory, and the schemes of annexation, and the purposed extension of slavery and the slave power, prevented the same results in our Mexican difficulties on the south? As "a masterly inactivity" had averted an Oregon war with Great Britain, so might it have averted a Texas war with Mexico. Never was a finer argument supplied to the cause of peace, as demonstrating the superiority of her counsels to those of war, than is afforded by the beginning of the contest with Mexico. Never was there a more conclusive exhibition of the truth that what the advocates of war call "the necessity" of hostilities, is a necessity of their own creation, or, at least, of their own exaggeration, and has no reasonable foundation in national honor, rightly understood, or patriotism, truly felt.*

* "Mr. Webster's admirable letter to Lord Ashburton on the subject of Impressment, did more to settle that question than a hundred battles could have done." — DR. DEWEY'S PEACE ADDRESS, May 29, 1848, p. 9.

The contrast of our conduct towards Great Britain and that towards Mexico, is very marked. It was said that "our title to the whole of Oregon was clear and unquestionable," but the fleets and armies of the United States were not immediately despatched to take possession. The final decision was delayed till the next session of Congress, and submitted to their wisdom. It was finally settled by negotiation, and, notwithstanding the claim to 54° 40′, the line of the treaty was fixed at 49°. It was conceded, on the other hand, that the boundaries of Texas were not "clear and unquestionable," but were matters of future negotiation; the final ceremonies of annexation were not concluded till Dec. 22, 1845; but the forces of the United States had already taken up threatening positions in the Gulf, on the Pacific, and upon the Nueces; rumors of war were rife; and although Congress was in session at the time, a secret order was despatched to Gen. Taylor, on Jan. 13, 1846, — less than a month after annexation was finally adjusted, — to advance up to the Rio Grande, into a country which the articles of the Joint Resolution themselves implied was debatable ground. Could any key to such different measures in the two cases be detected in the fact that Great Britain was strong, and that Mexico was weak? or, in the further fact, that Oregon was free territory and was not wanted, and that Texas was a slave State and was wanted, and wanted, too, up to the extreme limit to which she had ever swelled her revolutionary pretensions?

It is very true that Mexico was deeply incensed against us on account of the annexation of Texas, that her Minister called for his passports and returned home after that measure was passed by Congress, and that the further payment of the claims was suspended, and that Mexico refused to accredit Mr. Slidell as a Resident Minister. Many statesmen of all parties in the United States did not blame her indignation. A former President of the Republic of Texas said in the Senate of the United States, that we "annexed war," when we annexed Texas. But though war might exist *de jure* in the judgment of the Mexican Government, since it was through the instrumentality of citizens of the South and West that Texan independence was secured,* yet war did not exist *de facto*. The return home of Almonte, the Mexican Minister at Washington, did not necessitate the interruption of all friendly relations between the two countries; witness the recent dismissal of the English Minister, Bulwer, from the court of Spain. No declaration of the final non-payment of claims, still due, had been announced on the part of the indebted nation. Three instalments out of twenty had been punctually paid, and the fourth was receipted for, but not received. Mexico but paused to see what would be the end of these things. She did not reject a commissioner † empowered to settle the question of boundaries, but she refused a resident minister, as his reception would imply that the relations between the two countries were entirely amicable. The questions at issue must first be settled, and then she would be prepared to resume all the forms of a mutual good understanding.

We see, therefore, by this rapid glance, that although there were serious irritations and recriminations between the parties, there was no actual war; not a sword had been drawn. There was still hope, that by reason and forbearance on both sides, the term "sister republics" would not cease to be even a figure of speech.‡ Similar difficulties

* The language of Mr. Van Buren in his letter to Mr. Hammett, April 20, 1844, on the Texan question, was, "Nothing is either more true or more extensively known than that Texas was wrested from Mexico, and her independence established, through the instrumentality of citizens of the United States."

† 30th Congress, 2nd Session, House of Representatives, Executive Documents, No. 60, pp. 16, 17, 24, 25, 29, 30, 31.

‡ "*General Worth.* Has Mexico declared war against the United States?

had been peacefully despatched before in our international history, and none presumed to doubt that the same result would follow now. It was the nineteenth century of the Christian era. The world had grown wiser and better. Christian ideas had begun to enter cabinets and congresses. Negotiations were more satisfactory, as well as more innocent instruments than bayonets. War was an unpopular game, and public opinion had joined with the higher voices of a Christian civilization in branding it as the master crime of the earth. So most men felt, wrote, and spoke.

There appeared to be no pressing exigency that required an instantaneous settlement of the long-standing difficulties. No new invasion of Texas was seriously meditated by her old enemy.* Mexico had not the sinews of war. Time would heal her wounded honor and pride. A handsome bonus for the brilliant gem, plucked from her coronet, might be found in remitting a portion or the whole of the instalments still outstanding. We had waited with other nations until they had recovered their reason; why could we not do the same with Mexico? We had borne long and patiently with the old monarchies of Europe, we should naturally treat, it might be supposed, with unusual tenderness and long-suffering the young republic at our side.

But the military forces of the United States were first

" *General Vega.* No

" *General Worth.* Are the two countries still at peace?

" *General Vega.* Yes. — *Minutes of an Interview between General Worth, of the United States' army, and General Vega, of the Mexican army, at Matamoras, March* 28, 1846. 30th Congress, 1st Session, House of Representatives, Ex. Doc. No. 60, p. 136.

"*Hostilities*" (still not declared war) "may now be considered as commenced." — *General Taylor's Letter to the Department, April* 26, 1846. same Documents.

* Mr. Kaufman, of Texas, said in the Senate, July 27, 1848, that "the annexation of Texas was the cause, but not the immediate or necessary cause, of the late war with Mexico."

advanced to Corpus Christi in the summer of 1845, with the ostensible purpose of protecting the new State of Texas.* Not that any imminent danger threatened. No army of invasion was mustering against her. At the most, only some windy menaces, which the sagacious estimated at their true value, were aimed at her security. Mexico was deeply engaged in her own affairs at home. She had little time or means to attend to truants abroad. Revolution chased revolution, and leaders rose and fell on the stormy sea of her politics. She was in no state to wage a war of re-conquest; and we believe most firmly that it was not in her heart to win back her lost province at the tremendous hazard of a war with the strongest power on the western continent. Therefore, although Dr. Channing had said in 1836, that "to annex Texas is to declare perpetual war with Mexico;"† though Mr. Forsyth, Secretary of State, when the plan of annexation was proposed by Texas in 1837, had replied, that "so long as Texas shall remain at war, while the United States are at peace with her adversary, the proposition of the Texan Minister Plenipotentiary (for annexation) necessarily involves the question of war with that adversary;"‡ and Mr. Van Buren had written, that "we cannot avoid the conclusion, that the immediate annexation of Texas would draw after it a war with Mexico;"§ and Mr. Clay, in the same year, had used the words "annexation and war with Mexico are identical;"‖ and though a Texan chief magistrate had, as already quoted, declared the same, after the deed was consummated; yet no immediate acts of war did follow. Mexico did not refuse to receive a

* 30th Congress, 2nd Session, House of Representatives, Ex. Doc. No. 60, pp. 79 – 93.

† Works, vol. 2, pp. 206, 207.

‡ 28th Congress, 1st Session, Senate, No. 341, p. 114.

§ His Letter to Mr. Hammet, April 20, 1844.

‖ Mr. Clay's Raleigh Letter.

special commissioner to treat of disputed questions and boundaries, and we affirm what will be the eternal verity of history, as we believe, when we say that facts demonstrate there would have been no war after the erection of Texas into one of the States of the American Union, had Gen. Taylor never removed his camp from the banks of the Nueces to those of the Rio Grande. It was peculiarly a case for cool, calm deliberation, negotiation, dignified forbearance, in which the greater power would lose no honor, but would gain much, by a temperate and conciliating course with the weaker one. No final door of conference was closed, and much was to be hoped from that healing efficacy of time, which soothes at once the griefs of a nation as those of the humblest of its citizens.

But on the 13th of January, 1846, as before stated, the fatal order was issued by the American Executive, by which Gen. Taylor was directed to advance and occupy, with the troops under his command, "positions on or near the east bank of the Rio del Norte," as soon as it could be conveniently done. How little this measure was necessary for the protection of Texas, or to ward off any threatened or suspected invasion, is apparent from the letters of the commander-in-chief, who was on the spot, and knew what was going on, written to the Secretary of War at home.* Aug. 15, 1845, Gen. Taylor writes, "Nor do I fear that the reported concentration of troops at Matamoras is for any purpose of invasion." Aug. 20th, "Caravans of traders arrive occasionally from the Rio Grande, but bring no news of importance. They represent that there are no regular troops on that river, except at Matamoras, and do not seem

* See this whole correspondence in 30th Congress, 2nd Session, House of Representatives, Ex. Doc. No. 60. The President said in his annual message, Dec. 1845, that the forces of the United States were in a position (on the Nueces) "to defend our own and the rights of Texas." Why then were they advanced to the Rio Grande?

to be aware of any preparations for a demonstration on this bank of the river." Sept. 6th, "I have the honor to report that a confidential agent, despatched some days since to Matamoras, has returned, and reports that no extraordinary preparations are going forward there." Oct. 11th, "Recent arrivals from the Rio Grande bring no news of a different aspect from what I reported in my last." Jan. 7, 1846, "A recent scout of volunteers from San Antonio struck the river near Presidio, Rio Grande, and the commander reports everything quiet in that quarter." Feb. 16th, "Many reports will doubtless reach the Department, giving exaggerated accounts of Mexican preparations to resist our advance, if not indeed to attempt an invasion of Texas. Such reports have been circulated even at this place, and owe their origin to personal interests connected with the stay of the army here. I trust that they will receive no attention at the War Department."

If all were thus tranquil, and hopeful of peace, why did the world hear that thunder-clap in a clear sky, that the American army had changed their quarters 150 miles further West? But, to those who had fathomed the deep purpose of the Annexation of Texas, "the trumpet gave no uncertain sound," as it heralded the march over that desert prairie; for its every note rang of conquest, new additions of territory, and the expansion of Southern institutions. Is not this true? and, if true, should it not now be as fearlessly spoken, as it was then daringly done? We are no sectionists, or disunionists, or partisans; but the truth must out, else it were better that every lip were cold, and every tongue dumb. We consider the war had virtually begun, the moment Gen. Taylor had struck his tents at Corpus Christi. The door of conciliation might then be considered as shut and barred. The Rubicon was crossed.

The next step in this argument for peace, drawn from the commencement of the war, is to consider the boundary question. Who was the aggressor? Difficulties existed, but not war *de facto*. Who applied the spark that fired the magazine? On which side was war an offensive, and on which side a defensive act? And here it is to be observed, that whichever party in such a case first assumes active hostilities, has much to answer for. It is no light matter to "Cry havoc; and let slip the dogs of war." And though in such events both sides are always to be blamed for pushing their quarrels into the neighborhood of such an awful extremity, yet a peculiar guilt rests upon the invader, who strikes the first blow.

It is conceded, in all quarters, that there *was* a boundary question between Mexico and the United States. The official documents, on both sides, demonstrate this fact in the strongest manner. The Resolutions that authorized Texas to annex herself to the Union, bore this fact on their face. The language of one was: "First, said State to be formed, subject to the adjustment by this Government of *all questions of boundary*, that may arise with other governments." The clause "other governments," can have no reference to any power but Mexico; because Texas borders upon no other country, except the United States, to which it was annexed.

Mr. Ashley, of Arkansas, when advocating annexation in the United States Senate, said:* "The third (his own resolution) speaks for itself, and enables the United States to settle the boundary between Mexico and the United States properly. And I will here add, that the present boundaries of Texas, I learn from Judge Ellis, the President of the Convention that formed the Constitution of Texas, and also a member of the first Legislature under that Constitution, were fixed as they now are, (that is, extending to the Rio

* Appendix to the Congressional Globe, 28th Congress, 2d Session, p. 288.

Grande,) solely and professedly *with a view of having a large margin in the negotiation with Mexico*, and not with the expectation of retaining them as they now exist in their statute book." Even Texas had not yet ventured to grasp such a lion's share, except as an advantageous position to occupy when she went into negotiation.

When the project of annexing Texas by a treaty was in process, Mr. Calhoun, Secretary of State, wrote to Mr. Green, our chargé d'affaires at Mexico: "You are enjoined, also, by the President, to assure the Mexican Government that it is his desire to settle all questions between the two countries, which may grow out of this treaty, or any other cause, on the most liberal and satisfactory terms, including that of boundary; and, with that view, the minister who has been recently appointed will be shortly sent, with adequate powers." And again, in the same letter, he says: "The United States have left the boundary of Texas without specification, so that what the line of boundary should be might be an open question, to be fairly and fully discussed and settled, according to the rights of each, — the mutual interests and security of the two countries."

Mr. Benton, and Mr. Silas Wright, of the Senate, both spoke and voted against the Treaty of Annexation, partly on this very ground of boundary. "I wash my hands," said the former, "of all attempts to dismember the Mexican Republic, by seizing her dominions in New Mexico, Chihuahua, Coahuila, and Tamaulipas. The treaty, in all that relates to the boundary of the Rio Grande, is an act of unparalleled outrage on Mexico. It is the seizure of two thousand miles of her territory, without a word of explanation with her, and by virtue of a treaty with Texas, to which she is no party." And he closed his speech by offering the following resolution: "Resolved, That the incorporation of the left bank of the Rio del Norte into the American Union, by virtue of a treaty with Texas, comprehending, as the said incorporation would do, a portion of the Mexican departments of New Mexico, Chihuahua, Coahuila, and Tamaulipas, would be an act of direct aggression upon Mexico, for all the consequences of which the United States would stand responsible."

Mr. Wright, in a speech at Watertown, N. Y., said: "I felt it to be my duty to vote against the ratification of the Treaty of Annexation. I believed that the treaty, from the boundaries that must be implied from it, embraced a country to which Texas had no claims, over which she had never asserted jurisdiction, and which she had no right to cede."

The intention was, however, as is evident from the letter of Mr. Calhoun, for the United States, as Mr. Ashley had said of Texas, to have "*a large margin in the negotiation with Mexico.*" And finally, as a conclusive and unanswerable proof that there was a question open relative to the boundaries, we have the Message of President Polk, Dec. 1845,* in which it is said that Mr. Slidell was authorized, as "an Envoy Extraordinary and Minister Plenipotentiary to Mexico, clothed with full powers to adjust and definitely settle all pending differences between the two countries, including those of boundary between Mexico and the State of Texas." The matter was so understood by Mr. Donelson, diplomatic agent to Texas, who wrote to Gen. Taylor, during the summer of 1845: "I would by no means be understood as advising you to take an offensive attitude in regard to Mexico, without further orders from the Government of the United States."

"The occupation of the country between the Nueces and the Rio Grande, you are aware, is a disputed question."

In 1836, an agent, Mr. Morfitt, was despatched by Gen. Jackson, the President of the United States, to examine and report upon the condition of Texas, which had then

* See, on this and other points below, the official documents of Congress, and the Appendix to the Congressional Globe.

established an independent government; and in his report, dated in August of that year, he stated: that "the political limits of Texas proper, previous to the last revolution, were the Nueces River on the west, along the Red River on the north, the Sabine on the east, and the Gulf of Mexico on the south."*

Again; Mr. Donelson, in a letter to justify his refusal to order Gen. Taylor to occupy the east bank of the Rio Grande, writes, July 11, 1845, to Mr. Buchanan, Secretary of State: "The Joint Resolution of our Congress left the question (of limits between Texas and Mexico) an open one."

"I have been far from admitting that the claim of Texas to the Rio Grande ought not to be maintained. This was not the question. It was, whether, under the circumstances, we should take a position to make war for this claim, in the face of an acknowledgment on the part of this government, (Texas,) it could be settled by negotiation. I at once decided that we should take no such position, but should regard only as within the limits of our protection that portion of territory actually possessed by Texas, and which she did not consider a subject of negotiation." "What the executive of Texas had determined not to fight for, but to settle by negotiation, to say the least of it, could as well be left to the United States upon the same condition."

Mr. Woodbury, in his speech in favor of ratifying the Treaty of Annexation, says: "Texas, by a mere law, could acquire no title but what she conquered from Mexico, and actually governed. Hence, though her law includes more than the ancient Texas, she could hold and convey only that, or at the uttermost only what she exercised clear jurisdiction over."†

* House Journal, No. 35, 2d Session, 24th Congress; 24th Congress, 2d Session, Ho. of Rep. Ex. Doc. No. 35, p. 12.

† Appendix to Congressional Globe, June, 1844, p. 768.

Mr. Gallatin says: "The Republic of Texas did, by an act of Dec. 1836, declare the Rio del Norte to be its boundary. It will not be seriously contended that a nation has a right, by a law of its own, to determine what is or shall be the boundary between it and another country. The act was nothing more than the expression of the wishes or pretensions of the government. As regards right, the act of Texas is a perfect nullity."*

Up to the last moment before the war broke out, Gen. Taylor acknowledged that the question of boundaries was open; for, in his reply to Gen. Ampudia, who commanded him to retire beyond the Nueces, he said, April 12, 1846:† "I have been ordered to occupy the country up to the left bank of the Rio Grande, until *the boundary shall be definitively settled.*"

A work, entitled The Republic of the United States of America, embracing a review of the war and defending it, says, p. 112: "By the act of annexation, the question of boundary between Mexico and Texas was left an open one, to be decided by negotiation between the governments of Mexico and the United States."

The Message of the President of the United States, in relation to the territories of New Mexico and California, of July 24, 1848, states: "That the province of New Mexico, according to its ancient boundaries, as claimed by Mexico, lies on both sides of the Rio Grande. That part of it on the east of that river was *in dispute* when the war between the United States and Mexico commenced. * * * *

"Though the republic of Texas, by many acts of sovereignty which she exerted and exercised, some of which were stated in my Annual Message of December, 1846, had established her clear title to the country west of the Nueces, and bordering on that part of the Rio Grande which lies *below*

* Peace with Mexico, p. 7.

† 30th Congress, 1st Session, Ex. Doc. No. 60, p. 139.

the province of New Mexico, she had *never conquered or reduced to actual possession, and brought under her government and laws*, that part of New Mexico lying *east of the Rio Grande*, which she claimed to be within her limits. On the breaking out of the war, we found Mexico in possession of *this disputed territory*. As our army approached Sante Fé, (the capital of New Mexico,) it was found to be held by a governor under *Mexican* authority, and an armed force collected to resist our advance. The inhabitants were *Mexicans*, acknowledging allegiance to *Mexico*. The boundary *in dispute* was the line between the two countries engaged in actual war, and *the settlement of it*, of necessity, depended on *a treaty of peace*."*

Observe, this was a region *east* of the Rio Grande. Observe, too, that as Santa Fé, on the Upper Rio Grande, was confessedly *not brought under the government and laws of Texas;* so was neither the port of Point Isabel, nor other towns and villages on the Lower Rio Grande. All that can be predicated of one can be of the other, so far as their being "*conquered and reduced* to the actual possession" of Texas was concerned.

Finally, we quote at length a most significant passage on the special subject of the boundary, and the general question of the war, from "the author" of annexation himself, Mr. Calhoun, whose sincerity in declaring his opinions, whatever we may think of their nature and bearing, never has been called in question.

He says:† "It is true Mexico claimed the whole of Texas; but it is equally true that she recognized the difference, and showed a disposition to act upon it, between the country known as Texas proper and the country between it and the Del Norte. It is also true, that we and Texas recognized the same difference, and that both regarded the

* The italics are ours.

† Printed speech, United States Senate, Feb. 24, 1847, pp. 12, 13.

boundary as unsettled; as the resolution of annexation, which provides that the boundary between Texas and Mexico shall be determined by the United States, clearly shows. It is worthy of remark, in this connection, that this provision in the Joint Resolution is understood to have been inserted, in consequence of the ground taken at the preceding session by the Senator from Missouri, on the discussion of the treaty, that the Nueces was the western boundary of Texas, and that to extend that boundary to the Rio del Norte would take in part of Tamaulipas, Coahuila, and New Mexico. What, then, ought to have been the course of the executive, after annexation, under this resolution? The very one which they at first pursued, — to restrict the position of our troops to the country actually occupied by Texas at the period of annexation. All beyond, as far as the executive was concerned, ought to have been regarded as subject to the provisions of the resolutions, which authorized the government to settle the boundary.

* * * * *

"Why negotiate, if it were not an unsettled question? Why negotiate, if the Rio del Norte, — is, as it was afterwards assumed, — was the clear and unquestionable boundary? And if not, upon what authority, after the attempt to open negotiation had failed, could he determine what was the boundary, viewing it as an open question? Was it not his plain duty, on such an occurrence, to submit the question to Congress, which was then in session, and in whom the right of establishing the boundary and declaring war was clearly invested? Had that course been adopted, I greatly mistake if the sense of this body would not have been decidedly opposed to taking any step, which would have involved the two countries in war. Indeed I feel a strong conviction, that if the Senate had been left free to decide on the question, not one-third of the body would have been found in favor of war. As it was, a large majority felt themselves compelled, as they believed, to vote for the bill recognizing the existence of war, in order to raise the supplies of men and money necessary to rescue the army under Gen. Taylor, on the Del Norte, from the dangers to which it was exposed."

CHAPTER VII.

THE SAME SUBJECT CONTINUED.

"'Let us hope, then, that the law of nature, which makes virtuous conduct produce benefit, and vice loss to the agent, in the long run, which has sanctioned the common principle, that honesty is the best policy, will in time influence the proceedings of nations as well as individuals; that we shall at length be sensible, that war is an instrument entirely inefficient toward redressing wrong; that it multiplies, instead of indemnifying losses.' — JEFFERSON.

NOTWITHSTANDING the foregoing irrefragable proofs that the boundary between Texas and Mexico was in dispute, it has been asserted that the Louisiana purchase, of 1803, extended to the Rio Grande. So it *was* claimed, as it is customary to have "a large margin for negotiation." But it was a trick of diplomacy. Western Florida was laid claim to, as a part of the same purchase, but the claim did not stand. So Oregon was claimed, to 54° 40′, but the treaty reduced the line down to 49.° These large margins of claims are the last things a reasonable being would suppose that nations would be willing to carry before the bar of the Public Opinion of Christendom, as adequate causes of war. If annexation was but re-annexation, why did the United States sleep so many years, and allow an independent republic of Texas to swallow up the claim, and put in peril of perpetual alienation, or of foreign domination, the rights of the American Union, from the Sabine to the Rio Grande? *

The defence that is set up on the ground that Texas, when she became independent, claimed to the Rio Grande, and that Santa Anna, in 1836, allowed the claim, is equally futile. Why Texas aspired so far, is confessed in the quotation already made from Mr. Ashley, in which he vouches for the reason why that was done, on the very competent authority of the President of the Texan Convention that formed the Constitution. The fact that Santa Anna was a Texan prisoner of war, which is stated at the very head of the preamble of the alleged treaty, and in imminent danger of having his head cut off † if he did not concede all that was required of him, is a sufficient answer to that branch of the argument.‡ A compulsory obligation of that kind,

* Hon. J. Q. Adams said, in the House of Representatives, May 13, 1846, "I wrote that despatch as Secretary of State, and endeavoured *to make out the best case I could for my country, as it was my duty.* But I utterly deny that I claimed the Rio del Norte as our boundary, in its full extent. I only claimed it a short distance up the river, and then diverged to the northward some distance from the stream." — *Appendix to the Congressional Globe*, p. 907, 29th Congress, 1st Session.

† Article 8th of the "Treaty." "The President and Cabinet of the Republic of Texas, exercising the high powers confided to them by the people of Texas, do, for and in consideration of the foregoing stipulation, solemnly *engage to refrain from taking the life of the President, Santa Anna, and of the several officers of his late army,*" etc. And article 11th threatens, in case of refusal to enter into such an agreement, such treatment as Texas might deem proper in view of Mexican cruelties!

‡ Gen. Lamar, Secretary of war of Texas, says, in a letter to the President, Burnet, May 12, 1836, "What good can they hope to result from an extorted treaty? General Santa Anna is our prisoner of war. * * * What he assents to whilst a prisoner, he may reject when a freeman."

loses its binding force from the very nature of the circumstances which give it birth. Besides, he could not constitutionally act for the whole Mexican Government, although he was President; and one of the first acts the government did when he returned home, was to disown the so-called "treaty" of San Jacinto.

It is true that Texas had exercised some acts of "sovereignty and jurisdiction" west of the Nueces. Corpus Christi was on that side of the river. But power was one thing, and right was another. She might and did exercise such power *west of the Nueces;* but that was a very different jurisdiction *from going to the Rio Grande,* 150 *miles, in the use of her prerogatives.* She had an imperfect revolutionary title to certain places and parts,* as just stated; but the documents already quoted make it as plain as noon-day that both Texas and the United States, before and after annexation, regarded the Rio Grande only as a negotiable, not as an established line. The Texas of annexation was not a definite, but an indefinite territory. Every speech, every resolution, every letter, every message declared it without a dissenting voice *before the war began.* To go to war with Mexico for debatable land, was what Texas did not expect or require, as Mr. Donelson stated; for the question was not one to be settled by war, for war settles nothing, but unsettles everything; but it was a legitimate subject for diplomacy, and Mexico consented to meet the United States in the person of a commissioner appointed for that purpose, and for none other.

* The Texas county of San Patricio was west of the river Nueces, and lay in the immediate neighborhood of Corpus Christi. The official language of Mr. Donelson was, "Corpus Christi * * * is the most western point now occupied by Texas."

"The occupation of the country between the Nueces and the Rio Grande, you are aware, is a disputed question. Texas holds Corpus Christi; Mexico, Santiago, near the mouth of the Rio Grande."

The fact that certain gazeteers, geographies, and atlases, from 1820 to the present time, stated the Rio Grande as the boundary of Texas, are all of suspicious authority, for they are chiefly American works; and they no more prove that such was the real boundary of that province, than Mitchell's outline map, extending the northern line of Oregon to 54° 40′, proves that that was the true limit of the United States in that direction. Claims and rights are different terms. The blue and red of geographical lines are often the negotiable, rather than the adjusted limits. Let them pass for what they are worth; but they cannot shake one documentary fact, one diplomatic concession. Another conclusive proof that the left bank of the Rio Grande was not "American soil," in any other sense than that it was North American soil, is furnished by the facts that Mexican custom-houses were recognized at Brazos Santiago, or Point Isabel, and at Santa Fé, by the United States; and that duties were paid by its citizens at those places after the annexation of Texas. An official order was issued by the Secretary of the Treasury regulating exportation to, and importation from Santa Fé, as a Mexican town within the period, when, according to other statements of high authority, it must have constituted an integral portion of Texas, and, therefore, of the United States, after annexation.*

* An act of Congress was passed, May 3, 1845, "allowing a drawback upon foreign merchandize exported in the original packages to Chihuahua and *Santa Fé, in Mexico*," etc. And Mr. Walker, Secretary of the Treasury, says, in his annual report, December, 1845, that it had "gone to some extent into effect." — See the *Official Documents.*

The Austin Democrat, of 1848, in arguing the claims of Texas to Santa Fé, puts the case with great strength: "If Santa Fé is a province taken by force of arms from Mexico, (and, therefore, belonging to the United States as a territory, and not to the State of Texas), so was the country between the Nueces and the Rio Grande; and the very moment Gen. Taylor set foot on the western bank of the former

This point was so indisputable, that it was freely admitted before the war, though, after the war broke out, it seemed to be, in spirit at least, denied. Thus the Secretary of War, July 8, 1845, in a letter to Gen. Taylor, wrote as follows:—"This Department is informed that Mexico has some military establishments on the east side of the Rio Grande, which are, and for some time have been, in the actual occupancy of her troops. In carrying out the instructions heretofore received, you will be careful to avoid any acts of aggression, unless an actual state of war should exist. The Mexican forces at the parts in their possession, and which have been so, will not be disturbed as long as the relations of peace between the United States and Mexico continue." *

On July 30, 1845, the Secretary again wrote to the American General as follows:—"You are expected to occupy, protect, and defend the territory of Texas, to the extent that it has been occupied by the people of Texas. The Rio Grande is claimed to be the boundary between the two countries, and up to this boundary you are to extend your protection, only *excepting* any posts on the eastern side thereof which are in the actual occupancy of Mexican forces, or *Mexican settlements*, over which the Republic of Texas did not exercise jurisdiction at the period of annexation, or shortly before that event. It is expected, in select-

stream, he committed an aggression upon a foreign soil, and hostilely invaded a country with which his country was at peace. If Laredo was ours, so was Santa Fé; if Santa Fé was not, neither was Laredo."

We give a list of the following towns and hamlets then belonging to Mexico on the east side of the Rio Grande, taken from Mr. Davis's speech in the House of Representatives, Dec. 22, 1846, and from Lieut. Emory's Map:—Embuda, Canada, Nambe, Pojuaque, Santa Fé, Agua Fria, San Juan, Zandia, Alameda, Albuquerque, Valencia, Tome, Las Nutrias, Parida, Valverde, Prenido, Laredo, and many others.

* 30th Congress, 1st Session, Ex. Doc. No 60, p. 82.

ing the establishment for your troops, you will approach as near the boundary line, the Rio Grande, as prudence will dictate. With this view the President desires that your position, for a part of your forces at least, should be west of the river Nueces."*

And on Nov. 10, 1845, the American Executive instructed Mr. Slidell, envoy to Mexico, to offer a relinquishment of the claims of the United States against that nation, and $5,000,000, provided she would allow the Rio Grande to be established as the western boundary of Texas.†

It were easy to quote from Mexican authorities numerous declarations to the effect that the occupation of the left bank of the Rio Grande was an act of invasion, and, therefore, of war, on the part of the American troops. But it will be more to our purpose to show, at some length, that such was unconsciously, and even against stout disclaimers, the feeling and natural expression of the Americans, as well as of the Mexicans, and even of the prime agents and actors in the annexation of Texas, and the war with Mexico. "Nature cannot be driven out with a pitchfork." What men really feel, they will unconsciously, and unfavorably to their own cause, express, if not directly, yet at least incidentally.

We pass by in this connection the declaration of Mr. Benton in the Senate, that to occupy the east bank of the Rio Grande, "would be an act of direct aggression on Mexico," and quote that of Mr. Ingersoll in the House of Representatives,‡ that "the stupendous deserts between the Nueces and the Bravo (the Rio Grande or del Norte) rivers, are the natural boundaries between the Anglo-Saxon and the Mauritanian races. There ends the valley of the west.

* 30th Congress, 1st Session, Ex. Doc. No. 60, pp. 82, 83.

† Ibid. No. 52, p. 78. $25,000,000 were to be offered for California, and $20,000,000 for that province, provided the line of boundary should not include Monterey on the Pacific. p. 79.

‡ 29th Congress, 1st Session, Appendix to Cong. Globe.

There Mexico begins. Thence, beyond the Bravo, begin the Moorish people and their Indian associates, to whom Mexico properly belongs, who should not cross that desert if they could, as on our side we ought to stop there; because interminable conflicts must ensue from either our going south, or their coming north of that gigantic boundary. While peace is cherished, that boundary will be sacred. Not till the spirit of conquest rages, will the people on either side molest or mix with each other; and whenever they do, one or the other race must be conquered or extinguished."

Mr. Calhoun, too, in a letter dated Aug. 12, 1844, to Mr. King, the American minister to France, says, "Nature herself has clearly marked the boundary between her (Mexico) and Texas, by natural limits too strong to be mistaken." *

We come then, first, to an incidental and unconscious testimony of the commander of the American troops himself. When he met on the river Colorado on his march, the Mexican officer, who forbade his crossing that river, and declared that the act would be regarded as an unwarranted aggression on Mexico, how did Gen. Taylor conduct the matter? Did he act and speak as if the Mexican troops, by advancing some thirty miles east of the Rio Grande, had violated the territory of the United States? Did he charge them with invasion, and order them to retire into their own country on the right bank of the Rio Grande? Not at all. He manifests no zeal to repel invasion. He kindles with no indignation that they should threaten to shed "American blood on American soil." His whole mien and behavior wear the most indubitable and natural semblance to that of an invader. He does not order off the opposing troops, as if they had no right there, but he manifests a deter-

* 28th Congress, 2nd Session, Appendix to Congressional Globe, p. 5.

mined spirit to go whither he was ordered, right or wrong, and no matter through what opposition. He had none of the passion with which he would have met a British force advancing in hostile array into New York or Illinois. His whole bearing says in words that could not lie, "My march is an aggression on Mexico, or at least an advance upon disputed territory. If the Mexicans are invaders, so much more am I. But a soldier must obey orders." If these things were not so, why did not the brave commander fire on these presumptuous aggressors, who had penetrated so far into an American State under the protection of the Union? Once at least Gen. Taylor so far forgot himself as to write thus, "It was my earnest desire to execute my instructions in a pacific manner, to observe the utmost regard *for the personal rights of all citizens residing on the left bank* of the river, and to take care that the religion and customs of the people should suffer no violation."* Truly a very worthy spirit. But why this exceeding care, if these were citizens, not of Mexico, but of the United States, as the pretended boundary claim made them?

A similar undesigned, and therefore altogether more powerful, evidence that Gen. Taylor had advanced upon Mexican, or at least disputed, soil, is afforded by his officers and men, writing home to their friends, or by letter-writers, who were in favor of the Mexican war, and who did not see the bearing of their own statements. We quote high Executive authority to the same effect.

In his annual message of Dec., 1846, the President says, "by rapid movements the province of New Mexico, with Santa Fé, its capital, has been *captured* without bloodshed,"

Again, he says in the same message, "in less than seven months after Mexico commenced hostilities, at a time selected by herself, we have taken possession of many of her

* 30th Congress, 1st Session, House of Representatives, Ex. Doc. No. 60, p. 145.

principal posts, driven back and pursued her invading army, and acquired military possession of *the Mexican provinces* of New Mexico, New Leon, Coahuila, Tamaulipas," * etc. But all these provinces extended *east* of the Rio Grande, except New Leon.

T. B. Thorpe, author of "Our Army on the Rio Grande," and other works, in describing the approach of Gen. Taylor's army to that river, says, "Large droves of splendid horned cattle were now frequently seen; and occasionally a small cotton field, hedged in by thorn bushes, strengthened by trunks of trees set in the ground, gave welcome evidence of a settled country. Scattered *Mexican* huts next appeared." Could this have been a part of Texas proper?

The author of "the Life of General Zachary Taylor, and a History of the War in Mexico," published in the "Brother Jonathan, Battle Sheet, 1847," an advocate of the war, uses the following language: "The administration at Washington, on the 13th of January, 1846, ordered Gen. Taylor to move forward, and occupy the east bank of the Rio Grande, opposite Matamoras, but not disturb any of the *Mexican* settlements, or any military posts that might be on this side of the Rio Grande, and to purchase every thing needed for the army at the highest price."

Again, "on setting out on this march, he (Gen. Taylor) embodied the above instructions in one of his general orders, which he caused to be circulated among the *Mexicans* on the east side of the Rio Grande."

Again, "on the 24th, Gen. Taylor, leaving the main command with Gen. Worth, and taking with him Col. Twiggs, and his dragoons, approached Frontone, a small *Mexican* village at Point Isabel, *in the department of Tamaulipas*,

* The Legislature of Tamaulipas has demanded two millions of dollars of the Federal Government, as indemnity for the territory North of the Rio Grande, ceded to the United States by the treaty of Gaudalupe. — *Newspaper*, 1848.

where Gen. Garcia was stationed with two hundred and fifty men."

And once more; "but three or four inoffensive *Mexicans* were found in the place (Frontone)." *

We ask how could all these things have been, if this were American, Texan, or United States soil?

Capt. W. S. Henry, of the U. S. Army, wrote a work, entitled "Campaign Sketches of the War with Mexico," in which the following passages, unconscious witnesses of the truth, are found:

"Friday, August 1, 1845. After enjoying the delightful view from the bluff, a party of us strolled over the beautiful plain, on the borders of which many *Mexican* families reside." Observe that this was in the immediate vicinity of Corpus Christi.

"March 19, 1846. Passed many pens in which the *Mexicans* confine their droves of cattle and horses."

"March 23d. "This part of the country is really beautiful, and I am not surprised that the *Mexicans* are loath to part with it."

"March 28th. As we approached the bank we passed through a long line of *Mexican* huts."

"Two hours after our arrival a flag-staff was erected, under the superintendence of Colonel Belknap, and soon the

* A law was passed by the Congress of the United States, after the annexation of Texas, Dec. 29, 1845, "That the State of Texas shall be one collection district, and the city of Galveston the only port of entry, to which shall be annexed Sabine, Velasco, Matagorda, Cavello, La Vaca, and Corpus Christi, as ports of delivery only." No port routes were established beyond the valley of the Nueces until after the commencement of the war.

By an additional act of Congress, passed March 3, 1847, Saluzia was made the only port of entry, and Matagorda, Aranzas, Capano, and Corpus Christi, the only ports of delivery in that collection district of Texas.

Why were Brazos, Santiago, and Point Isabel left out, if they belonged at that time to Texas?

flag of our country, a virgin one, was seen floating upon the banks of the Rio Grande, proclaiming in a silent but impressive manner that the 'area of freedom' was again *extended.* As it was hoisted, the band of the 8th Infantry played the 'Star-spangled Banner,' and the field music 'Yankee Doodle.' There was not ceremony enough in raising it. The troops should have been paraded under arms, the banner of our country should have been hoisted with patriotic strains of music, and a national salute should have proclaimed, in tones of thunder, that 'Liberty and Union, now and forever, one and inseparable,' had *advanced* to the banks of the Rio Grande." Then it is certain that they had not reached that river before Gen. Taylor pitched his camp there, by this writer's own testimony.*

The same author says, under date of March 30th, "our situation is truly extraordinary: right in the *enemy's* country (to all appearance,) actually occupying their corn and cotton fields, the people of the soil leaving their homes,† and we, with a small handful of men, marching with colors flying and drums beating, right under the very guns of one of their principal cities, displaying the star-spangled banner, as if in defiance under their very nose; and they, with an army twice our size at least, sit quietly down and make no resistance, not the first effort to drive us off."

In a "Life of Major-General Zachary Taylor, with an account of his brilliant achievements on the Rio Grande," etc., etc., by C. Frank Powell, is the following passage; ‡ "we

* The Italics are ours.

† "The population fled at the approach of your army. I wish to know if it has come to this, that when an American army goes to protect American citizens on American territory, they flee from it as from the most barbarous enemy? Yet such is the assumption of those who pretend that on the east bank of the Rio Grande, where your arms took possession, there were Texas population, Texas power, Texas laws, and American United States power and law." — *Corwin's Speech in the Senate, Feb.* 11, 1847.

‡ p. 13.

shall not make it our province to question the policy of taking forcible possession of a territory known to be held *in dispute* by two free and independent republics; but nothing is clearer than that the commander of the American forces but complied with implicit instructions of the Department, which were his guaranty and justification."

"We cannot say, that neutrality would have been preserved had possession not been taken; and it would seem that the acquisition of the republic, — but in equal part interested in the dispute, — by a third power, did not change the position of affairs, or authorize such power to invest the territory. Be this as it may, however, on the 28th of March, 1846, the United States' army took up its quarters opposite Matamoras, and planted the United States' flag *in the ancient department of Tamaulipas.*"

Gen. Taylor wrote to the Adjutant General,* April 6, 1846: "On our side, a battery for four 18 pounders will be completed, and the guns placed in battery to-day. These guns bear directly upon the public square of Matamoras, and within good range for demolishing the town. Their object cannot be mistaken by the enemy."

The force of these quotations from active agents or advocates of the war, is to prove that acts of invasion and hostility, if committed by either party up to the date of these extracts, were chargeable on the American authorities. They had pushed their troops into a debatable region. They had penetrated among Mexican villages and fields, and planted their cannon in hostile array, commanding a Mexican city. If these were not acts of war, (casus belli,) they were acts provocative of war; and, if not designed, yet, assuredly, they were perfectly adapted, to plunge the two countries into a sanguinary conflict. Had pacific counsels prevailed in both governments, we can now see how

* 30th Congress, 1st Session, House of Representatives, Ex. Doc. No. 60, p. 133.

easily and honorably those occasions and steps might have been shunned, which resulted at last in such terrific evils, both to the victor and the victim. Far be it from us to exempt either Mexico or the United States from deep guilt, in bringing on the contest; but which government was chiefly instrumental in springing the mine at last, has been made sufficiently clear by the preceding remarks.

In this connection it will be proper, as a part of the history of the war, to state, that it had actually begun, and two principal battles, those of Palo Alto and Resaca de la Palma, had been fought, before the Congress of the United States, the war-making power, was apprized of what was going forward, and the steps which had been taken to bring matters to a crisis; or had been favored with an opportunity to pronounce on the merits or causes of a war with Mexico. Their vote, therefore, was but a foregone conclusion. They but registered the decision that had gone forth from another branch of the government. While, accordingly, the House of Representatives of the 29th Congress, on May 13, 1846, voted, by a majority of 173 to 14, that, "by the act of the republic of Mexico, a state of war exists between that government and the United States;" on Jan. 3, 1848, the newly chosen House of Representatives of the 30th Congress voted, in a Joint Resolution of thanks to Gen. Taylor, his officers, and men, by a majority of 85 to 81, that the war was "unnecessarily and unconstitutionally begun by the President of the United States;" and this vote was subsequently sustained against reconsideration, on Feb. 14th, by a majority of 115 to 94.

Having thus far discussed the beginning of the war, as an argument for peace, as a precedent, illustrating the saying of the Wise Man, that it is better to "leave off contention before it be meddled with;" we now proceed to make a few remarks on the termination of the contest, as also bearing witness in behalf of the cause of peace.

Various proposals were made to the Mexican Government, during the prosecution of the war, to enter into negotiations of peace. Offers were addressed, at different periods, by the superior commanders, acting under directions from home, to treat of matters in dispute between the two countries; but Mexico, feeling herself deeply wronged and aggrieved, and clinging to the principle of the integrity of the national domains, rejected with scorn all pacific counsels.

It was with this view, that an armistice of eight weeks formed one of the articles of the capitulation of Monterey. And, after the battle of Buena Vista, Gen. Taylor sent an officer to Gen. Santa Anna, "to express to him the desire still cherished by the American Government, for the re-establishment of peace." "Say to Gen. Taylor," was the reply, "that we sustain the most sacred of causes, — the defence of our territory, and the preservation of our nationality and rights."

After the battle of Cerro Gordo, Gen. Scott addressed a letter to the Mexican people, to persuade them to entertain propositions of peace, and to understand their true interests. But the effort was fruitless.

Finally, the sword, drunk as it was with human blood, proving an ineffectual instrument of pacification, a more hopeful plan suggested itself to the American Government. N. P. Trist, Esq., as before stated, was appointed, on the 15th of April, 1847, an agent, by the President, unconfirmed and unauthorized by the Senate, the confirming and treaty-making power; and his commission stated that he was invested, "in the fullest and most complete manner, with ample power and authority, in the name of the United States, to meet and confer with any person or persons, who shall have similar authority from the republic of Mexico, and between them to negotiate and conclude an arrangement of the differences which exist between the two countries — a treaty of peace, amity, and lasting boundaries. Mr. Trist carried with him to Mexico, from the department of State, "a project of a treaty." Its principal features were, the cession to the United States of the disputed territory between the Nueces and the Rio Grande, with the adoption of the latter river as the boundary line; the cession of New Mexico, and both Upper and Lower California; and the free right of way forever across the isthmus of Tehuantepec. Three millions of dollars had been placed, by Congress, at the disposal of the President of the United States, by which the provisions of a treaty of peace might be concluded, and its objects fulfilled. Mr. Trist accompanied Gen. Scott and his army to the Valley of Mexico; and, after the battles of Contreras and Churubusco, he met Mexican commissioners, specially appointed to negotiate a treaty. From the 27th of August, 1847, to the 7th of September, the commission thus jointly constituted was in session, at a small village in the immediate vicinity of the capital. Mr. Trist laid his project before the Mexican commissioners, who also proposed conditions of peace, that rested essentially on these points: the adoption of the Nueces as the boundary; thence west to the eastern boundary of New Mexico; thence north with that boundary to the thirty-seventh degree of latitude; thence west with that parallel to the Pacific; and that the country between the Nueces and the Rio Grande should be left as an uninhabited country. But the commission could not agree; the failure turning wholly on the claim of the south part of New Mexico, which neither party would yield; while Mr. Trist was willing to concede Lower California, and to refer the question of the Nueces territory to the cabinet at Washington. On the 7th of September the discussions closed, and on the 8th Gen. Scott opened his cannons on Molino del Rey.

Mr. Trist was subsequently recalled, by the President of the United States, and his authority as a peace commissioner declared to be at an end. But he remained in Mexico, with the army; and, on the 2d of February, 1848,* he negotiated, with commissioners appointed by the Mexican Government, the treaty of peace, which has already in the preceding chapter been mentioned, as receiving finally the ratification of the lawful powers of both governments. The articles of pacification are too well known, to be repeated at length. It is sufficient to state, that the troops of the United States were to withdraw from Mexico; the blockaded ports to be opened; the Rio Grande to be the boundary line on the Gulf of Mexico, and on the Pacific the line between Upper and Lower California; the payment of fifteen millions of dollars to Mexico, in consideration of the territory thus acquired; and the exoneration of Mexico from all claims of citizens of the United States for spoliations, to the amount of several millions more.

The conclusion of the war thus demonstrates the superior power and blessings of peace. Both parties were tired of the contest; the one of being defeated and ravaged, the other of losing thousands of lives, and millions of money. So far as the peace was a measure forced by the sword, it is as dishonorable in the light of humanity and Christianity to the victorious, as it is humiliating to the vanquished nation. For Fenelon, noble champion for his day of the humane spirit in international intercourse, says, in his "Directions for the Conscience of a King," that "a treaty of peace, that is made from necessity, because one party is the stronger, is like that which is made with a robber, who has a pistol at your head." And so far as the power of money prevailed, where the power of the bayonet had failed, so far as the negotiation, though unauthorized at the time, succeeded, where the bravest general had been frustrated in "conquering a peace," the treaty might as well have been negotiated in February, 1846, as in February, 1848.

* 30th Congress, 2d Session, House of Representatives, Ex. Doc. No. 50, on the Treaty of Peace. Also, Senate, Ex. Doc. No. 52.

CHAPTER VIII.

THE EXPENDITURES OF THE WAR.

"I said one day in Venice, in a company which was very clamorous for a war, I wish that each of the great men and great women present was ordered by the emperor to contribute, at the rate of four thousand ducats a head, to the charges of the war; and that the other fine gentlemen among us were made to take the field forthwith, in person." — PRINCE EUGENE.

WE devote this chapter to "the waste of treasure," produced by the Mexican War, to both the nations concerned. There are men of reputed wisdom and high standing, who scorn the consideration of the cost of a war. They deem it a sordid act to put money into one scale, to weigh against national glory in the other. We confess that money is not the chief good of life, and that wasting it by millions is not the chief evil of war. We confess that there are things which a nation should hold infinitely dearer than an overflowing exchequer, and for which it should pour out its gold and silver with the bountifulness of the rains of heaven. Such are the maintenance of its just rights by Christian means, the diffusion of education and religion among its people, and the contribution of food and clothing for the famished and naked abroad, as well as to build up every good institution, asylum, and public work, that will insure the physical, domestic, and moral improvement of its masses. But we do not recognize this war as among these objects; it belongs to a very different category.

When we look, too, on one hand, at the horrid destitution and consequent degradation and wretchedness of extensive strata of society in the old world, and then witness, on the other, the fruitful cause, direct or indirect, of this incalculable woe, in the war-debts which hang like Alps and Andes around the necks of the European powers, we would utter a cry that should pierce the hearts of our countrymen, and warn them from the ambition of copying into their unwritten history so dark a chapter. Vice and misery need be no riddle or wonder in England or France, after we have read the history of their battles. Doubtless, many other causes besides war have contributed to dry up the sources of public prosperity, to make the rich richer, and the poor poorer, and multiply pauperism and crime to an almost boundless extent. We, as citizens of a republican government, think we can identify these causes in some measure with the old feudal, monarchical, and ecclesiastical institutions that yet have a footing beyond the Atlantic. But it is still our conviction that these causes, bad as they may be in themselves, have derived tenfold virulence of evil from the omnipresent and overshadowing institutions and customs of War. For war, not only in a time of war, with its ruinous drain, near or remote, upon every branch of production and industry in the state; but war, contradictory as the terms may be, in a time of peace, has swallowed up many millions more than the civil list. The treasury of the richest country on the earth, thus becomes, like the sieve of the Danaides, always filling and always empty. And the fortune of the state is repeated in miniature in the fortune of the humblest citizen. For the waste of war is not half enumerated when we have summed up the huge public expenditures, which are as much beyond our imagination adequately to conceive, as the distance to one of the fixed stars, but we must gather up a countless heap of items, each minute in itself, but constituting a mountain of aggregate loss, — the poor man's garden trampled by the hoofs of the war-troop, the corn-fields cut up for forage, the little improvements on his acre ravaged, the one " ewe-lamb " taken, the widow's cow driven away, or the widow's son wrested from her side to bleed and languish in foreign parts. These, — and the catalogue might be run to any length, — constitute "a waste of treasure" and of human comfort in their lowlier aspects, which are never registered in the national legers of the contending powers, but which are all recorded with a pen of iron in the book of human life and of God, where every leaf is a broken heart. There need be some great cause, "known and read of all men," to justify the infliction at home and abroad of such manifold woes, else they accumulate and darken into a crime, before which all ordinary guilt is but a breath of air.

But the expenses of this war, great as they are, will not be too great a price to pay, if they shall serve to awaken any considerable portion of the people to the wrongs and barbarities of this old-world institution. We may rejoice, in one sense, in the heavy burdens men bring upon themselves for their sins. It is of a piece with the great retributive Providence of God, as good as it is just. Fearful indeed would it be, if we could carry on such a contest with a powerful nation, and not have a mete recompense of reward following after it, to the pecuniary, as well as other interests of the country. We cannot act in this world under an exhausted receiver, in which we are cut off from the great vital atmosphere of humanity, nor disconnect ourselves from the compound system of life, in which mutual action and reaction throughout are reigning principles. Thus viewed, the cost of our Wars, our Slaveries, our Intemperance and other vices and vicious customs, is a wise and kind punishment, inflicted upon us to remind us how far we have strayed from the ways of our God, and how hard and harder, the farther he walks in it, becomes the way of the transgressor.

Property is one of the trusts of God to man, and though it is, of and by itself, one of the inferior blessings of life, yet the spirit in which the trust is discharged, and the uses to which money is applied, are matters of the first importance. As we use or abuse its magic power, we can kill or make alive, raise or sink, bless or curse, ourselves, our family, our town, our state. Property is one of the momentous trusts of government, and it may be transformed into camps or schools, bullets or books, destructive armies, or pacific exploring expeditions. It may be cast into the scale of civilization or barbarism. It may be employed to convert the goodly earth into a Pandemonium, or to hasten the Millennial ages.

When, accordingly, the revenues of a people are expended in war, and a debt of fearful magnitude is saddled upon posterity, it is right to demand that a strong and sufficient reason be made out to justify such extraordinary measures. Much as men may be enamored of military glory, and passionately as they may resent any infringement upon their rights, yet war is a ruinous game to the winner as well as the loser. Every battle is as truly the destruction, by its immediate and its ramified influences and effects, of millions of the earnings of the laboring and producing classes, as if the balls were of silver, and the wadding Treasury notes. And somewhere and upon somebody the loss will fall, and fall with the certainty of gravitation. Far away it may be; and mixed up and mystified with endless details of currency, and tariffs and income-taxes, it probably will be; but upon the rich man's property, upon the poor man's sinews even more surely, the reckoning will come, and the money, the mines and mints of money that were absorbed into mighty fleets and armies, and that went down at Trafalgar, or were blown into the canopy of smoke that shrouded Cerro Gordo, must all be paid, cent for cent, and dollar for dollar. Such is the waste and profligacy of war. Such is the tremendous responsibility of those who set in motion its destroying agencies of fire and sword, famine and pestilence.

The figures used in calculating the expenses of wars in general, are so vast that they are blunted in their force by their very magnitude. For when we say, as is said on good authority, that the American Revolution cost Great Britain $680,000,000, that the French Revolutionary war of nine years from 1793, cost $2,320,000,000; that the contest with Napoleon, from 1803 to 1815, cost $5,795,000,000, or an average of $1,323,082 every day, or more than a million of it for war-purposes alone every day; that Europe spent $15,000,000,000 for the wars that raged from 1793 to 1815; and that we of the United States expended in a period of forty-one years, from 1791 to 1832, during which time we had only two years and a half of actual war, the sum of $842,250,891, of which sum only $37,158,047 belonged to the civil list, the rest used for war purposes; when we have read a few statistics of this appalling kind, we seem to lose in the indefiniteness of such inconceivable sums of money the vivid impression which even the loss visibly of a single dollar out of our own pocket would occasion. And it is perhaps somewhat to this intellectual incapacity of comprehending the billions of the war-tax, as well as to moral apathy, that we may fairly attribute the ease with which every government satisfies the mass of its subjects in its outrageous expenditures for forts, and ships, and armies. And the marvel is, after we have surveyed the devastations of war upon man's prosperity, not that he starves, rebels, or speculates wildly about his condition on earth, not that multitudes suffer and perish in pauperism, famine, ignorance, and sin, but that society has any life left at all, that every vein of circulation is not stagnant, and every nerve of motion palsied.

Though much of the property thus expended by a nation is not actually annihilated, but only passes from one hand to another in purchasing the articles of war, yet when we have added to the qualified public account the innumerable private losses that go unrecorded, the sum total would exceed rather than fall short of the above statements. And here observe, that nothing of all that man does under the sun, is so purely, so prodigally wasteful as war. It is killing, burning, exploding, consuming, wasting, cheating, in all its processes. It has no producing power. If called, in company with other trades and guilds to show the results of his labors, the warrior can only point to the smoking battle-field, to the shattered city, to the trampled fields, to dead and dying men and horses, to broken weapons and dismounted batteries, as the most consummate material trophies of his skill. His implements till no soil but "the dark and bloody ground," and his arm gathers no harvest but the harvest of death. His messengers are missiles of destruction, and his arm rests when he has done his weary day's work on a pyramid of human skulls. "Thrifty, unwearied Nature, ever out of our great waste educing some little profit of her own," may "shroud-in the gore and carnage," and "next year the Marchfeld will be green, nay greener;" but for every ear of wheat that waves over the unnatural field, some tear was shed, some heart was broken, some life was lost. The productiveness of war would furnish a new chapter for Smith or Say on the wealth of nations and the laws of political economy.

From the enormous outgoes of other wars we readily draw the expectation, that our frugal republican habits have suddenly launched out into the most spendthrift ways in our recent contest. The Florida war of six years with a handful of naked Seminoles cost $42,000,000. The French war with Algiers has for sixteen years cost $20,000,000, annually, making a grand total of $320,000,000. The Affghan war, short as it was, cost Great Britain $65,000,000. For with all their inventions men have not yet discovered how to wage a cheap war. They invent labor-saving and ingenious machinery for every other work, but the horrid work of battle requires to be done by the practised hand and the steady eye of an intelligent agent. Hence with all the increased means of destruction, man has still in a great measure to do the bloody drudgery himself, and work his own hellish engines ; he cannot drag the reluctant steam or electricity into his service to tend his cannon, or propel the serried array of his lances. General Taylor is thought to have given a heroic command to his troops in his General Orders on the day preceding the battle of Palo Alto in saying, " he wishes to enjoin upon the battalions of Infantry that their main dependence must be on the bayonet ;" but it shows the manual labor, so to speak, of a battle, and the impossibility, as in the arts of peace, of shifting off a large amount of the toil upon the spontaneous forces of nature. It requires men to kill men by the hundreds and thousands. The business cannot be done by machinery.

The time of reckoning the cost of the Mexican war has not yet come. The most that can be done now is to make some general estimates from what is known and authenticated to what is unknown, and to what never will be known. But from documentary statements we learn that this war has not proved an exception to the general rule. It has consumed millions upon millions of American, and what to the philanthropist and Christian will be deeply, if not equally deplorable, millions upon millions of Mexican property. The capital that the two chief young republics of the earth could ill afford to lose, has been squandered. Heavy debts that will require years for their disbursement have been contracted. The energies of many thousand men in both countries have been diverted from industrial and productive occupations. Many have taken up the profession of arms, and will not return again to the pursuits of peace, but will seek to find, in some "Buffalo Hunt on the Rio Grande," or some "Fox Hunt in Canada," the chosen theatre of their adventures.

The cost of the war to Mexico has probably on the whole

been as great as it has been to the United States.* For though her troops did not leave their own soil, nor require to be transported thousands of miles by land and water, yet she had three or four times as many in the field, and the killed and wounded men, cut off in the prime of life from all occupations, were far more numerous. The United States in most cases honorably paid the inhabitants where the country was conquered for all the articles consumed by the troops, but Mexico lost an immense sum by the blockade of every port in the Gulf and on the Pacific, the diversion of her maritime revenues into the coffers of her enemy, and the heavy military contributions that were levied upon the respective provinces, invaded both by General Taylor and General Scott, and by the commodores on the several naval stations. She also lost an incalculable amount of public stores, and the *material* of war of every description. So far as conquest was concerned and the fruits of conquest, all the gain was on the part of the United States, and all the loss on the part of her helpless victim.†

* Three causes have been mentioned by some periodical writer, why the United States have suffered less pecuniary loss in this war, than nations ordinarily do in such contests; 1. The distance of the active warfare from our own soil. 2. The perfect security and freedom of our commerce. 3. The influx for a time of foreign specie, owing to the famine in Europe.—*Advocate of Peace, March and April*, 1848, pp. 176—178.

† The Quarter Master General reports, Nov. 24, 1847, the receipt of $46,960,82 captured in Mexico, or accruing from customs.

The Secretary of the Navy reports, Nov. 17, 1847, the collection by officers of the United States of $530,810,46 in the four cities of Vera Cruz, Tampico, Matamoras, and Saltillo, as military contributions levied upon them.

The General Orders of Scott, dated Mexico, Dec. 31, 1847, assessed $3,046,568, on the several States of Mexico, according to their ability, being " quadruple of the direct taxes paid by the several States to their Federal Government in the year 1843 or 1844." It was not, however, nearly all collected.

The actual destruction of private and public property must necessarily have been immense in the path of the invading armies, and at the sieges of Monterey, Vera Cruz, Puebla, Atlixco, and Mexico, to say nothing of the bombardment of other places, Tuspan, Tobasco, and Huamantla. It will let us into the secrets of war-making a little to read such as the following items of intelligence taken at hazard. Edwards, in his sketch, entitled "Doniphan's Campaign," pp. 153, 154, writes, "at this same Ceralvo we arrived on the twenty-ninth. It is one of the *few* places which Taylor did not destroy along the road:—he had been compelled *to lay waste most of the ranchos and small towns*, on account of their affording concealment to parties of guerillas who would occasionally rob the waggon trains." General Taylor in a letter to the War Department, dated Monterey, Sept. 28, 1846, says, "The command left by Colonel Harney at the Presidio crossing, having been fired upon by the Mexicans with the loss of one killed and two wounded, *set fire to the public stores* they were left to protect, and retreated to San Antonio." The bombardment of Vera Cruz was computed to have destroyed between one and two millions of property.* These facts may serve to show the losses which probably ensued to a

The Secretary of War reports, Dec 1, 1848, that the amount of "contributions, and avails of captured property" cannot at that time be fully and accurately ascertained, but $3,844,373,77 were reported as received, and more was expected from New Mexico and California. — 30th Congress, 2nd Session, House of Representatives. Ex. Doc. 1, p. 80.

An officer, on board the United States' man-of-war Independence, wrote under date of April 15, 1848, Mazatlan, that "we have collected or secured at the Custom House here duties to the amount of $150,000."

* It was computed by some that the bombardment of Vera Cruz destroyed property to the amount of $6,000,000; and Mexican authorities asserted an equal loss at the capital, but it was no doubt exaggerated.

greater or less extent at every point, touched or occupied by the American arms. When to these considerations we add the loss of part of her provinces of Tamaulipas, Coahuila, Chihuahua, and the whole of New Mexico, and Upper California, we shall stand justified in the opinion that notwithstanding what she has received in indemnity, viz. the relinquishment of the claims, and the payment of $15,000,000, as a make-peace, the loss to Mexico has been fully equal to that of the United States.

We proceed to state what that is, according to the most reliable documents and estimates; premising, however, that many years must pass, before any one can say what the expenses are in full; since all the incidentals, — as pensions, bounties, and private claims, — of neither the Florida war, nor that of 1812, nor even that of the American Revolution, have as yet been ascertained and paid. The details, too, in official documents, are so difficult to analyze and understand, that none but an accomplished financier can do the subject full justice. Even Mr. Gallatin himself, one of the ablest and most experienced of living men in his day, in this department of affairs, in his Treatise of 1848, entitled "War Expenses," is obliged, sometimes, to confess himself at fault.

War was declared by the President of the United States, May 13, 1846, and peace was ratified by the Mexican Congress, May 25, 1848. The two nations were, therefore, embroiled with each other about two years. The fiscal year of the United States ends June 30th, and the two years of the war may be regarded as covering, in some measure, two fiscal years. The expenses of the war extended, however, materially into the fiscal year beginning June 30, 1848, and ending June 30, 1849.

The whole expenditures * of the Government of the United States, for the year ending June 30th, 1847, were	$59,451,000
Whole expenditures of the year ending June 30th, 1848	,58,241,000
Estimated expenditures of the year ending June 30th, 1849	54,195,000
	$171,887,000
The expenditures of the three previous years, however, viz., 1844, 1845, and 1846, were only . .	90,957,000
Leaving the round sum of . . . . . . which may chiefly be attributed to the war with Mexico.	$80,930,000
If to this sum we add the money to be paid to Mexico for new territories	15,000,000
Extra pay for three months, allowed by Congress, July 19, 1848, to all soldiers, computed by the Secretary of War at from 80 to 100,000, engaged in the war, say . . , ...	2,000,000
Claims, for which the Government is liable . .	3,250,000
We have the sum of . . . . as the direct expenditure of the war.	$101,180,000

If we take another,† more specific method, we arrive at nearly the same result.

Expenditures of 1845 - 6 over those of 1844 - 5, attributable to Gen. Taylor's movements . . .	$4,299,000
Expenditures of army and navy proper, 1846 - 7, over those of previous years	30,777,000
Ditto, 1846 - 8	31,715,000
Other increased expenditures of the War Department over those of previous years . . .	15,217,000
Expenditures after June 30th, 1848, for return of troops, etc. etc.	4,000,000
For new territories	15,000,000
Extra pay	2,000,000
Claims	3,250,000
By which we have . . . . as the sum of the positive expenditures, independently of the endless array of bounties, pensions, and claims, which will now pour like the Gulf Stream into Congress.	$106,258,000

* See Official Documents.

† See Official Documents.

When to this sum, which has been a *direct* cost, we add the long array of indirect expenditures, that will stretch through the next half century, to reward the officers and soldiers engaged in this war; the injury to the business of the country, by withdrawing so many millions of capital, and scattering it over a foreign land; the destruction of so many thousand lives, the loss of health to so many thousand more, thus sinking a large amount of the productive labor of the country; the employment of multitudes in the barren and unproductive work of equipping the warrior, the war-horse, and the war-ship, with their enginery of death, besides the using of military stores and arms in arsenals; and the interruption of business, consequent upon a state of war with one of our trading neighbors; then we shall not think it extravagant to say, that the *indirect* cost of the war, were it ferretted out in all its particulars, would equal the direct expenditure, and amount to $100,000,000 more; thus swelling the grand total to $200,000,000.

To fortify these results, we will adduce some other considerations, relative to the finances of the war. Thus the military and naval appropriations for the year ending June, 1847, were $40,863,155.96; for the year ending June, 1848, $31,377,679.92; and, for the year ending June, 1849, $42, 224,000; amounting, in all, to $114,466,835.88. A part of this sum goes for other expenditures than those of the Mexican hostilities; but this sum does not include the price paid for California and New Mexico, the claims which the United States have obligated themselves to pay, and the bounty of 160 acres of land* to every volunteer, making, as has been

* "The Mexican War land-warrants will greatly outnumber those of the Revolution, or the war of 1812, as there are many more soldiers. They are worth more, also, as there is a wider field allowed for selections. All the soldiers, who volunteered for twelve months, are entitled to one hundred and sixty acres of land, and the six months' volunteers are entitled to eighty acres. The wife, children, father, or

computed, for 60,000 men 9,600,000 acres, or $6,000,000 in Treasury scrip, if the soldiers or their heirs prefer to take the equivalent; to say nothing of the large sums which were voted by State Legislatures, or contributed by individuals, to equip and furnish the volunteer regiments and their officers, and the thousands and the tens of thousands expended in welcoming back, in a festive manner, the survivors, on their return home.

One Senator stated, in his official place, that the war was costing, at one period, at the rate of $500,000 per diem.

Another said: "I am satisfied, that one year of this war will cost us about $100,000,000." He then cited the appropriations, to justify such an inference. For the army alone:

By the Act of the 13th May, 1846	$10,000,000
By the Act of the 20th June	12,000,000
By the Act of the 8th August	2,200,000
	$24,200,000

Raised by loans, to meet war expenses:

By the Act of the 20th of July	$10,000,000
By the Act passed winter session, 1846-7 . . .	23,000,000
Surplus in the treasury when the war began, consumed,	12,000,000
The necessary appropriations, to be passed the same session	50,000,000
Total,*	$119,200,000

Such were the expenditures made, or estimated, up to

mother, of soldiers who died in the service, are allowed the same quantity of land." — *Newburyport Herald.*

* The Secretary of War says, Appendix to the Congressional Globe, 30th Congress, 2d Session, p. 22: "More than 60,000 claims have been presented under the Act of 11th Feb. 1847, for bounty land and treasury scrip About 40,000 have been acted on and allowed; 20,000 are now pending; and it is estimated that there are 40,000 yet to be presented." See, also, 30th Congress, 2d Session, Ex. Doc. No. 1, p. 369. 90,000 claims had been presented, May, 1849, as we learnt by personal inquiry at the War Department.

March 3, 1847, according to the uncontradicted statements of a United States Senator, made in his seat.

A distinguished Governor of Tennessee, an advocate of the war, declared, in a public address, that the expenses would be $8,000,000 per month.

Colonel Doniphan's regiment of mounted dragoons consisted of 1,000 men. They volunteered for one year. When they returned home, each of them received $560 for his pay, his horse, etc., and his land scrip in addition; making, in all, the sum of $750,000.

The claims of citizens of California against the United States, for money and supplies furnished by them during the war, amounted to $500,000 or $800,000.*

The President, in a Message to Congress, dated July 6, 1848, stated that the debt of the United States, before the war began, was $17,788,799.62; and that, in consequence of the war, it had been increased to $65,778,450.41; thus making the actual war debt $47,989,650.79. He then says, that $12,000,000 were to be paid to Mexico; and that the unliquidated claims, assumed by the United States, were $1,519,604.76, and the interest thereon; all which, added to the above sum, make the total of a direct debt of $61,509, 255.55, in July, 1848, according to the admission of the President of the United States.

From these and a variety of other facts of a similar character, we draw the conclusion that this war cost the United States, directly and indirectly, at a moderate computation, $200,000,000, and that it cost Mexico, directly and indirectly, an equal sum.

Suppose this sum were allotted to be paid by the people of this country at so much a poll, and reckon the population at 20,000,000, then each man, woman, and child, would

* 30th Congress, 1st Session, Senate, Rep. Com. No. 75, pp. 2, 7, 15, 50.

be laid under a direct tax of $10, or say, on an average, each family, of $50. Or, if we suppose the actual expen ses to come within the exceedingly moderate estimate of $100,000,000, we should then have a direct tax of $5 a head. And if the levy were made not according to heads, but purses, the burden would fall on men in proportion to their ability to pay, and every man of substance would ask with an increased interest, What is the Mexican war? Why was it fought? And what are its pleas and benefits?

As the war was ostensibly prosecuted, in part, for the ends of a suit at law, to recover a bad debt of an unwilling debtor, the result has taught the old lesson of the folly of going to law for a redress of grievances. The report of the commission that sat nearly two years on the United States' claims for Mexican spoliations upon her commerce, states that

The whole amount claimed was		$11,850,578.49
The two Mexican Commissioners agreed in allowance of only		630,406.76
The two American Commissioners allowed . .		3,846,311.00
Awarded by the Prussian umpire, Baron Roenne	$1,586,745.00	
Agreed by all the Commissioners . .	439,393.00	
Total finally allowed . .		$2,026,138.00

This was the original legal and conceded debt of Mexico to the United States. Her finances were embarrassed, and she did not meet her engagements. Nations, like individuals, find it hard to pay old debts; and the older the harder. Witness France, witness the United States, witness Spain, witness every nation. But in 1843 a new treaty was entered into, and Mexico agreed to pay promptly and in regular instalments, principal and interest. But she was poor and revolutionary, and the Texan difficulties, and her jealousy of the United States, increased the embarrassment, and perhaps, as was natural, the indisposition to pay. So is it explicitly declared by Mr. Voss, the American agent, in an official letter. Some of the instalments were promptly paid, all were declared good, but procrastination prevailed in the Mexican councils, and the United States naturally became indignant and impatient. This is one of the final and alleged causes of the war, that Mexico would not pay her honest debts. But even if she did not, it was a costly method to collect the dues, to send Generals Taylor and Scott, and Commodores Conner, Perry, Sloat, and Stockton, as sheriffs, with such an expensive *posse comitatus* to levy on the Mexican estate and pay the debt by such an *execution*. "It was," to use the homely phrase of the American philosopher, "paying too dear for the whistle." Then, too, it was not for us, who have waited long decades of years for the old European monarchies to pay up for the spoliations they committed on our commerce; and who, even when they did pay, delayed promptly to disburse to the private claimants; it was not for us, who have in too many States repudiated our debts; it was not for us, the stronger republic, to force to sharp practice and summary punishment, our younger, weaker sister republic. It was not a just or a magnanimous act, and, — what is mainly relevant to the object of this paragraph, — it was not a profitable business transaction; for we now pay for the war, pay for the new territory, and pay the claimants.

The master-evil of war-expenditures, however, is not, as before hinted, so much in the money that is lost, as the spirit that is left behind. This point has been so ably set forth by the *Democratic Review* of February, 1847, that we need not apologize for quoting its language. "It is not alone the war, and the expense, great though it be, that is to be dreaded. We are rich and industrious, and having plenty of resources, can pay any sums. A protracted war is, however, building up a great military interest heretofore unknown to our institutions. The great peril which destroyed Mexico we are about to encounter. The long Spanish war of independence stifled her industry and smothered her commerce. No interest flourished but the military, and her liberties ultimately perished in its giant gripe. This interest, having no sympathy with industrial pursuits, in its nature aristocratic, is already rapidly growing among us. A few years only will consolidate its strength, and spread its influence through all the ramifications of contractors and *employées*, dependent upon war expenditures. Such an interest is one to be dreaded, perhaps, more than any other, when we reflect upon the materials of strife within us, the rancor of party spirit, and the recklessness of fanaticism."

A further consideration which will impress upon us more vividly the wickedness of "the waste of treasure" in war, is the various beneficial uses to which such mighty sums of money might be devoted. If "moneys," as the old Roman said, "are the sinews of war," so are they also the sinews of peace. If the "dollar" be not "almighty," and the god of this world, it is at least an essential instrument in promoting every good word and work among mankind. Money builds the city, and beautifies the country. Money fills the sails and turns the water-wheel. Money tunnels the mountains, and barricades the rivers. Money speeds the loom, and propels the cars, and operates the telegraph. Money gives food to the well and medicine to the sick. Money clothes our bodies and raises our houses. Money erects the schoolhouse and the sanctuary, and puts a teacher in one and a preacher in the other. Money multiplies the Scriptures, and heralds the blessed news of salvation from clime to clime. It is money that is needed at this moment, as the great coöperator, to send civilization and Christianity to those who are now sitting in darkness and the shadow of death, as well as to re-civilize civilization itself, and to re-Christianize Christendom. Money, money, is the call of the educator, the reformer, the philanthropist, the missionary; and it is not a selfish call; for by this power the printing, and teaching, and speaking, and exploring, and travelling, are physically sustained, and "seed is given to the sower, and bread to the eater."

In this light, consider that the $200,000,000 of money squandered in this unjust, unnecessary, and unconstitutional war, would found a library in each of the ten largest cities of the United States, namely, New York, Philadelphia, Baltimore, Boston, New Orleans, Cincinnati, Brooklyn, Albany, and Washington, which should contain as many volumes as the largest library on the continent of Europe, and endow it with a princely fund sufficient to keep it in repair, and enrich it with the accessions of all living literature from every nation, thus opening inexhaustible fountains of knowledge for all future generations, and placing the interests of learning on a foundation worthy of the first republic on earth.

Or, suppose this sum devoted to the endowment of common schools, academies, and colleges, of agricultural, reformatory, scientific, normal, and professional seminaries of instruction; and to the establishment of Lyceums, Lowell Institutes, Adult Schools, Teacher's Institutes, and then a magnificent apparatus of means and agencies of every description would be provided to cultivate what the poet has called

"Acres of untilled brains,"

to develope the mighty mind and the great heart of our America, and to prevent the hourly repetition of that pathetic "tragedy," of which the prose-poet speaks, "that there should one man die ignorant who had the capacity for knowledge."

Imagine such a sum employed in the industrial and material improvements of a country, to give security to its navigation and commerce; to facilitate domestic and foreign intercourse; to bind city to city, and State to State, and nation to nation, in harmonious coöperation; to develope the physical and mineral resources of the earth, and make her not the step-mother, but the own mother, of her children; and how many millions of naked would be clothed, and how many millions of the hungry would be fed, and how much time would be redeemed from inexorable toil to devote to the higher culture of our nature, and to the making not of money, but of men, worthy to be called men!

Or, were it expended in the fine and the useful arts, to join everywhere in eternal union, beauty and utility; to stimulate and reward invention; to carry all the sciences, and, consequently, all the arts depending upon them, to a higher state of perfection; to multiply in the cities and habitations of a free people the rarest productions of architecture, painting, sculpture,—the works of genius baptized into the name of Christ; how ample would be the instrumentalities for developing such a national character as the world has never before seen, except in the dream of some rapt sage, or the vision of some inspired prophet!

Let it be consecrated on the altar of philanthropy, and what chain would not be broken, what prisoner not visited, what sick untended, what beggar unrelieved, what insane given over, what idiot abandoned, what blind, or deaf, or dumb, or maimed uncared for, what inebriate unreformed, what licentious not purified, and what criminal uninstructed and unrecovered!

Or, propose the sublimest of the works done, or to be done in this world, and the one in a manner comprehending all the other enterprises referred to, we mean the Christianizing of the whole world, the sanctification of the five human races; and in the interest alone of this gigantic war-bill we should find abundant means, so far as pecuniary resources are concerned, to set in operation forty-eight majestic missionary and Bible societies, as large as the American Board, and the British and Foreign Bible Society, to work with omnipresent and almost omnipotent power in every land, and shed the light of divine truth and mercy in every benighted heart and habitation, and plant the churches of the Redeemer on every hill-top and in every valley from pole to pole. Call it not folly or fanaticism to imagine such a Millennium. It was once the hope of prophecy; it was later the vision of Christ; and it shall one day be the Kingdom of God on earth.

If this be our strength and glory to raise money, and expend it in wicked and wasteful wars, tormenting our neighbors and ourselves, then is our strength weakness, and our glory shame. If a whole nation will expend without reluctance their kingly treasures, (that might constitute the moral lever to raise the earth,) in the arts of human butchery and misery, in conquest and invasion, what title has it to be called a Christian nation? It has none. It is a heathen people with a Christian cloak; heathen in spirit, and heathen in practice. We may cry, "Lord, Lord," but the use of holy words cannot save the *workers* of iniquity from the condemnation of the Judge of all.

In concluding this chapter, a practical question suggests itself; how shall the masses of a nation be made to feel the abomination of spending hundreds of millions in war? and how shall the future be exempted from the grinding injustice of having its labor and property mortgaged in advance, and forever crippled by the war-debts of the past? In one way, and we believe in one way only. Let these untold millions be paid at once by a direct tax. Pay as you go, should be the rule of nations as well as of individuals. We have no right to make our children settle with their toil and tears the debts of our folly. Now the war-expenses are not felt, because they come obliquely and stealthily, and are so mixed up with tariffs and indirect taxes, and the consumption of the proceeds of the public lands, that few understand their operation. But apply the principle of a direct tax, and every man in the community would inquire into the merits and demerits of a war, and would not fail to clamor loudly and effectually against all wars of aggression, invasion, conquest, and slavery. We are happy to strengthen our position by the opinion of one of the ablest Judges on the Bench of the Supreme Court of the United States.* "All wars should be accomplished by a system of direct and internal taxation. Nothing short of this can show, in addition to sacrifice of life, what we pay for military glory. This was the policy in the better days of the Republic."

CHAPTER IX.

THE DESTRUCTION OF HUMAN LIFE.

"Seek, — burn, — fire, — kill, — slay."

"Food for powder, food for powder." — SHAKSPEARE.

PHYSICIANS are accustomed to make an examination, after the disease has proved fatal, in order to ascertain more clearly its seat, causes, and diagnosis. It is not a grateful task to enter into the bloody chambers, where life was mysteriously hidden; but they do it for the sake of the living, and to prevent the repetition of like effects. The moralist and Christian, too, are sometimes obliged to make, so to speak, *post mortem examinations*, for however painful it may be to live over again scenes of violence and wrong, and to follow the track of armies, yet they feel it to be a duty if they can by this means obtain powerful evidences in behalf of the cause they advocate. They wish thus to call the surgeon, as well as the financier, to testify to the evils of war, and to invoke

* Judge McLean.

the hospital no less than the exchange, to pronounce its condemning sentence.

But here, as in the matter of war-expenditures, the very immensity of the suffering—wounds, maiming, sickness, death, caused by war, — staggers our conception, and paralyzes our imagination. When we read that a thousand men died in battle, that two thousand were sick in the hospital, we no more realize that infinite sum of misery than we do the length of eternity. But let only one image of personal agony rise vividly before us, — the active, hopeful, widely-endeared young man, reeling headlong from his horse, crushed and bleeding by the terrible cannon ball, — or the father on whom a whole family depends, languishing month after month in a foreign clime, anxious, weak, pained, dying by inches, with no hand of wife or child to bathe the fevered temples, or minister the healing cup; and we have a deeper impression of the unutterable miseries of war than solid pages of statistics could give us. And if we could then multiply one by many, and consider what a single hostile meeting of armies is, and does, could be *in* it, and yet not *of* it, could view it as a self-possessed spectator, could see all the cruel machines of death in "awful activity," the earth trembling with the thunder of artillery, the air rent with shrieks and shouts, the light of the sun shut out by sulphurous clouds, the waters running crimson with the heart's blood of thousands, every shot carrying away a limb or a life, every charge sweeping to the dust hundreds of poor wounded, dying creatures, we should pronounce a battle the very incarnation of hell on earth.

But men do not know what war is, how much of all that is most fearful in pain, and terror, and suffering, and death, is as surely drawn in its train, as any cause leads to any effect. Men at home who make war, do not know what they are doing, what mountains of misery and sin they are heaping upon their fellow men; for if they did know and had not hearts of flints, they would say, sooner than do this thing, this infinite evil, "perish our right arm from its socket, palsied be our tongue in our mouth!" Men in camp and field become mailed and triple-mailed in their sensibilities by their dreadful familiarity with exhibitions of suffering; and whereas they would once have fainted at witnessing the slightest surgical operation, they can at last look unmoved on the carnage of Waterloo. So that the history of war never has been written, and from the necessity of the case, never can be. We may get a glimpse here and there, where its thunder-clouds are parted, and we look upon the ground strewed with the dead and dying; or where we walk through its long range of hospital wards, and hundreds of ghastly faces start up at the sound of our steps; but its physical, like its other evils, are too vast to be comprehended by a finite mind.

We are accustomed to speak of the late war between Mexico and the United States, as if it were the conflict of two soulless generalizations, two historical or geographical bodies, that pitched their camp and arrayed their battle, one against the other. The terms are corporate, political, and insensible. Happy indeed were it, if it were the meeting of names on paper, and not of living men in the bloody field. Happy were it, even if the old custom of more chivalrous days were revived, and they, the historical personages who make the war, should themselves do the fighting, king meeting king, or president, president, either in their own persons, or in the representatives, and substitutes of their respective choice and country. Rivers of blood would thus be spared, and the question subjected to an equally fair mode of arbitrament and decision. But the nature of war, as it is now carried on, is far different. It is the personal conflict of thousands of Mexican men against thousands of United States' men. It is the raising of hand against hand, and the baring of hundreds of human bosoms to the awful hail of balls, and sabre strokes, and lance and bayonet thrusts. It is upon bodies keenly sensitive to the least wound, in every vein, and nerve, and fibre of which the Almighty has set the seal of his creative wisdom and goodness, and which he has made capable of vast enjoyment, and suffering; it is upon head and heart, upon life and limb, that the bruises and lacerations come, smiting, crushing, snapping the bones as if they were worth no more than pipe-stems, rending open the flesh as if it were the meat of the shambles, and battering to pieces the image of God as if it were the common clay of the potter. It is not Mexico that suffers by the war; it is some thousands of her people, many of them innocent men, women, and children, who happened to come within the reach of the destroying ball and bomb, in the battle and siege. It is not the United States, that has been visited by pain, grief, loss of life, of health, friends, morals, through the instrumentality of this conflict; but it is certain men, families, living hearts, suffering bodies, agonized souls. In looking then at the tremendous devastations of war, let us remember that they all fall on individual human beings, and not on soulless corporations, insensible nations, or geographical names.

This destruction of human life in any aspect in which we can view it, is a complex evil. It has branches of mischief shooting in all directions. Existence is the free gift of God, and not lightly or unnecessarily to be trifled with or squandered. Every man born in a civilized community, reared to manhood, and armed and equiped with the requisite training, experience, and principle to act well his part in society, is to be considered as so much capital, invested for the best good of the land he lives in, and paying the rich percentage of usefulness and reciprocity to a large circle of fellow creatures. When prematurely taken away, before he has lived out half his days, by accident or sickness, we feel that it is an inscrutable Providence. But when by suicide he cuts short his probation, or when by the exposures and dangers of war, another species of suicide in one sense, he dies before his time, there is a great and positive loss to every interest of the community. Here is a world of work of every kind to do, the season is pressing, time does not halt, the harvest is white unto the sickle, but the laborers that should enter into this rich and varied field, and reap fruit unto eternal life, are taken from their families, and far away are made "food for powder," or mowed down by disease, as if they were so many worthless animals. Little calculation is made to save their lives, except as constituting one of the prime materials for war. In making good a battle or forcing a siege, the aim is not to save the men but to gain the victory. Napoleon never hesitated to sacrifice any number of lives, provided he could thereby carry his point. Every general, in order to be successful, must adopt more or less the same principle. But every man that is offered upon the bloody plain to the god of battles, is one heart, one head, one life less, to do the great work for which men were placed temporarily on the earth, — to glorify their Maker, and benefit one another. So much has been subtracted out of the most valuable capital of a country, which no money can replace. A nation's life has been abridged; a nation's heart has bled some great drops of blood. Human life is the basis and condition to all other good, and in proportion as any considerable amount of it is violently abstracted from the community, do all the great interests of humanity receive a sensible shock.

In immediate connection with the above considerations upon the evils resulting from the loss of life in war, it should be added that it has especially a barbarizing influence upon the humane and moral sentiments of a people. This is true even of the wholesale mortality produced by the plague, cholera, famine, earthquake, or volcano. The heart of a community is apparently stunned by the frequent presence of death. Defoe, in his history of the plague in London, records with graphic simplicity the dreadful brutality and wickedness of the survivors, even while they were admonished every instant that death was at the door, if not rioting in the house. Much more does the waste of human life by agencies of man's own choosing and operating, harden the heart, and paralyze the conscience. War is the most formidable of these agencies. It is " Death on the pale horse," seen by the Revelator,* " and hell followed with him." " And power was given unto them over the fourth part of the earth, to kill with sword, and with hunger, and with death, and with the beasts of the earth." In proportion as a Christian civilization has made its beneficent way among men, it has raised the value of man, shown his worth, and dignity, and set a higher price upon his life. Gross and savage customs have been ameliorated, or done away. All that relates to human comfort, and welfare, has been invested with a new and sublime interest, because of the nature and destiny of the being in whom it centres. But war, waged under the most favorable circumstances, and with all possible palliations and neutralizing influences, arrests these humane movements, revives the barbarian estimate of life, and all that appertains to it, and strides on to its infernal revelry of blood and glory, though it send the voice of lamentation and woe through the homes of a whole people. The oft-repeated spectacle of death under every shocking mode of agony, mutilation, carnage, and disease, steels the heart of the spectator. The news of it, also, sent far and wide on the wings of a war-literature and a martial press, produces a demoralizing influence upon a whole nation. Human life becomes cheap in view of these immense butcheries, and then human virtue too is undervalued. Men care less what they say, or do, or how they live. A spirit of recklessness is engendered. Crimes increase in number and in turpitude. Offences against person and life are multiplied by the contagion of the camp, and the brilliant examples of the battle-field. Many are ready to dispute the maxim, that one murder does make a villain, if millions make a hero. They emulate the daring spirit, and the summary Indian justice of war, that demands eye for eye, and tooth for tooth, and life for life. A whole Christian people may thus be sensibly degraded by the

* Rev. 6: 8.

waste of human life, and the means by which it is effected, and fall to a lower standard of morals and public order. This is not one of the least evils of war.

It is quite as difficult to ascertain accurately the mortality, as it is the cost of the Mexican war. Persons of different views and temperaments will give different estimates. All that we can accomplish in either of these matters, is an approximation to the reality. National governments do not feel it to be a duty to render such an account of their doings, that the people at large can see how much is the cost in life, limb, and dollars of their "glory." No open and intelligible debt-and-credit account is kept. Besides, the books cannot be "posted up," till many years after the war. We have to glean therefore, the census of death from many unsatisfactory sources, but we shall endeavor to avoid the common sin of exaggeration, and to justify all inferences by well-authenticated facts.

There were some causes which rendered the late conflict peculiarly fatal to life. The scene of strife was not, as in the Revolutionary war, that of 1812, or the Florida war, within our own borders. We were invaders of a foreign land. We dared the burning Line. A long march by land, or a voyage by sea, transported the combatants to the scene of action. Their food, climate, habits were changed. If sick or wounded, they were too far from home for wife or sister to visit them, too far to be easily restored to their friends. The process of acclimation had to be encountered under the most unfavorable circumstances. Fever, vomito, dysentery, erysipelas, and other disorders raged among the troops with terrible virulence. Far more perished in the hospitals than in the field. The deaths at the city of Mexico among the American soldiery averaged a thousand a month for a considerable time after they occupied "the halls of the Montezumas," and three or four hundred a month afterwards. The wounded very generally died by the effects of the climate, and the access of sickness. The fact, too, that so large a portion of the troops were raw volunteers, wholly unused to a soldier's life, and often unwilling to submit to the necessary sanitary regulations of the army, accounts in part for the almost incredible expenditure of life. Many, also, that escaped death brought home broken constitutions, and hacked and shattered frames, and will linger out a species of living death the rest of their days. The dissipation of the camp, too, prostrated hundreds, and returned many a once athletic young man to his friends decrepit in mind and body.

While on the side of the Mexicans, (whose woes and losses now at least, if not before, we may consider and regret, since we are at peace, and friends again,) the loss in battle was very great from the precision and rapidity of the American fire, and the greater number of troops they had in the field. They were also ill provided with the necessary supplies of food and clothing, and camp equipments. The army of Santa Anna was in great destitution before the battle of Buena Vista; and after its retreat, the road-side was encumbered for sixty leagues with those who were dying of hunger and thirst. We have no accurate statements of the number of soldiers on the side of Mexico engaged in the war; but we should set the estimate no doubt within very moderate bounds, if we should say, that three times the number compared with our troops were in the field, and that the loss in battle averaged three times as much; and that the loss in battle and sickness together was as much or more than that of the Americans.

The Northern States, according to one statement, furnished 22,136 volunteers, and the Southern States 43,213, in all, 65,349. The Northerners generally enlisted for the war; the Southerners for one year or a less term.

The Report of the Adjutant General, April 5, 1848,

to the Secretary of war * "makes the whole number of *the regular army* employed everywhere in the prosecution of the war, inclusive of December 1847, about 26,690, besides a battalion of marines, (350.)" "Twenty-nine thousand men have been recruited since the 13th of May, 1846." The whole number of *volunteers* mustered in the service, from May, 1846 was 71,309, of which 56,926 were finally accepted. The naval force was 8,000 at least. When to these numbers we add at least 5,000 teamsters, and "the large number of *recruits*," which Gen. Jones says, "arrived at Vera Cruz and other places in Mexico," and were never reported or accounted for, we deem it a very moderate statement to make, that 100,000 Americans were in Mexico during the war. †

Suppose that only one man in five of the 100,000 men, who first and last have been in the war, has perished, and the very moderate computation gives us 20,000 dead. It has often been stated in Congressional speeches, that the American loss could not be less than that number, and we believe it to have been even far more.

The hospital often proved more destructive even than the battle-field.

On Sept. 3, 1846, Gen. Taylor wrote from Camargo, "there has been great sickness and mortality in some of the volunteer regiments."

He writes on June 30, 1847, at the camp near Monterey, "it is confidently hoped that the troops in that camp (near Mier) will escape, in a great measure, such excessive sickness as prevailed last year at Camargo, and which is now beginning to be felt there."

From the same place he says, on July 27, 1847, "great

* 30th Congress, 1st Session, Senate, Ex. Doc. No. 36.

† In August, 1846, Congress authorized an increase of the Navy, from 7,500 to 10,000, but owing to various circumstances it was not increased to more than 8,000.

sickness and mortality have prevailed among the volunteer troops in front of Saltillo."

He adds the following, in a letter dated Camp, near Monterey, Aug. 10, 1847: "There continues to be much sickness among the new troops, both at Mier and Buena Vista, accompanied by an unusual share of mortality. Nearly twenty-five per cent. of the force *present* is disabled, at this moment, by disease."

We see, by these declarations, that the great warrior dreaded the sweeping scythe of disease, far more than he did the sword of the enemy. Indeed he declared, in a speech made at Port Hudson, La., on occasion of the return of the volunteers, reported in the newspapers, 1848, that, "of those who have died in active service in Mexico, the proportion of those cut down by disease to those who fell on the battle-field, *is about five to one!*"

Besides the losses on the field and in the hospital, on Gen. Taylor's line of operations, many perished by the hand of violence,—either in private, or by armed parties of guerillas.

The sickness on the Vera Cruz line was even more formidable than on that of the Rio Grande. It was a more southern latitude. The *tierra caliente*, or hot region, of the sea-coast, and the *tierra templada*, or table land, of the interior, and the valley of Mexico, were all found to be fatal to the American soldier. Gen. Scott writes from Puebla, June 4, 1847, as follows: "The effective strength of this army has been surprisingly reduced. Besides the discharge of seven regiments, and two independent companies, of old volunteers, we had to leave in hospital about 1,000 men at Vera Cruz, as many sick and wounded at Jalapa, and 200 sick at Perote. Here we have on the sick report 1,017. Not a corps has made a forced march, except in the pursuit after the battle of Cerro Gordo, and every possible attention has been given to the health of the troops. The general sickness may be attributed to several causes: 1. The great contrast in climates, above and below Cerro Gordo; 2. The insufficiency of clothing, but little having arrived when the army marched from Vera Cruz; and 3. The want of salt meats, the troops not having had any oftener than one day in nine, since we reached the elevated country; as our insufficient means of transportation allowed us to bring up only small quantities of bacon and no mess pork. The prevailing diseases have been chills and fevers, and diarrhœa."

On July 25th, Gen. Scott reported the sick at Puebla at 87 officers and 2,215 men; in all, 2,302.

Mansfield, in his History of the Mexican War, states that Gen. Scott left Puebla, on Aug. 7 - 10, with 10,738 men, and that 3,261 were left in garrison and in hospitals. Of the last, the largest part were in hospital, where there were, at one time, no less than 1,900 sick! Of these, 700 found their graves at Puebla!

With 3,217 sick in the hospitals at Vera Cruz, Jalapa, Perote, and Puebla, early in June, at the very beginning of the sickly season, and 2,302 at Puebla alone, the last of July, and 1,900 in August, we can imagine what must have been the later scenes of the same summer, as the army fought its way, through quadruple its own numbers, to the capital of the country. The accounts of the mortality there, before referred to, thus become perfectly credible. The names have been published of no less than 700 men, who died at Perote in a few months. Even on Dec. 4, 1847, Gen. Scott stated officially, that there were 2,041 sick, exclusive of officers, in the city of Mexico.

Let us now consider what have been the losses of individual regiments and companies, and how they sustain the above estimate.

Of 80 Sappers and Miners, who left West Point for the battle-fields of Mexico, only 24 returned home; all the rest having found graves in that distant land.

Of the 730 in the Ninth Regiment of Infantry, that left Fort Adams, in 1847, there were but 105 or 106 that returned home, in 1848: 14 died on the voyage from Vera Cruz home, between July 11th and August 14th.

The South Carolina Regiment, of 1,100, had, at the end of nine months, only 80 or 90 remaining, to enter with Scott the city of Mexico. "The destruction of life in Napoleon's march to Moscow did not equal this."

Col. William B. Campbell's First Regiment of Tennessee volunteers, returned only 350 of the 1,000 it carried into Mexico. The average loss was 50 men a month.

"The North Carolina Regiment," says an officer writing from Buena Vista, in Sept. 1847, "was paid off the last of August on muster-rolls made two months previous; and almost every fifth man had died since muster. The Mississippi Regiment had suffered still more. Companies, that came into the field 85 and 90 strong, now number scarce 30 men on parade."

Another officer writes from the city of Mexico: "Of nearly 400 men, who left Columbus (Georgia) in the five companies, we have not more than 40 fit for duty. About 35 are in hospital at Jalapa, and the remainder in that of Perote."

Of 648 men, in the regiment commanded by Gen. Pierce, only 120 remained fit for service in the city of Mexico.

Col. Baker, Member of Congress from Illinois, declared in the House of Representatives, that his regiment of volunteers of 820, lost 100 in six months, in the Rio Grande Valley; dismissed 200 more, to die by the way, or find their way home, with constitutions broken down. He also said, that the bones of nearly 2,000 young men, in whose veins flowed some of the best blood of the country, who had never seen the face of an enemy, were now resting in the mould on the banks of that river.

The Adjutant General, in answer to a resolution of Congress, reported, Feb. 1847, that of the volunteers who had joined the army up to that time, there had, in a period of from sixty to ninety days, 331 deserted; 76 been killed in battle; died of disease, 637; and discharged, in consequence of sickness or disability, between 2,000 and 3,000 men; or, as stated by Mr. Hudson, in a speech in the House, Feb. 15, 1847, a loss of 20 per cent. in about two months and a half, or about eighty per cent. a year.

But it is needless to accumulate such reports. The conclusion is obvious. Many put the loss at 20,000, on the part of the United States; others raise it to 30,000; we are safe in saying it was between 20,000 and 25,000.

And, as we have already seen, if we turn to the other side, we can have no doubt that Mexico suffered an equal mortality. For if the sickness, which was great even among the natives, was less, the destruction in battle was treble or quadruple, if the American bulletins speak the truth.

Owing to the limited medical and surgical appointments of the Mexican armies, and their poverty of means, great multitudes of the wounded perished. When we have added to the above list the deaths by disease, we can have no doubt that 20,000 is a very moderate estimate for the Mexican waste of life. Gen. Scott computed that 7,000 Mexican officers and men were killed and wounded in the several battles in the vicinity of the capital alone.

We conclude, from these various considerations, that the mortality on both sides, during the two years of the existence of the war, reached no less than 40,000; or 20,000 a year, or 10,000 annually on each side. The reports of the generals, the climate, the great number of the battles, sieges, skirmishes, being about twenty-eight, the proportion lost in single regiments and companies, and the great proportion that died by sickness, assure us that this immense loss of human life, with all its attendant evils, and woes, and pains, is chargeable upon the authors and abettors of this stupendous system of legalized murder.

CHAPTER X.

THE HOSPITAL AND THE BATTLE-FIELD.

"Woe to the hand that shed this costly blood;
Over thy wounds now do I prophesy, —
Which, like dumb mouths, do ope their ruby lips,
To beg the voice and utterance of my tongue; —
A curse shall light upon the limbs of men." — SHAKSPEARE.

BUT besides the catalogue of the dead, there is the great army of the wounded and the broken down, whose lot is often more pitiable than death.

We find either reported, or moderately computed, Americans wounded	3,968
Mexicans	7,210
Total	11,178
Add as many more sick and otherwise disabled	11,178
Total	22,356

No one who read the newspapers during the progress of the war, can doubt that we set the number very much within bounds when we estimate the wounded and the ruined in health on both sides, at 22,000. For scarcely a public print came to hand that did not record the ghastly return of the once robust young man, the horrid apparition of gaunt, and maimed, and cadaverous forms, that were once called fathers, or brothers, or sons. A returned volunteer at Brighton, Mass., could not make for a long time his own mother know him, as his appearance was so much changed, and he had lost his voice. He came home but to rest his anguished head on her bosom, and die.

The reasons have already been given why such ravages were made by disease; but the number of Americans wounded in the battles, who survived to return home, was less than in most wars; first, because the barbarity of the Mexican troops instigated them often to kill the prostrate foe when opportunity offered; then, because the slightly wounded in that hot climate, were often snatched away by the intervention of some disease; and, finally, because the distance was so great home, both by land and sea, that many perished in the act of removal. The forces of the United States had not time to be acclimated; and at the very period when that process was in its most critical stage, they were hurried on with all the daring impetuosity of the American character, from march to march, and from battle to battle, travelling in some instances on foot forty miles in a day. Col. Baker, of the Illinois volunteers, and also a member of Congress, stated in his place in the House, during the session of 1846-7, that "of 2,400 Ohioans who left Cincinnati in June, 1846, 900 are no longer in their regiments,—dead, or with ruined constitutions. The number of dead, dying, or lost, will make about the proportion of forty per cent in one year. Out of 18,000 volunteers of June and July, 1846, 7,000 are already dead or gone." There were at one time in a single hospital in New Orleans, 680 of the returned volunteers sick.

In attempting to form any adequate idea of the sufferings of the sick and wounded in hospitals, we must consider that they are away from home, and often home-sick; that they are in general nursed, if nursed at all, not by the natural kindred of home and neighborhood, or by the tender hand of woman, but by strangers and men, and, perhaps, foreigners, who were often indeed more kind than their own people; that medicines are often wanting; delicacies that win a sick appetite are unknown; ill-conditioned and unventilated rooms, poor furniture, bedding, and changes of garments, and the lack of the indescribable atmosphere of home; uneducated and inexperienced physicians and surgeons, according to the testimony of high official authority; the assemblage together of large numbers of the sick and wounded, with all their groans, insanity, loathsomeness, contagion, and scenes of death, in large apartments; the morbid imagination generated and aggravated by such environments of discomfort and danger. When we have summoned up these and similar circumstances of the war-hospital, we wonder not that death resorts thither as to the chosen hall of his revelry, and the inscription seen by Dante, in his awful vision, might well be supposed to be written over the door,

"No hope to those that enter here."

A writer, speaking of a large number of discharged volunteers sent home by the ship "Virginia," and dating his letter Nov. 13, 1846, Balize, La., says, "Half these were wounded or sick, some having lost their legs, others their arms, others being wounded in their arms and legs. Will you believe me when I tell you that with all these sick and wounded, and dying men, not a surgeon or nurse was sent along to attend upon them, not a particle of medicine furnished, not a patch of linen for dressing wounds? Such is the truth, and such, I understand, is the usual manner in which the men who have been out to fight our battles, but who are unfortunate enough to get wounded or become sick, are sent home, like old horses turned out to die."

The testimony of another eye-witness is as follows,—and we should bear it in mind that most American writers and correspondents who went into Mexico, were advocates, defenders, or at least palliators of the war:—"I left our sick at Matamoras yesterday. It makes one's heart bleed to witness the sufferings of these poor fellows. In camp, you must know, few of the conveniences considered necessary to the ill at home, can be had. A man gets sick, and he is carried to the hospital with his blanket and his knapsack.

Bed and bedding there are none, and as the country is destitute of lumber, bedsteads are not to be had. A blanket and the ground is, therefore, the couch upon which the volunteer lies sick, and dies, if he does not recover. If he dies, the same blanket forms his winding-sheet and coffin,— plank is not to be had."

A shell from one of Gen. Scott's batteries struck the Charity Hospital at Vera Cruz, in the siege of that city, penetrated the roof, bursting in the room where the sick inmates were lying, and killed twenty-three.

At the siege of Puebla, the less severely sick and wounded of the hospital were obliged to take an active part in protecting the American quarters; and the list of the physician and surgeon numbered, according to the report of Col. Childs, 1,800.

A young soldier writes to The *Philadelphia Inquirer*, from Perote, in November, 1847, "Oh, the misery of this hospital life, who would believe it! * * *

"Imagination cannot picture to you a military hospital. It cannot be given to you on paper. Tall, bony skeletons, torn and racked by disease, struggling to make a step, tottering along like Hamlet's ghost! A year ago they were among friends smiling upon them. Here they are sick and dying in this Lazar-house of slaves, once freemen! See there! keep back, and let that once manly, now decrepit form pass between the arch. His assistants can hardly support him. That arch he is passing for the last time. To-morrow sees him borne along on the barrow. He looks around, the tear glistening in his eye, but, his manly spirit yet unsubdued, brushes it away. That deep sigh proclaims all hope fled. His shattered mind dwells on by-gone days. He raises his sunken eyes to heaven, and mutters all his earthly joys, — Home, — Father, — Mother! Others, in idiocy or raving lunacy, sink into the slumbers of death. Others, with the loss of a leg or an arm, or perhaps both, are still thankful that they have life. And there are no charms or enjoyment to make them feel their loss. Fame, glory, ambition, have brought many here, but I assure you that bane of society, *rum*, has had a large share in the business; many, many have told me so.

"These few disconnected lines may serve to give you some idea of the state of things here, but my powers of description are not sufficient to show up the realities of every-day life. Were I an Irving, I could picture scenes that would distress you, but which I hope none will ever see again.—It is a noted fact, that many who die here, have their fate hastened, if not caused, by thinking and grieving about home. And all this for Fame. I think she will break her trumpet ere she can honestly sound *the glories of the Hospital!*"

A soldier from Maine stated that he was allowed by the Government twenty cents per day for his support from New Orleans home. The Volunteers from Massachusetts were subsisted home from the same place at about the rate of one cent per mile,—many sick and suffering! Said a Western editor, "we spent some hours in conversation with those poor fellows, endeavoring to understand the meaning of such overwhelming squalor, want and misery; for we do not exaggerate when we say, that we never beheld its parallel except at the Irish emigrant sheds in Canada last summer. The condition of these poor creatures was outrageously offensive to every human sense, as well physical as moral." Said another editor, "Private Avery died yesterday; and the sick receive no attention, except those who are so fortunate as to have friends who visit them. All are broken; many are destitute; and individual charity and friendship constitute the only succor which has yet been bestowed upon those who have found relief."

But not to make these details of wretchedness tedious, let us pause a moment before we conclude, and contemplate this tremendous spectacle of death, sudden or lingering, in war. What but the voice, at which the dead themselves shall live, has potency enough, or can plead trumpet-tongued against the deep damnation of *such* a taking off of thousands of our fellow-men? Life, as well as property, is a great trust from the Creator, to be held, preserved and employed, according to the will of the principal. We have no right to lay violent hands on it ourselves, nor to suffer, if we can prevent it, and keep a clear conscience, any other man to do it harm or hazard. Moses proclaimed from Mount Sinai, Jesus from Mount Zion, "Thou shalt not kill." It is the law of the moral and social world, and it cannot he openly, frequently, and flagrantly broken, as is done in war without involving one or both the parties concerned in a most solemn responsibility, both to God and man. We are pained even at the sight of an animal killed; what should be our horror then at the contemplation of a battle where men meet in vast numbers with all the skilful enginery of destruction, for the express aim of setting this law of God at the utmost defiance, and imbruing one another's hands in the blood of children of the same Heavenly Father, and disciples of the same Saviour! The following is from an actor in the battle of Buena Vista: "The morning of the 23d came. The fight was renewed, and soon the battle became general. The hissing shot swept like a hurricane through the serried ranks, opening huge gaps, instantly to be closed by fresh victims; the shell, with its fearful surging noise, flew over the plain, leaving a blue streak behind, and after cutting down several, would burst, its fragments disemboweling and tearing off heads and arms alike; the flesh would be rent from a soldier's body and hurled in a million shreds, into the face of his comrade, who would shrink as if struck by the ball itself. Brains, and bones, and blood flew in the air over a fighting line like drops of water lashed from its current by a falling tree.

Here the opposing forces stood in speaking distance, and piteously poured a wasting fire into one another's breasts; there the work was hotter and deadlier, and as the column surged forward and back, the thrust of the bayonet was to decide the victory. In a few instances, men threw down their guns, and grappling the hair or throat, plunged their long knives into their enemy, and may be, while the reeking blade was raised for a second blow, the strong and blood-dyed arm fell lifeless. A man would rise from the close embrace of the death-struggle, and, ere he was erect, a sabre stroke had cleaved his skull and crushed through his face. In the rear and on the flanks, heavy squadrons of cavalry hung, and flew in thundering gallop, eager to detect some assailable point, that they might trample to death a broken line. Oh! it was a cruel and heart-sickening sight to look upon that dense impassioned mass of men rioting in blood and carnage like demons."

It is the unspeakable aggravation of the loss of life in war, as compared with the mortality of a famine, or a disease, that it is man killing man, brother lifting up sword against brother, and repeating the example of Cain, in each one of a hundred or a thousand legalized murders. The chief evil of war is its sinfulness, its unholy motives, its fiendish passions, its repeal of every thing good, and its encouragement of all the worst feelings and desires of the carnal man. Its battles, fought on the shores of time, send their hellish influences through eternity. According to the ingenious mathematical demonstration of a great Natural Philosopher of the present day, whatever sound is made, goes on and on resounding and reverberating in never-ending echoes;—the shriek of the murdered, "the confused noise of the warriors," rolling forever through the universe, and repeated to the last syllable of time. This is a faint image of the everlasting evils that will follow on earth and in futurity, the convulsions of war.

The loss of life in this manner is attended, also, with the two-fold painful feeling, that many who perish are not candidates for this change in the ordinary course of nature, but that they are often the young, the vigorous, and the enterprising ; fathers, sons, brothers, who can ill be spared from the sphere of active life. War feeds on some of the most active of our race. But a yet more affecting idea to the Christian and moralist associated with this mode of death, is that it takes place oftentimes not only in the absence of all suitable preparation, but in a state of the most extreme disqualification and violent unfitness ;—the soul agitated with the most tumultuous, if not the most diabolical passions; the weapons of death clenched in the grasp of a dreadful resolution, "the human face divine" lighted up with the fires of ambition or revenge, the eye kindling with exultation at seeing a brother fall, and the word of impiety and undying hate still trembling on the lips. What a state in which to bid adieu to this solemn life of earth, and to enter on the more solemn scenes of an eternal world!

CHAPTER XI.

LEGITIMATE BARBARITIES OF THE WAR.

"Were not the mercies of God infinite, it were in vain for those of the military profession to hope for any portion of them, seeing the cruelties by them permitted and perpetrated are also infinite."—Mouluc, Marshal of France.

War, in its nature, is a barbarism. It implies a return to the brute force, that governs men in the savage state.

It is a substitution of might for right. The parties do not rest the strength of their cause upon the weight of their arguments, but the calibre of their cannon. Since the whole system combines physical violence, in all its varieties and most shocking displays, we must expect to find, in each separate act and scene, the marks of its atrocities and cruelties. Every battle, from the necessity of the case, must be a reign of the Furies. Every camp must be a school of abominations. Every march, though "the land is as the garden of Eden before," must leave "behind it a desolate wilderness." *

These are natural and necessary results. We cannot wound and kill men without hurting them. War is the god of cruelty. It is the embodiment of inhumanity. It cannot be carried on, for a single day, upon Christian principles. It militates against every social precept of the Gospel. Its aim is not to love, but to hate our enemies; to do them evil, not good; to destroy men's lives, not to save them; to return not good for evil, but evil for evil, a greater evil for a less evil, or even evil for good; to curse, not bless our enemies; to see how far it can make mankind, not the children of "the Highest, who is kind unto the unthankful and to the evil," but the children of "him who was a murderer from the beginning."

In bringing, therefore, the Mexican War before the bar of public opinion and the religion of Christ, we shall expect to find it, like all other wars, a system of barbarities, — a reversal of civilization and Christianity. Though carried on between two nominally Christian nations, and with loud professions, at its outset, of humanity, we shall soon discover, by the testimony of unimpeachable witnesses, that it is the same old "trade of barbarism," as Napoleon called war; and that, while it was a contest not particularly embittered

* Joel 2: 3.

by religious animosities, though fought between a Catholic and a Protestant power, and while its period was the nineteenth century of the era of the Prince of Peace, the boasted age of intelligence, science, refinement, and philanthropy, yet that its outrages and horrors are equal to those of any war, of any age, in proportion to its duration and the number of its combatants. Its evils, in other respects, have fitly corresponded to its amazing waste of treasure and life.

There are, in the first place, what may be called the *legitimate and inevitable horrors* of the battle, the siege, the camp, and the hospital. These we have already adverted to; but they deserve a more emphatic consideration, that our readers may realize, in some measure, what a war is, and for what kind of a thing they vote or speak, when they advocate a war. Then there are what may be called *the illegitimate barbarities;* those which military men themselves condemn, and which, even they feel, dim the beauty of their great idol, the glory of arms, and wither the laurels of the victor. To the examination of the evidence, on both these points, we will now direct our attention; and, if testimony summoned from these fields of blood possess any credibility, — if language convey any meaning, — and if the human heart be alive to human pains and sins, — we must feel that we stand in the presence of calamities that ought not to be allowed to drop into oblivion, without giving us their most solemn lessons of peace, and admonitions against war.

Here, also, let it be remarked, that we have, in these accounts, a more unbiassed description of war, as it is, than can often be obtained, from the fact, that those who went into it were, for the most part, not hardened and professional soldiers, but men fresh from peaceful pursuits, and, in not a few cases, ardent patriots and worthy citizens, though they might not, to use the Western phrase, stop "to see whether they were right," before they "went ahead." The letter writers, too, were generally spectators, rather than actors, in the scenes they portray. The two leading generals, whose reports we shall quote, were also humane and kindly-hearted men, so far as the profession of arms will allow. We have, therefore, a fair chance to know something of the real character of war, from the declarations of those whose bosoms had not become wholly steeled to its miseries.

Palo Alto and Resaca de la Palma. A correspondent of the *Boston Courier*, says: "That night was to me a terrible one, which I shall never, never forget. The screams and groans of the wounded and dying on both sides, mangled and torn as they all were, with the grape and six-pounder shots — the conflagration of the battle-ground, fit emblem of the awful work of death which had so long been going on, — the moans of the poor oxen and horses, so terribly mangled, — and the dreadful uncertainty of the extent of our loss, and how many of our friends, who were alive at dinner, were then asleep forever, — the night-work of our surgeons, with their horrible instruments all besmeared with human blood, — were sights, and sounds, and thoughts, I pray God, in his mercy, may never visit me again."

An officer of the army writes from Matamoras, May 23, 1846: "I went over the field, after the battle of Resaca de la Palma; and the sight which met my eye there was one which imagination can scarcely depict. Bodies of Mexican soldiers were lying about in every direction; some with their heads entirely or partly shot off, others without legs or arms, others with their entrails torn out. One man, a fine-looking fellow, was lying on the ground, with a cartridge in his fingers; having evidently been killed while in the act of priming his musket. I crept about on my hands and knees through the chapparal, and at every few paces I would come across dead bodies; and, at one spot, I discovered the body of a beautiful Mexican girl, staked through the heart."

"Go where you would," says T. B. Thorpe, in "Our Army on the Rio Grande," "and there were evidences of the artillery. Ringgold had written the strength of 'his arm' with terrible distinctiveness. Arms and legs gone, shattered bodies, ghastly wounds, all too hideous for the musket, were everywhere to be seen. It was surprising that men could live, thus torn to pieces. And yet the greatest suffering, apparently, was from a musket ball. Had it been grape, or of heavier material, it would have done its work effectually, and left its victim painless in death. As it was, it had gone through the breast, tearing the fine machinery of the lungs to pieces, and yet left vitality enough to have them move on in their ruins, poisoning the whole frame with impure blood, and leaving the patient to suffer beyond the power of imagination to conceive. Poor soldier! His breath rattled and tore away at his vitals; his sufferings were, indeed, a dark spot on the bloody page of war."

He also describes the awful scenes at the Rio Grande, during the retreat and crossing of the Mexicans, and the confusion at the city of Matamoras: "The water was covered with the miserable beings, who, confused and desperate, plunged about in the waves, calling on God to help them, or venting their impotent maledictions upon those who had forced them to a watery grave. They sunk by scores, clutching each other in the agonies of death; and the "mad river" fairly boiled, with the expiring breath of those who had sunken under its dark waves!

"In the midst of the panic, Father Leary arrived at the bank, and by his presence restored order, in a certain degree, among the fugitives. He took his place on the flat, already crowded with troops. It was about shoving off, when down the bank swept a flying column of cavalry. Goaded by their riders, the steeds madly leaped into the boats; crushing to death scores of their victims, and driving the remainder into the river. The holy father raised his crucifix above his head, muttered an ejaculatory prayer, and disappeared, with the mass of his fellow-beings, under the waves.

"Nothing could exceed the consternation that reigned in Matamoras, on the night of the 9th. Between 4,000 and 5,000 lawless soldiers were wandering, panic-struck, about the streets. * * *

"The night was made hideous, by the constant arrival of the wounded, in sacks; many yelled like fiends, as the rough carriage and contracted form started afresh their bleeding wounds; others were found dead in their sacks, having been drowned while crossing the river on swimming mules. * * *

"The more substantial citizens hurriedly gathered together their effects, and fled into the country; many of these fell by the hands of unorganized troops, and their property was divided among the murderers. Hundreds of soldiers were scattered over the country, who pillaged all within their reach, and attacked the defenceless that came in their way. Social, civil, and military order was scattered to the winds; dark crime and unbridled passion rioted in the terrible confusion that followed this terrible defeat.

Monterey. The attack on this place had the character of a battle, a siege, and an assault, and combined the horrors of all. Let us call the witnesses, remembering that they are war-men, and observing that their stories have internal marks of genuineness and authenticity.

Young Wynkoop, of Zanesville, Ohio, writes, "During the fight of the second day, a flag of cessation was sent to the Mexicans, requesting a few hours to bury the dead which were strewed in frightful piles over the field. This was refused, and the wounded and dead lay where they fell, beneath the rays of a scorching sun till the battle was ended. It was then almost impossible for our men to endure the stench, while they heaped dirt over the poor fellows where they lay. The bodies of the dead were as black as coals. Many of them were stripped of their clothing by the Mexicans during the night. Several of those who were wounded during the first day's fight, crawled into ditches and holes to avoid the balls which were rolling like hailstones over the field, whence, exhausted by the loss of blood, they were unable to crawl, or give signs of distress. As a consequence, many perished, though some who were found in this condition were removed, and are recovering.

"I am satisfied with glory, if it is to be obtained only by butchering my fellow-men; and I wish some of our valorous friends at the North could see a little more of the realities of war, and they would not be so anxious to rush into one on every trivial occasion. It makes me sick now, when I think of the scenes I witnessed. They were perfectly horrid. On the night of the 23d, as our shells exploded in the city, they were followed by the most *terrific cries*, perhaps from *women* and *children*, which did not cease till morning. Thank God! I only threw two shells that night, on account of being told the Texans were on the roofs of the houses immediately in my line of fire, and as I was about to open in the morning upon the principal *plaza*, which was filled with four thousand troops, I was stopped by the appearance of a flag of truce, and the result was the capitulation of the city, and a suspension of arms for two months, which I *hope* may terminate in a general peace, and that we may be permitted again to see our families."

But what heart, though it be of stone, is not pierced and thrilled with the following tragedy of real life! To think that an humble, disinterested heroine like this woman should perish in her work of humanity! Hers was the true glory. The warrior's fame is a sham and a cheat. She shall live in the eternal memory of history. We may say, without irreverence, of her, as was said of the woman of the new Testament, that wheresoever this battle shall be spoken of "in the whole world, there shall also this, that this woman hath done be told for a memorial of her."

The following is an extract of a letter addressed to the "*Louisville Courier*," dated Monterey, Oct. 17, 1847:—"While I was stationed with our left wing in one of the forts, on the evening of the 21st, I saw a Mexican woman busily engaged in carrying bread and water to the wounded men of both armies. I saw the ministering angel raise the head of a wounded man, give him water and food, and then bind up his ghastly wound with a handkerchief she took from her own head. After having exhausted her supplies, she went back to her house to get more bread and water for others. As she was returning on her mission of mercy, to comfort other wounded persons, I heard the report of a gun, and saw the poor innocent creature fall dead! I think it was an accidental shot that struck her. I would not be willing to believe otherwise. It made me sick at heart, and, turning from the scene, I involuntarily raised my eyes toward heaven, and thought, Great God! *is this war?* Passing the spot the next day, I saw her body still lying there, with the bread by her side, and the broken gourd, with a few drops of water still in it,—emblems of her errand. We buried her, and while we were digging her grave, cannon balls flew around us like hail."

Buena Vista. "At one time during the fight," says an eye-witness, writing from Saltillo, "we returned over the ground on which we made our first charge. We there saw the mangled bodies of our fallen comrades, and, although animated by the excitement of the fierce contest which was just then renewed, yet I think there was not a heart among us which did not for a moment cease to beat on beholding that horrible scene. But for his straw hat, and a few other articles of clothing which the ruffians had left on him, I should have failed to recognize the body of young Eggleston.

He was shot, stabbed, and otherwise abused. This was, indeed, the fate of all whom I saw. Lieut. Moore, and a man named Couch, of our company, were the only persons whose bodies I easily recognized.

"After the battle, I rode over the whole field. Parties were engaged in burying the dead; but still there were hundreds of bodies lying stiff and cold, with no covering save the scanty remnant of clothing which the robbers of the dead found too valueless to take from them. I saw the human body pierced in every place. I saw expressed in the faces of the dead almost every expression and feeling. Some seemed to have died defending their lives bravely to the last. Some seemed to have died execrating their enemies, and cursing them with their last breath; others had the most placid and resigned expression and feeling; while others evidently used their last words in supplicating for mercy. Here lay youth and mature age calmly reposing in untimely death.

"Among the hundreds of the dead whom I saw there, I was much touched by the appearance of the corpse of a Mexican boy, whose age, I should think, could not have exceeded fifteen years. A bullet had struck him full through the breast, and must have occasioned almost instant death. He was lying on his back, his face slightly inclined to one side, and although cold, yet beaming with a bright and sunny smile, which eloquently told the spectator that he had fallen with his face to his country's foe.

"Saltillo is one vast hospital. Besides our own wounded (four or five hundred in number), Gen. Taylor has collected all the wounded Mexicans who were left by their army, and put them in hospital. It is most disgusting to visit one of these places. All the Mexicans are badly wounded; for those who were slightly wounded went off. They are dying every hour in the day."

Says Capt. Carlton, in his work called "The Battle of

Buena Vista,"—"We imagined that during the battle, and upon the field when the conflict was ended, and afterwards upon the road over which the enemy had retreated, we had witnessed human suffering in its most distressing forms. But such was not the case. The scene presented to our eyes on entering within the walls of Encarnacion, was so filled with extreme and utter agony, that we at once ceased to shudder at the remembrance of any misery we had ever before looked upon. There were 300 men crowded together in that wretched place, 222 of whom had been wounded at Buena Vista, and brought thus far. There were five officers amongst them. As they had received but little surgical attention, and had been harassed and worn down by travelling so far while debilitated with pain and loss of blood, their wounds were nearly all either gangrened or highly inflamed. Many of them were enduring the most excruciating torments; many were delirious from excess of anguish; while others, whose wounds had become mortified, were perfectly composed, and yet were even more piteous to behold, as their very quietness was but a more certain indication of speedy dissolution. In fine, the whole hacienda presented at one glance a picture of death, embracing all the degrees, from the strong man bearing up with fortitude against the sure and speedy fate which awaited him, down to the poor mortal struggling in the last throe of existence. And all intermixed with them, were the bodies of those who had just commenced the long journey, yet warm, and lying in the various positions they were severally in when life departed. Poor fellows! No beloved eye had beamed tearfully upon them in their last moments. No voice of affection had murmured in their ear little gentle words of hope, or that touching comfort, "*we shall meet again.*" And there was no kind hand to honor their remains by straightening them for the grave."

Such is war, Christian war, or war carried on by one

Christian nation against another, as described by its colonels, captains, and soldiers! It is not perhaps in good taste to call up such horrid and loathsome images; but better, infinitely better it is, that we should have our sensibilities even painfully aroused to feel the unutterable horrors of war, than that we should ever by our guilty indifference or unremonstrating silence allow or encourage those causes to go into operation, by which all these miseries are produced, or should exert a direct and interested part in bringing them to pass. What indeed must be the magnitude and terror of those evils in their reality, when the mere description of them on paper is so abhorrent and disgusting! Let us be willing to encounter a horrid image of distress in our reading, if it shall move us to seek by all means in our power to arrest some father, son, brother, fellow-man, from falling into that distress in actual life, or to stay a nation's myriad-handed power from embarking in the business of human butchery.

It was in reference to the action at Buena Vista in particular, and other battles in general, that the highest military, executive, and legislative authorities in the nation used the phrases, — "the grateful task of congratulating the troops upon the brilliant success which attended their arms," — "a great and glorious victory," — "a success which commands universal admiration," — "a glorious triumph," — "brilliant successes," — "gallant army," — "brilliant series," "glorious actions," and many other terms of a like import. But would it not be more in harmony with the dictates of humanity and the Gospel, and with the proper feelings in a free and prosperous nation, that this "exultation of success," to use the language of the American commander-in-chief, should be "checked by the heavy sacrifice of life which it has cost;" and that even if wars are necessary things, which we are not yet prepared to concede, the heart-rending scenes which are exhibited on its fields of death, and in its hospitals of anguish, should have no such epithets as "great," "glorious," "gallant," "brilliant," appended to them? Far be it from us to undervalue courage, patriotism, and many of the qualities which the soldier may manifest in the hour of danger, but the spirit of glorification is not in good taste, either intellectual or moral, in these awful scenes. Fiends in the regions of woe may exult over the fallen and the lost, the sorrowing and the despairing; but it is not for man, frail, suffering, dependent man, needing mercy himself, be he king or president, general or senator, to glory in war and the exploits of war; but if necessity requires such inconceivable atrocities and agonies, to veil his face and bow his head, and pray for mercy on the victims, as he would at the foot of the gallows supplicate for the malefactor.

Vera Cruz (True Cross!). According to the statements of official authority, Gen. Scott gave permission for the foreign consuls and their families to retire to neutral ships in the harbor, or other places of safety, and allotted time before he opened his cannon and completed his investment, for all women and children, and non-combatants, who desired to do so, to depart from danger into the country. But all chose to take their chance in the besieged and bombarded city. The scenes which followed,—behold them!

The General-in-chief writes to the War Department, March 25, 1847, "All the batteries, Nos. 1, 2, 3, 4, and 5, are in awful activity this morning. The effect is no doubt very great, and I think the city cannot hold out beyond to-day."

The British, French, Spanish, and Prussian Consuls, in a letter to Gen. Scott, March 24th, speak of "the frightful results of the bombardment of Vera Cruz during yesterday and the day before."

The following is an extract from the *New York Herald:*—"The bombardment of four days placed the town in ruins, under which great numbers of non-combatants, men, women, and children, were buried.

"The bombardment is represented to have been terrific, and to its thunders succeeded the moans of the dying in every part of the town for several days afterwards."

The *New Orleans Commercial Times* says, "A shell from one of our mortars passed through the dome of one of the churches, and exploded on the altar, killing ten or fifteen women who had gathered there for protection."

A correspondent of the *Alton Telegraph*, writing from Vera Cruz, says, "The French families in the city were the greatest sufferers. I heard a great many heart-rending tales which were told by the survivors with breaking hearts; but I have neither the inclination nor the time now to repeat them. One, however, I will name. A French family were quietly seated in their parlor the evening previous to the hoisting of the white flag, when a shell from one of the mortars penetrated the building, and exploded in the room, killing the mother and four children, and wounding the residue. Another shell struck the charity hospital, penetrated the roof, bursting in the room where the sick inmates were lying, and killed twenty-three. Thus rushed into eternity, in the twinkling of an eye, not only the invalid, but the innocent and unoffending. Such are a few of the horrors and fearful calamities that have marked the progress of this siege and capture."

Sketches still more graphic and heart-rending are given in the *Advertiser*, Auburn, N. Y., from E. C. Hine. "After penetrating some distance," he says, "I paused and looked around me. Save our little party, not an American was to be seen. We were literally alone in an enemy's city. We were the first of our countrymen who had entered Vera Cruz.

"Never had I beheld such destruction of property. Scarcely a house did I pass that did not show some great rent by the bursting of our bomb-shells. At almost every house at which I paused to examine the destruction occasioned by these dreadful messengers of death, some of the family, if the house did not happen to be deserted, would come to the door, and, inviting me to enter, point out their property destroyed, and, with a pitiful sigh, exclaim, *La bomba! la bomba!* (the bomb! the bomb!) My heart ached for the poor creatures.

"During my peregrinations, I came to a lofty and noble mansion, in which a terrible bomb-shell had exploded, and laid the whole front of the house in ruins. While I was examining the awful havoc created, a beautiful girl of some seventeen came to the door and invited me into the house. She pointed to the furniture of the mansion torn into fragments, and the piles of rubbish lying around, and informed me, with her beautiful eyes full of tears, that the bomb had destroyed her father, mother, brother, and two little sisters, and that she was now left in the world alone. O war! war! who can tell thy horrors!

"During the afternoon I visited the hospital. Here lay, upon truckle beds, the mangled creatures who had been wounded during the bombardment. In one corner was a poor, decrepit, bed-ridden woman, her head white with the sorrows of seventy years. One of her withered arms had been blown off with the fragment of a shell. In another place might be seen mangled creatures of both sexes, bruised and disfigured by the falling of their houses and bursting of the shells. On the stone floor lay a little child, in a complete state of nudity, with one of its poor legs cut off just above the knee! The apartment was filled with flies, that seemed to delight in the agonies of the miserable creatures over whom they hovered; and the moans were heart-rending."

"We are yet ignorant," says a Mexican paper, "of the exact number of the killed and wounded; but, by the best data we have obtained, estimate both at not less than 1,000 persons. The damage done to dwellings and edifices is *five or six million dollars*, — which cannot be repaired for many years."

The same authority says: "In a short time the hospitals were crowded with the wounded, the dead being simultaneously buried. The bombs entered the walls of the church of Santo Domingo, killing the unfortunate wounded, frightening away the nurses and doctors, who, after arriving with haste and risk at the church of San Francisco, and the chapel of the third order, encountered the same dismal fate, as well as at the hospitals of Belen and Loretto, where, it is well ascertained, one bomb assassinated nineteen innocent persons. In all quarters perished unfortunate persons, seeking a shelter from this frightful desolation; while the wounded retaining strength enough to raise themselves, fled as cripples, and sprinkled the streets with their blood. Most of the families, whose houses had been destroyed, had lost everything; all the property remaining to them being the clothes on their backs, because what the flames did not consume was buried under the ruins. Hundreds of persons, as well as fathers of numerous families of children, heretofore relying upon certain incomes, to-day find themselves without a bed to lie upon, without covering or clothing to shelter them, and without any victuals. Having been a target, during five entire days, for 6,000 or more projectiles, which separated when they exploded, forming, without counting the stones and rubbish thrown up, other elements of destruction to the amount of 2,500,000 shots, — after sustaining this attack, we remain reduced to the most frightful misery, without any one knowing how, to-morrow, to feed his family."

Tobasco. "In view of this scene, Commodore Perry ordered the vessels again to be cast loose from the steamers, to retake their position for raking the town, and now gave the order to open it, in vengeance and retaliation. Two hours were spent in throwing shot, round canister, and grape, and musket balls, into the place, demolishing parts of those houses from which Mexicans were seen to fire; and, at random, but always with certain accuracy, on some part of the town, the balls and shells fell; and wo was borne with them, even to the sickening of the hearts of those who sent them. Signals, at length, were made by the commodore, to unite the tow of the different schooners to the steamers, — the steamers taking a schooner under each wing. The anchors of the steamers were then weighed, and they stood near in to the town, as they passed up the stream, and raked the buildings as they went by. Winding ship, they came down again, discharging their other battery continually, and, in a naval point of view, *beautifully*, 'as they glided by the town, and now left it in its injuries, blood, and sorrow.'"

Mexico. One of the surgeons of the army, (who has since been dangerously wounded,) writing to a friend after the battles of Contreras and Churubusco, says: "After operating, with my assistants, till three o'clock in the morning, I left the building of which I had made a temporary hospital, to take an hour's rest in the open air. *I turned round, to look at my amputation table; under it was a perfect heap of arms and legs;* and, looking at myself, I was covered with blood from head to foot."

"We are permitted," says the "*Syracuse Daily Journal*," "to make the following extracts from a letter, written by one of the most distinguished officers of the army, to his wife:

"The sight of one battle-field cures one of a desire for military life. If he could see the literal piles of mangled corpses of the slain, — some without heads, some without legs or arms, some with their bowels torn open, the ground strewn with the wounded, dead, and dying, — he would be content with his lot.

"The most heart-sickening spectacle I ever beheld was the arch-episcopal palace at Tacubaya, converted into a hospital on the day of Molino del Rey. The floors of the spacious apartments were covered with wounded officers and men, to the extent of many hundreds, who were suffering horrid agonies, while the corps of surgeons were actively engaged in amputating limbs; some of the victims screamed with agony, while others sustained themselves with heroic fortitude. I had occasion to go through the spacious building twice that day, and witnessed many operations. I saw the amputated limbs quivering with life, while the gutters of the court were filled with streams of human blood. It was heart-sickening, and enough to cure any man of a taste for war."

A Mexican writes as follows, of the taking of the Capital: "On the morning of the 14th, before day-light, the enemy, with a part of his force, commenced his march upon the city. Our soldiers, posted behind the arches of the aqueducts, and several breast-works which had been hastily thrown up, annoyed him so severely, together with the trenches which he had to bridge over, that he did not arrive at the gates until late in the afternoon. Here he halted and attempted to bombard the city, which he did during the balance of the day and the day following, doing immense damage. In some cases, whole blocks were destroyed, and a great number of men, women, and children killed and wounded.

"The picture was awful. One deafening roar filled our ears, one cloud of smoke met our eyes, now and then mixed with flame; and, amid it all, we could hear the various shrieks of the wounded and dying.

"Many were killed by the blowing up of the houses; many by the bombardment; but more by the confusion which prevailed in the city; and altogether we cannot count our killed, wounded, and missing, since the actions commenced yesterday, at less than 4,000, — among whom are many women and children. The enemy confesses a loss of over 1,000; it is, no doubt, much greater."

CHAPTER XII.

ILLEGITIMATE BARBARITIES.

"War is also the fruitful parent of crimes. It reverses, with respect to its objects, all the rules of morality. It is nothing less than a temporary repeal of the principles of virtue. It is a system out of which almost all the virtues are excluded, and in which nearly all the vices are included." — Robert Hall.

But there is another picture, — not of fierce and cruel passions, clothing themselves in the garb of the laws of war, or riding on the whirlwind of battle, but bursting forth, without any law, restraint, or sanction, unless vengeance have a law. Here, too, we see the natural fruits of war, — the natural accompaniments, more or less, of every war. For, when the passions are aroused to their maximum, they cannot be checked at any particular point of propriety, morality, or even military subordination; but are ready to break over all bounds, and rush into the most ungovernable extremes of cruelty and lust.

In order to substantiate the facts under this branch of the subject, we shall quote the testimony of the soldiers and letter-writers, and confirm their statements by the authentic reports of the commanding generals on both sides. We shall thus see that the Mexican War, waged in the nineteenth century, between two professedly free and Christian nations, was in most respects no better, and probably no worse, than the wars of past times. We have said all that can be said, when we call it WAR.

In relation to the march of a body of troops from the Rio Grande towards Monterey, a correspondent of the *Louisville Journal* writes as follows, in vindication of severe language used by Gen. Taylor, respecting the volunteers: "The march of the regiment, from the lawless character of some of those composing it, was everywhere marked by deeds of wanton violence and cruelty. Along the whole extent of the march, ranchos were burned, cattle were shot, hogs and poultry were killed, and even pet pigs were slaughtered at the very feet of the women and children that owned them. The shooting of cattle was often done in utter wantonness; the marauders either suffering them to lie just as they fell, or merely cutting out their tongues and leaving their carcases to rot; thus showing that it was not the want of food that incited them to outrage. These outrages were all reported to Gen. Taylor, before his arrival at Marin, and can be substantiated by Col. Fauntleroy, of the 2d Dragoons; Col. Randolph, of the Virginia Volunteers; Col. Belknap, Inspector General of the U. S. Army; Lieut. Patterson, of the Mississippi Regiment, and many others, if necessary.

"At Marin itself, where the severe language of Gen. Taylor is said to have been used, the conduct of the advanced guard of Col. Curtis's regiment was marked by similar atrocities. The night before the arrival of the Ohio Regiment there, Gen. Taylor had slept in the town and seen the Alcalde, had been the guest of some of the principal citizens, had broken bread with them, and had promised them protection. But the advanced guard of Curtis's regiment entered the town; and instantly the work of pillage, robbery, and devastation was begun. At least four houses were set on fire by them."

The Monterey correspondent of the *Charleston Mercury*, after the capitulation of the city, says: "As at Matamoras, murder, robbery, and rape, were committed in broad light of day; and, as if desirous to signalize themselves, at Monterey, by some new act of atrocity, they burned many of the thatched huts of the poor peasants. It is thought that more than one hundred of the inhabitants were murdered in cold blood; and one Mexican soldier, with Gen. Worth's passport in his pocket, was shot dead at noon-day, in the main street of the city, by a ruffian from Texas. But for the moral influence, and the finally exerted physical force of the hirelings of government, the dark deeds of Badajoz would have been repeated at Monterey. Guards of 'mercenaries' are now placed in every street, and over every building, in the city; to prevent depredations being committed by those who come here from devotion to 'the land of the free and the home of the brave.'

"The Mexicans themselves admit, that before the arrival of the volunteers upon the Rio Grande, all Eastern Mexico was ripe for revolt, and annexation to the United States. Now there is no portion of the country so bitterly hostile to us and our institutions."

The army correspondent of the *New Orleans Picayune*, Mr. Haile, writing from near Mier, Jan. 4, 1847, says: "Below Mier we met the 2d regiment of Indiana troops, commanded, I believe, by Col. Drake. They encamped near our camp, and a portion of them were exceedingly irregular in their behavior; firing away their cartridges, and persecuting the Mexican families at a rancho near by."

"On arriving at Mier we learned, from indisputable authority, that this same regiment had committed, the day before, outrages against the citizens of the most disgraceful character; stealing, or rather robbing, insulting the women, breaking into houses, and other feats of a similar character! We have heard of them at almost every rancho up to this place.

"Gen. Taylor has issued proclamations, assuring the inhabitants of the towns in the conquered territory that they should be protected and well treated by our troops. Since this place has been garrisoned by volunteers, the families have been subjected to all kinds of outrages. At Punta Aguda it has been the same; most of those who could go, have left their houses. Some have fallen into the hands of the Camanches, while flying from the persecutions of our volunteer troops. Recently, the troops have received treatment from men stationed here, (I do not know who commands them,) that negroes in a state of insurrection would hardly be guilty of. The women have been repeatedly violated, (almost an every day affair,) houses are broken open, and insults of every kind have been offered to those whom we are bound by honor to protect. This is nothing more than a statement of facts. I have no time to make comments; but I desire to have this published, and I have written it under the approval of Capt. Thornton, Major Dix, (who has in charge $250,000 of the United States' money,) Capt. De Hart, Col. Bohlen, Lieut. Thorn, Mr. Blanchard, and my own sense of duty; and I am determined, hereafter, to notice every serious offence of the above mentioned nature."

In confirmation of these anonymous and other statements, we cite, from the Reports and Orders of Gen. Taylor, as follows. He writes from Monterey, Oct. 6, 1846, to the department at Washington: * "I have respectfully to report, that the entire force of Texas volunteers has been mustered out of service, and is now returning home by companies. With their departure we may look for a restoration of quiet and order in Monterey; for, I regret to report, that some shameful atrocities have been perpetrated by them, since the capitulation of the town."

* 30th Congress, 1st Session, House of Representatives, Ex. Doc. 60. pp. 430, 512, 513, 521.

Again; he issues orders, from the same place, Nov. 27, 1846, that "The many outrages, that have been recently committed in the city of Monterey, and elsewhere, upon the persons and property of Mexican citizens, render it necessary to restrict the extensive use of riding animals among the rank and file of the army." So it appears that the Texans were not the only peccant soldiers in the camp.

On Dec. 2, 1846, orders are again sent out, to the following effect; "Grave complaints have come to the commanding general, touching depredations alleged to have been committed near Marin and Ramos, by troops and armed parties passing on the road. The general is therefore under the necessity of calling the attention of all officers, commanding escorts or other bodies of troops, and of all discharged men or others who may travel armed, between this point and Camargo, to the great importance of respecting the rights of all Mexican citizens. The good faith of the country and the army has been pledged to this course; and it is the interest of all to see that the reputation of neither be disgraced, by scenes of plunder and marauding. The troops are well supplied with the subsistence and forage allowed by law, and nothing can justify the wanton destruction of private property."

On Oct. 5th a Mexican lancer was shot in open daylight in the streets of Monterey, according to the report of the commander in chief.

The Special Orders of Dec. 7, 1846, relate to a "court of inquiry, convened at the request of Captain C. W. Bullin, 1st Kentucky regiment, to investigate the imputations against Company D, as connected with the violent death of a Mexican."

A published letter from Monterey, dated Nov. 30, 1846, says, "The tables have been turned on the Mexicans, and for those who have been assassinated of the volunteers, a double number of the enemy have suffered within a day or two. It is reported this morning, that Gen. Taylor has ordered the 1st Kentuckians to Ceralvo, to prevent this killing."

"The war," says the same writer, Dec. 1, 1846, "between the Kentuckians and Mexicans, as it is familiarly termed, has created no little excitement both in town and the camp. It is thought that not less than forty Mexicans have been killed within the last five days, fifteen of whom, it is said, were killed in one day, and within the scope of one mile. From this, you will see that the boys are determined to have and to take revenge for the assassination of their comrades.

"Ever since the occupation of Matamoras by our troops, the Mexicans have been cutting off our men, whenever they could be found in convenient places for the job; and the compliment has been invariably returned, generally two for one."

A letter from Camargo, Jan. 8, 1847, says, "assassinations, riots, robberies, etc., are so frequent that they do not excite much attention. Nine-tenths of the Americans here think it a meritorious act to kill or rob a Mexican; and as large or larger proportion of the latter think it is doing 'God service' to retaliate in kind. Sometimes one side, and then the other are the aggressors. Intense and bitter hatred exists on both sides; and the impunity with which crimes are committed operates as a license. There exists a kind of military authority and a species of civil power, neither well defined, nor of much efficiency.

"To enumerate the various acts of violence committed, would fill a column or two of your paper, and probably not do much good. In the newspaper published here, they are occasionally briefly stated. Two days since, a Mexican, well known here, was found in the public road about two miles from town, mortally wounded. He lived long enough to state that he had been met by two young men with muskets and bayonets. They demanded his blanket; he gave it up, and as he was riding off, one of the men deliberately shot him through the body. He leaves a widow and five or six young children. Murders equally cruel, have been perpetrated on our people, and no one can be discovered as the guilty person."

The horrid tale below is from a letter published in the *St. Louis Republican.*

"*Camp of the Army at Agua Nueva*
Mexico, February 13, 1847.

"Some most unfortunate events have transpired in our column lately, which will arouse the vengeance of the 'paisanos' (peasants) in this country against our troops, and will furnish the disaffected at home with new food for vituperation against the war. Occasional murders of our men have been perpetrated ever since we have been in this country,—all killed by the lasso. The Arkansas regiment of horse, from their having been employed as scouts, and occupying the outposts, have been particularly exposed to this guerilla warfare, and have lost four or five of their men. The day before yesterday, it was reported that one of their number had been killed by the Mexicans, as he had been missing from camp since the day before, when he went out to look for his horse.

"Search was made for the body, and it was found about a thousand yards from our camp, with a lasso * around the neck, and tied to a prickly pear, having been dragged some hundred yards upon the face through the chapparal. It presented a horrible sight: the name of the young man was Colquitt, a nephew of the senator. The Arkansas men vowed vengeance, deep and sure. Yesterday morning, a number of them, some thirty perhaps, went out to the foot of the mountain, two miles off, to an 'arroyo' which is washed in the side of the mountain, to which the 'paisanos' of Agua

* The "lasso" was in use among some of the wild troops in Xerxes' army in his invasion of Greece. *Herodotus*, 7. 85.

13

Nueva had fled upon our approach, and soon commenced an indiscriminate and bloody massacre of the poor creatures, who had thus fled to the mountains and fastnesses for security. A number of our regiment being out of camp, I proposed to Col. Bissel to mount our horses and ride to the scene of carnage, where I knew, from the dark insinuations of the night before, that blood was running freely. We hastened out as hastily as possible, but owing to the thick chapparals, the work of death was over before we reached the horrible scene, and the perpetrators were returning to camp glutted with revenge.

"Let us no longer complain of Mexican barbarity, — poor, degraded, 'priest ridden' as she is. No act of inhuman cruelty, perpetrated by her most desperate robbers, can excel the work of yesterday, committed by our soldiery. God knows how many of the unarmed peasantry have been sacrificed to atone for the blood of poor Colquitt. The Arkansas regiment say not less than thirty have been killed. I think, however, at least twenty of them have been sent to their eternal rest. I rode through the chapparals, and found a number of their dead bodies not yet cold. The features, in every instance, were composed and tranquil, —lying upon their backs, eyes closed, and feet crossed. — You would have supposed them sleeping, but for the gory stream which bedewed the turf around them. In some instances, after the vital spark had fled, in the overflow of demoniac vengeance the carbine ball dashed out the brains of its clayey victim."

The following is an extract from one of the Orders of Gen. Taylor in relation to this barbarity. "The Commanding General regrets most deeply that circumstances again impose upon him the duty of issuing orders upon the subject of marauding and maltreating the Mexicans. Such deeds as have been recently perpetrated by a portion of the Arkansas cavalry, cast indelible disgrace upon our arms, and the reputation of our country. The General had hoped that he might be able in a short time to resume offensive operations, but if orders, discipline, and all the dictates of humanity are set at defiance, it is vain to expect any thing but disaster and defeat. The men who cowardly put to death unoffending Mexicans, are not those who will sustain the honor of our arms in the day of trial."

Gen. Taylor showed his sagacity in this prediction, for it was precisely those troops that a few days afterwards were the first to fly from the field of Buena Vista.

It was in reference to these and similar barbarities that Santa Anna said to Gen. Taylor's messenger at Agua Nueva on the day after that battle; "the Americans wage against us a war of Vandalism, whose excesses outrage those sentiments of humanity which one civilized nation ought to evince toward another. In proof of this assertion, you have but to go outside of this apartment to see still smoking the dwellings of this recently flourishing village; you passed the same vestiges of desolation at La Encantada on your route hither; and if you will go a little farther on, there, to Catana, you will hear the moans of the widows and orphans of innocent victims who have been sacrificed without necessity."

We gather the following from the *Boston Daily Times* of May 11, 1847:—

"By a letter from Gen. Taylor of the 4th April, it appears that a party of Americans, under Col. Mitchell's command, the 1st Ohio U. S. Dragoons, and Texas Rangers, made prisoners of twenty-four Mexicans at Guellapea, gave them a mock trial by night, and then shot them through the head!"

The above narrative will lead us to believe, that the Mexican accounts of the war are not wholly exaggerations. They refer to "the thousand and ten thousand assassinations committed by our troops;" "multitudes of Mexicans wandering in the woods, and pursued like wild beasts in their own country, robbed of their property, and driven from their families; the multitude of peaceable and honorable men, who have been insulted, seized and beaten in presence even of a beloved daughter, or idolized wife; the proud barbarity, the shameless cruelty required to burn the village, to slay the simple rustic, the feeble woman and the innocent child, as we beheld at Agua Nueva, Hidalgo, and other towns of the North."

So outrageous was the conduct of the United States troops, that General Mora y Villamil, commander at San Luis Potosi, wrote a spirited remonstrance to Gen. Taylor, dated May 10, 1847, in which he says;* "that the treacherous assassinations of Agua Nueva, Catana, and Marin have not been the only ones;" and that the "ruin, devastation, and conflagration of towns mark every where the march of the invading army." In his reply of May 19, 1847, Gen. Taylor acknowledges the facts referred to, and says that "they were in truth unfortunate exceptions, (to the mode in which the war was generally conducted in that part of Mexico) caused by circumstances beyond my control." He also states the violent provocations which led to the above mentioned barbarities, and says also, "Mexican troops have given to the world the example of killing wounded men upon the field of battle." In a letter to the War Department at Washington, dated May 23, 1847, he discusses the unpleasant subject, confesses the facts, attributes them to the volunteer troops, and says, "while no one can regret their occurrence more than I do, yet I have not to reproach myself with the omission of any precaution to prevent them. Without a sufficient regular force even to guard our magazines and depots, I have found it entirely impossible to enforce, in all cases, the repeated orders which have been given against marauding and other irregularities."

Still later, June 16, 1847, we have the following somewhat "rough and ready" † sentences from the same pen; "I

* 30th Cong. 1st Sess. Ex. Doc. 60. House of Rep. pp. 1139—1142.

† "Rough and Ready;" this phrase occurs in Carlyle's edition of "the Letters and Speeches of Oliver Cromwell," First Parliament, Speech Second. 1845.

deeply regret to report that many of the twelve months' volunteers in their route hence of (to) the lower Rio Grande, have committed extensive depredations and outrages upon the peaceful inhabitants. There is scarcely a form of crime that has not been reported to me as committed by them; but they have passed beyond my reach, and even were they here, it would be found next to impossible to detect the individuals who thus disgrace their colors and their country. Were it possible to rouse the Mexican people to resistance, no more effectual plan could be devised than the very one pursued by some of our volunteer regiments now about to be discharged.

"The volunteers for the war, so far, give an earnest of better conduct, with the exception of the companies of Texas horse. Of the infantry I have had little or no complaint; but the mounted men from Texas have scarcely made one expedition without unwarrantably killing a Mexican. I have, in consequence, ordered Major Chevallies' command to Saltillo, where it can do less mischief than here, and where its services moreover are wanted. The constant recurrence of such atrocities, which I have been reluctant to report to the department, is my motive for requesting *that no more troops may be sent to this column from the state of Texas*." *

A few items respecting the invading "Army of the West" will give a like melancholy picture of unbridled passions and cruel and disgraceful excesses, at which every feeling of common justice and humanity cries out with horror. But we record these things not to heap opprobrium upon individuals, but to demonstrate the abominableness of a system; we do it not, because we love our country less, but because we love peace and right more.

F. S. Edwards in his work, "A Campaign in New Mexico," says, when at Ceralvo, "I have been credibly informed that when these rangers are sent out on scouting parties, a

* 30th Cong. 1st Sess. Ex. Doc. No. 60. p. 1178. The italics are ours.

Mexican guide is generally provided, but that he never returns; the Texans always shooting him on some pretext or other before he gets back. * * *

"One of the most dastardly acts I ever heard of was perpetrated by half a dozen Texan officers a short time before we came down. They had lost their way, and hired a Mexican to show them to their camp, which he faithfully performed; but when they came in sight of it, they drew lots who should shoot their faithful and unsuspecting guide;—the one on whom the lot fell, immediately drew a pistol and shot him."

The same author relates that in his march from Camargo to Reinosa, one of the party incautiously advanced two or three hundred yards ahead of the guard, and was shot by some Mexicans who were seen riding off at full speed. His comrades when they arrived at the next small town, searched for the murderers, and having as they supposed found them, killed seven men, and burned down the house in which they were found.

Dr. Wislizenus, in "a Memoir of a Tour to Northern Mexico," published under authority of Congress,* writing under the head of Parras, May 14, 1847, says; "one of our waggon drivers, a very quiet man, had been assaulted by a Mexican loafer, and received several wounds, from the effect of which he afterwards died. As the prefect of Parras was not able to find out the guilty person, the friends of the wounded man took revenge on some Mexicans, and more disturbance would have grown out of it, if we had stayed longer."

We quote another passage from the same book. "About six miles from Marin, is the spot where General Canales, with his guerilla bands, had captured, some months past, a rich train of the American army, and killed most of the unarmed waggon drivers. The bones of these ill-fated

* 30th Congress, 1st Session, Senate. Miscellaneous, No. 26. p. 73, 78.

men, which were either not buried at all, or dragged out by the wolves, were scattered about in all directions. Another more horrid spectacle offered itself to our eyes near Agua Negra, a deserted village, where a man (and to judge from pieces of clothing, an American) had been burnt to ashes, some bones only being left. In seeing such horrors, known only in old Indian warfare, can any one blame the American troops for having sought revenge, and burning all the villages and ranchos on their route which gave refuge to such bands of worse than highway robbers? The right of retaliation,(?) as well as expediency, command, in my opinion, such measures against such unusual warfare; and when carried out with some circumspection, it will break up those guerilla bands much sooner than too lenient a course."

He states that at Ceralvo on May 22, 1847, Nicholas Garcia, a well known chief of a guerilla band, "who was said to have committed many cruelties against Americans," was captured by some Texan Rangers, and shot the same day in the public Plaza; "dying like a brave man."

The following extract from the orders of Gen. Wool will speak for itself.

Headquarters, Army of Occupation,
Monterey, Mexico, February, 27, 1848.

"A band of American robbers, composed principally of deserters (chiefly from the Texas Battalion, and Captain Mear's company of Volunteer Cavalry,) dishonorably discharged soldiers, and followers of the Army, have been ravaging the country from Parras to the Presidio de Rio Grande, ravishing the women, and committing every species of atrocity on the defenceless inhabitants.

"A similar party has recently robbed an entire village, under the pretence of being a detachment of the American Army, sent to levy contributions on the place.

"These acts so criminal in themselves, and reflecting so much approbrium on the American name, call upon every one to make all possible exertions to apprehend the villains, and bring them to punishment. The officers commanding at Monclova, Presidio, Laredo, Mier, and Ceralvo will endeavor to effect this object by every means in their power."

By command of brigadier General Wool,

IRVIN McDOWELL, A. A. G."

It is unnecessary to go into California and New Mexico, and adduce testimony of a like ignominious character against some of the actors in the Mexican war. It might be said that in those remote and barbarous regions nothing but outrage and revenge could be expected. We will come then to the theatre of Gen. Scott's operations from Vera Cruz to Mexico, and substantiate the general truth of the statements made, by his own indignant words.

The difficulties began at the very outset of the Campaign. Gen. Scott reports to the Department at home, in a letter dated Vera Cruz, April 5, 1847 ;* "the seven old volunteer regiments with me, now become respectable in discipline and efficiency, cannot fail to give us much trouble when the time of their discharge and transportation back to their homes, shall arrive."

* * * * * *

"The inhabitants of this city, under the excellent government of Brevet Major General Worth, are beginning to be assured of protection, and to be cheerful. Those in the vicinity have suffered more from green recruits, who much dilute the regular companies, and from volunteers. My last orders, No. 87, herewith, against outrages, have rallied thousands of good soldiers to the support of authority. In the mean time, claims for damages, principally on the part of neutrals, through their consuls, have been many.

* 30th Congress, 1st Session, Ex. Doc. No. 60. pp. 910, 914.

I am without authority or means to indemnify, and can only feel and deplore the disgrace brought upon our arms by undetected villains."

These extracts are from the orders above mentioned, dated Vera Cruz, April 1, 1847. "Notwithstanding the strong provisions of printed general orders, No. 20, proclaiming *martial law*, many undoubted atrocities have been committed in this neighborhood, by a few worthless soldiers, both regulars and volunteers, which, though stamping disgrace upon the whole army, remain unpunished, because the criminals have not been seized, and reported by eye-witnesses of the atrocities. * * *

"One more appeal is made to the ninety-seven honorable men, against, perhaps, the three miscreants in every hundred. Certainly the great mass ought not to allow themselves to be dishonored by a handful of scoundrels, who scout all religion, morals, law and decency. Therefore let every bad man be denounced in his act of guilt, seized, and reported for trial, and this army will march in triumph, and be every where kindly received, and supplied with necessaries and comforts by the peaceful and unoffending inhabitants of the country."

We have spoken in another connection of the hanging of Isaac Kirk, a free colored citizen of the United States, at Vera Cruz, April 10, 1847.

It is needless to encumber these pages with detailed accounts of the outrages to persons, property and liberty, which marked the course of the American Army, and the horrible deeds done by bands of the Mexican guerillas. They are a part of the history of the war, but they find little space for memory except on the tablets of those bruised and broken hearts that encountered the storm of invasion.

The American commander writes from the city of Mexico, Oct. 13, 1847: "I have heard of many outrages and disorders said to have been committed by Major Lally's detachment about Jalapa. I trust that the rumors greatly exaggerate the facts ; or rather that they are entirely false. I will tolerate no disorders of any kind, but cause all to be rigorously punished. No officer or man, under my orders, shall be allowed to dishonor me, the army, and the United States with impunity."

In a letter, dated Dec. 25, 1847, he says further ; "I do not mean to accuse the reinforcements generally of deficiency in valor, patriotism, or moral character. Far from it ; but among all new levies, of whatever denomination, there are always a few miscreants in every hundred; enough without *discipline* to disgrace the entire mass, and what is infinitely worse,—the *country* that employs them. My daily distresses under this head weigh me to the earth."

The following extract from an American correspondent in the city of Mexico will illustrate the nature of some of Gen. Scott's "distresses."

"On Sunday night a Texan Ranger named Adam Alsence, of Capt. Robert's company, was attacked by a number of Mexicans in the suburbs of the city, and killed. He was mangled in a brutal manner, and the Texans, exasperated at the cruel death of their comrade, sallied into the streets the next evening, to the number of fifteen or twenty, and proceeding to the quarter where Alsence was killed, took fearful vengeance upon a party whom they found armed with pistols and knives. Seventeen of the Mexicans are reported killed, and forty wounded. Alsence was a German, and served in Bonaparte's Cavalry and was a good and faithful soldier."*

* The following is an extract from a letter in the *New Orleans Delta*, dated City of Mexico, Dec. 13, 1847. "About an hour ago, some of them, (Texans) were quietly passing through one of the streets, when a crowd of leperos gathered around them, and commenced

The following is an extract from a letter to Gen. Scott from Santa Anna relative to the renewal of hostilities after the armistice and the fruitless attempt to negotiate a peace. He says, and with the above declarations of the American General in our recollection, we shall probably think that he does not speak altogether *a la Mexique ;* "I have with pain and indignation, received communications from the cities and towns occupied by the army of your excellency, upon the violations of temples consecrated to the worship of God ; upon the robbery of the sacred vessels, and profanation of the images, venerated by the Mexican people. I have been profoundly afflicted by the complaints of fathers and husbands upon the violation of their wives and daughters. Those same cities and towns have been sacked, not only in violation of the armistice, but even of the sacred principles recognized and observed by civilized nations. I had guarded silence until now, for the purpose of not chilling a negotiation that gave hopes of terminating a scandalous war, which your excellency has justly characterized as unnatural."*

A few words in conclusion. The dark and dismal pages through which we have led our readers in these chapters are but too easily interpreted. They are the old story of war. They are the picture, not only of stately battles, in which horror is legitimated, but of a running warfare, embittered by old Texan feuds, and waged between the half-savage

throwing stones;—the result of which was, that in a very few minutes there were ten dead Mexicans lying in the street, and two men, badly wounded, taken to the guard-house."

Another paper records the following. "The *Arco Iris* says a detachment of American soldiers quartered at Medelin, started for a ball in the village about 11 o'clock at night. The ball party took alarm, and one of them discharged a pistol at the advancing Americans, who returned the fire, killing seven, and wounding nine, one of whom was a woman."

* 30th Congress, 1st Session, Senate, Ex. Doc. No. 52, p. 347.

guerillas of Mexico, and the lynch-gangs of the border and hunter emigrant population of the Western and South Western United States, whose conduct on their way to the seat of war, gave evidence to the cities through which they passed, what would be the fulfilment of their career when they were poured into Mexico. Beasts of prey are dangerous when they are set loose. The regular soldier may have a species of war-conscience, which is better than none at all. But they who go on a human hunt for the love of it, may be expected to dabble in blood even if it be a little out of the regular "orders."

But after crossing such streams of gore as we have now waded through, three questions arise which we would respectively offer to the consideration of both parties, the advocates of war, and the friends of peace.

1. What national right can be redressed by an infinite series of individual wrongs?

2. What true glory can be found in connection with the perpetration of endless injuries and miseries?

3. What "healing peace," to use an official phrase, can be cemented by a boundless expenditure of life and treasure, or based on the memory of ten thousand cruelties, sufferings, and wrongs?

CHAPTER XIII.

MILITARY EXECUTIONS.

"But grow like savages, — as soldiers will,
That nothing do but meditate on blood." — SHAKSPEARE.

ANOTHER list of the barbarities of the Mexican war includes the punishments inflicted upon deserters and other criminals. Many who have been most strenuous advocates of this war, are earnestly opposed to capital punishment. But their inconsistency will be apparent when it is recollected, that probably more persons have been shot and hung for various crimes by the American officers in Mexico during the last two years, than would be capitally executed in the whole United States in the ordinary course of justice during ten years. Some of these executions, too, have been conducted in a manner repulsive to every humane and Christian sentiment.

As the American army contained many Irish, German, and other emigrants from Europe, the Mexican generals issued proclamations, and employed every means in their power to entice away the soldiers from their allegiance. They offered large bounties to deserters, promising land and money to officers and soldiers, and giving the officers a guaranty that they should retain their former military rank.

These exertions were far from being in vain, for no sooner was Gen. Taylor encamped on the banks of the Rio Grande, than the desertions began, and according to the Report of the Secretary of War, made to the Senate, April 10, 1848, the enormous number of 4,966 men had deserted in Mexico from the troops of the United States. In fact, whole platoons in some instances either went over to the enemy, or returned home. The *Matamoras Flag* stated that on Dec. 22, 1847, about 25 Texan Rangers deserted at one time from Saltillo, and came home. Other cases occurred of a similar character.

To save the army from such disorders, severe punishment, as imprisonment, whipping, and other barbaric inflictions were resorted to, and a considerable number were put to death for desertion, murder, or other crimes.

T. B. Thorpe mentions, that two men were shot in the act of desertion at Matamoras, and that several were drowned in attempting to swim the river. Gen. Taylor, in a letter to the Department, dated May 30, 1846, confirms the account, and says, that soon after his "arrival on the Rio Grande the evil of desertion made its appearance, and increased to an alarming extent;" and that verbal orders were given to the pickets to hail those who were swimming the river, and if they did not return, to shoot them on the spot.

The *Matamoras Flag* states that five Mexican guerillas were hanged Dec. 19, 1847, in the main plaza of Saltillo for the murder of three discharged Mississippians at Rinconada Pass; and that an American named Neazum was hanged a few days previously, for having murdered a Mexican in the streets of the city.

The *Chicago Tribune* records the death of Lieut. James M. Stewart, of Niles, Michigan, who was hanged in Mexico for haying been enraged at a superior officer who struck him, and having run him through with his sword. It goes on to remark, that "an interesting family, consisting of a wife and several young children, are thus deprived of husband, father, and protector. This is another of the legitimate fruits of bloody, infamous, brutal, forever-to-be-detested war."

Isaac Kirk, a free man of color, according to Gen. Scott's Reports of April, 1847, was hung at Vera Cruz for "committing or attempting to commit a rape" upon a Mexican woman; and in an Address to the Mexican people, he appeals and says, "is this not a proof of good faith and energetic discipline?"

Two young Mexicans of rank and refinement were executed Nov. 24, 1847, in the city of Jalapa.

The *Vera Cruz Indicator* has the following account of the affair:—

"Gen. Patterson, while in Jalapa, governed with a rigid hand. The Mexicans complain bitterly of the recent execution, under his directions, of two young officers, Ambrosio Alcalde and Antonio Garcia, who were taken at Jalconumco with a party of guerillas, some time since, and who were alleged to have broken their parole. This the two officers and their friends denied, but the evidence was too strong against them to permit their escape.

"When the sentence was published, the whole city rose to beg for the lives of the young men, and deputations were sent to Gen. Patterson from the council, from the resident foreigners, from the clergy, regular and secular, from the ladies of the principal families, and the ladies of the convents, beseeching him to spare the lives of the unhappy youths, but without avail. They were hanged in the Plazuela de San Jose at noon of the 24th ultimo. Their bodies were delivered over to their friends, and after lying in state a few hours, were buried with the highest honors that public grief could devise. The whole city put on mourning, solemn processions lined every street, and the *miserere* was chanted in the churches. A gloom was thrown over the city which is not yet dissipated."

The *Arco Iris*, says that "Gen. Patterson's division left Jalapa on the 25th ult. Before his departure, he hanged, on the 23d, two American teamsters, for having killed a Mexican boy twelve years old."

Reynolds, an American soldier of the 8th Regiment of Infantry, was hanged at Jalapa on Dec. 29, 1847, for the murder of some Mexican women.

The *National Intelligencer* recorded the execution at Saltillo on Dec. 28, 1847, of Victor Galbraith, a bugler in Capt. Miers' company of volunteer cavalry, who was shot *for threatening the captain's life.*

But the most cruel and sanguinary scene that was probably ever enacted in war under the form of its Draconic code of laws, occurred at the villages of San Angel and Mixcoac in the valley of Mexico. On the 9th of September, 1847, 16 deserters were hanged at San Angel, and on the 10th, 4 were hanged at Mixcoac. But as if these victims were not enough to glut the cruel spirit of war, on the 13th, 30 more were hanged at Mixcoac, making in all 50 victims of capital punishment in four days. Without crediting the Mexican account that they were noosed by the neck and drawn up, and that they died by inches by being strangled with their own weight, their agony lasting more than an hour; it is nevertheless an unquestioned fact, that, in the last case of execution, the poor wretches, in order to slake the thirst of vengeance, and "to associate with the glory of their regiments the gloom of their tribunals," were pinioned, ropes put around their necks, and each man placed under a gallows, and *there made to wait nearly two hours*, with death staring them in the face, until, according to the declaration and promise of the presiding officer, a colonel, whose name shall not pass our pen, the neighboring heights of Chapultepec, then assaulted by the American troops, were carried; and that when the American flag was planted on that fortress, thirty men were instantly launched into eternity! We ask why have not the official reports of these transactions been published, with the other numerous documents of the war, if they are not too black and odious to bear the light of day, and the free judgment of a people, professing to be governed by the humane spirit of Christianity?

The rest of this battalion of San Patricio,* under the command of Reilly, who were captured when desperately fighting at Contreras and Churubusco against the Americans, were severely punished; some by being "whipped with fifty lashes each, the letter D. for deserter being branded with a red hot iron upon the cheek, and then condemned to wear an iron yoke weighing eight pounds, with three prongs, each one foot in length around the neck; to be confined at hard labor

* *Nativity of the Deserters.*—The *New York Police Gazette* contains "the names and places of nativity of the deserters recently recaptured by our army, from which we are sorry to learn that a large portion were Americans. They are classed as follows: Americans 54, Irishmen 34, Germans 17, Scotch 4, and one each from England, Nova Scotia, France and Poland."

in charge of the guard during the time the army should remain in Mexico, and then to have their heads shaved, and to be drummed out of the service;" and others were flogged with 200 lashes each, after being compelled to dig the graves of their companions, who were executed.

Several others, both officers and soldiers, by the names of Hare, Dutton, Madson, Wragg, Stewart, Wall, and others, were convicted at Mexico of burglary and murder, after the city was occupied by Scott, and sentenced to be hanged, but they were afterwards respited, or wholly pardoned.

Ruxton, in his "Adventures in Mexico," p. 230, says, in reference to the revolution in New Mexico, Jan., 1847, that "the troops marched out of Santa Fé, attacked their pueblo, and leveled it to the ground, killing many hundreds of its defenders, and taking many prisoners, most of whom were hanged." Another account states, that "fifteen Mexicans were executed as conspirators."

One man was executed at the town of Santa Cruz on Monterey Bay, in California.

We record then in all, 82 Americans and Mexicans, who were shot or hanged by the martial law, by the Americans, — and we probably have not ascertained all, — an amount of capital punishment, small indeed by the side of the wholesale slaughter of the battle-field, but worthy of being considered by those who are strenuous advocates of the repeal of the death-penalty, for it is, as we have said, a greater number than would suffer thus in the ordinary course of criminal justice in ten years in the United States.

CHAPTER XIV.

ILLEGALITIES.

"Laws are silent in war." — CICERO.

IT has already been strongly intimated, if not declared in so many words, that the laws of nations, and the constitution and laws of our own country, have been repeatedly and flagrantly broken in the war with Mexico. But in order to set this subject in a more vivid light, we propose to devote this chapter, if not the most important, at least one of the most curious, in the history of the day, to the various illegalities which have been committed. Other portions of this review will sufficiently demonstrate the opposition of the war to every principle of liberty and Christianity, but it will be the aim of these few pages to elucidate its equal antagonism to the laws of man, and to show that when even a civilized people burst through the enclosures of truth and right, they manifest in many respects the same reckless disregard of human statutes and constitutions, as is thought to belong to earlier stages of society.

Numerous unlawful acts preceded the war. The conquest of Mexican territory by citizens of the United States, with the connivance, if not the aid, of the national and State government, was contrary to the law of nations. The seizure of Monterey, in California, Oct. 19, 1842, by Commodore Jones, was a lawless act, disavowed indeed by the Government, but the perpetrator was never punished. The annexation of Texas, by a joint resolution, was contrary to our treaty with Mexico, to the comity of nations, and to the Constitution of the United States.

The act of war at first was illegal. It was a violation of the law of nations to enter a disputed territory, and hold it by force of arms, when it was fully conceded that it was debatable ground, and when we had recognized Mexican custom-houses within the year in that same territory by specific acts of Congress. Detailed proofs and illustrations of this point are contained in chapter seventh, and need not be recounted.

The origin of the war also was contrary to the Constitution of the United States. By this instrument it is reserved to Congress "to declare war, repel invasions." But by a vote of the House of Representatives, Jan 3, 1848, it was resolved, that the war with Mexico "was unnecessarily and unconstitutionally begun by the President of the United States;" and distinguished statesmen deliberately expressed their opinion, that he had brought himself within the peril of an impeachment. Mr. Calhoun said in the Senate, March 17, 1848, "I hold that the President had no more right to order the army to march into the disputed territory, than he had to order it to march into Mexico.*

The difficulties with Mexico were not brought before Congress, although then in session, until Gen. Taylor had commenced hostilities; and when the question was presented by an Executive Message, it was hurried to a decision in a surprise and panic, without the documents appended to it being allowed to be even read, and without any proper debate or deliberation.

The object of the war was an illegal and unconstitutional one. There are provisions in the Constitution to repel invasions, but not to make them. Far as heaven is from earth, was the thought of the framers of that instrument from sanc-

* Printed speech, p. 16.

tioning by one syllable of theirs the spirit of conquest. Besides, liberty is the spirit of that great charter, and a war to extend slavery, the slave-trade, and the political power of slavery, clashes with the genius of Independence. What is its preamble? "We, the people of the United States, in order to form a more perfect union, *establish justice, ensure domestic tranquillity*, provide for the common defence, promote the general welfare, *and secure the blessings of liberty to ourselves and our posterity*, do ordain and establish this Constitution of the United States of America."

The progress of the war was attended by many proceedings as much at variance with the laws of man as the laws of God. For the details we refer to other chapters of this work. The expedition of Fremont into California, in 1845 and 1846, was palpably unjustifiable, and its purpose but very thinly disguised. The absolution by Gen. Kearney of the inhabitants of New Mexico and California, from their allegiance to Mexico, his compelling the native officers to take the oath of allegiance to the United States,* and the execution as traitors by other commanders of those who rose and attempted to destroy their invaders, and shake off their control, were deeds that find no justification in the recognized laws of nations, however sanctioned by the bloody code of Mars. Many other illegitimate barbarities of the war are recounted in chapter thirteenth.

The introduction from abroad into Mexico, while the war was waging, by a written passport of the Executive, of the greatest General that country could boast, in the person of Santa Anna, who immediately placed himself at the head of large armies, and caused an immense loss of life and treasure to the Americans, was palpably against the rule forbidding to "give aid and comfort" to the enemies of our country, though the intention no doubt was to secure an

* 30th Congress, 1st Session, Ex. Doc. No. 41, pp. 27, 28.

earlier peace, and the cession of the territories which were coveted.

The annexation of the territories of New Mexico and California, by General Kearney and Commodore Stockton to the United States, before any treaty of peace had been made, and before Congress had passed any act to that effect, were high-handed violations of the Constitution, and also of the law of nations. They were too gross to be owned as acts of the Government even in this history of illegalities, and, like not a few of the other measures of the commanding officers in Mexico, were condemned at Washington.*

The establishment in Mexico of a system of tariffs and taxes by the dictation of the Executive of the United States, without any sanction or coöperation on the part of the popular branch of Government,† the appropriation of the moneys thus collected to whatever uses the Executive thought best, and the appointment under such a scheme of a multitude of custom-house officers and pay-masters, were measures declared both by Mr. Calhoun and Mr. Webster, to be invasions of the laws and constitution of the United States.

The dangerous march of Executive Power was further

* 30th Congress, 1st Session, House of Representatives, Doc. No. 60, p. 150; 30th Congress, 1st Session, Senate, Ex. Doc. No. 33, p. 410.

† "6. On the failure of any State to pay its assessments, its functionaries, as above, will *be seized and imprisoned, and their property seized, registered, reported, and converted to the use of occupation*, in strict accordance to the general regulations of this army. No resignation or abdication of office by any of the said Mexican functionaries shall excuse one of them from any of the above obligations or penalties." See also Art. 3, 30th Congress, 1st Session, Ex. Doc. No. 60, p. 1064. It would have been a very natural mistake if we supposed we had alighted on one of the military laws of Santa Anna, or some other chieftain, in the above severe enactment, not that it was in very truth a regulation *of one of those Generals who came professing to free the poor Mexicans from military tyrants!*

manifested by the creation of civil governments, the appointing of the various officers, magistrates, and judges, necessary to carry them on, and the allotment of their duties and salaries, without any reference to the authority of Congress, or any appeal to its judgment, any more than if that body had been non-existent.

The conclusion of the war was also in harmony with its commencement, object, and progress, tainted with the same disregard of forms and rules of law. Mr. Trist had been recalled by the power which appointed him as confidential commissioner to negotiate a peace, but he chose still to remain in Mexico on his own responsibility; and the plenipotentiaries of that nation, with a knowledge of that fact, did not hesitate to conclude a treaty with him.* The record of his name, therefore, as an officer of the United States, on that document, was not in accordance with the fact of the case.

The commissioners, Messrs Clifford and Sevier, conveyed the treaty of peace, as amended by the Senate, to Mexico, to procure its ratification by the Government of that country. The changes made by the Senate, were the substitution of the third article of the treaty of Louisiana in the place of the ninth article of this treaty, relative to the rights of Mexicans in the annexed territories; the entire suppression of the tenth article, relative to Mexican grants in the territories, and the alteration of the twelfth article, relative to the mode of payment by the United States of $15,000,000 to Mexico. The Mexican Government refused to ratify the treaty until the American commissioners had signed a protocol, declaring that no essential changes had been made, and explaining the ground of the several amendments.* The protocol was, however, regarded by many in Congress as

* 30th Congress, 1st Session, Senate, Ex. Doc. No. 52, pp. 5, 38; 30th Congress, 2nd Session, House of Representatives, Ex. Doc. No. 50, p. 11, et passim.

virtually involving a new agreement on the part of the United States, and its concealment by the Executive for nearly a year from the knowledge of Congress, was deemed another specimen of illegal and unconstitutional proceeding.

We have thus baldly and briefly indicated some of the gross and generally-conceded illegalities which have characterized the war. Monarchies may trample upon the laws, and live, because they are based upon might. Republics may trample upon their constitutions, but they will die, because they are founded upon right. The only loyalty possible in our country, is a loyalty to the Constitution and laws, always coupled with the liberty to amend them and square them by the laws of God, and when that sense of allegiance is gone, the sheet-anchor of the republic parts in twain. The laws of the land are not the perfect expression of the supreme right and truth. But they are the highest yet seen and realized by the mass of the people; and to lift a violent hand against them, to violate them with impunity, is to weaken the sole restraints that remain to hold in check the turbulent forces of the country. We are admonished by mobs in our Atlantic cities, and Mormon wars and lynchings in our western borders, and by the new plans of military adventure coming to light, hatched by this war, that this is no period in the history of our republic to relax, by word or deed, the sacred bonds of the Constitution and the laws.

CHAPTER XV.

POLITICAL EVILS OF THE WAR AT HOME.

"Of all the enemies of public liberty war is perhaps the most to be dreaded. It is the parent of armies; from these proceed debts and taxes; and armies, and debts, and taxes, are the well-known instruments for bringing the many under the dominion of the few. War is the true nurse of executive aggrandizement.——No nation could preserve its freedom in the midst of continued warfare. These truths are well established." — MADISON.

THE science of politics, wisely viewed, is a great and a good science. It highly concerns the welfare of states and nations. Its principles are noble when they are drawn from the laws of God. And the art of government, or the carrying out and realization of these lofty principles, is a glorious art. Politics, whether as an art or a science, have fallen into low esteem with many sensible people, simply on account of the chicanery of politicians, and not because the work of organizing and governing mankind is not in itself of the highest dignity and moment.

And if these declarations hold good of politics and government in general, then are they doubly true of the science and administration of republican institutions. For here government exists and is moulded by the consent and will of the governed. Castes, conventional ideas and arrangements give way before simpler and truer views of man's relation to man. Freedom is but one of the deep seminal principles of republican and Christian politics. Duties require to be considered as well as rights. Mutual help is as essential as personal independence. Love must be the vital air of a self-governing community. And he who, possessed and quickened himself by these life-giving sentiments, seeks by act and word, seeks above all by the just and benevolent conduct of public affairs, to diffuse them abroad and impress them on the heart of a whole nation, and give a high-toned moral character to its history and destiny, occupies the position of an archangel for doing good, — wide and lasting good to his race.

It is when we have taken this more elevated and comprehensive view of the real grandeur of human government, when rightly administered, that we descend to the consideration of such a chapter in our national career, as that of the Mexican war, with the most loathing and repugnance. We think no event has ever occurred, since the establishment of the Federal constitution, so ominous to the prospects of our country in particular, or free institutions in general, as this invasion. Not that we despair of the republic. Not that we have lost one jot of our faith in the capability of man for republican governments. Not that we see any immediate signs of the overthrow of any one of our chartered and constitutional rights and privileges. But we are taught by an impressive and tremendous example, that republics may, under all the forms of freedom, full-blown and flourishing, do deeds, incur responsibilities, hazard evils, and inflict injuries, at which any old barbaric monarchy might well stand aghast. Still more pungently has the solemn lesson been thrilled through our hearts, that if we would have a country worth the name of Liberty and the love and service of freemen, if we would save the name, — republic, — from becoming a hissing and a scorn in the earth, and if we would rescue this gigantic empire of the West from sinking into the Babylon of the nations, we need to ply in season and out of season, with all our characteristic energy as a people, the means of intellectual, social, and religious life, the school, the press, and the church, in all their purity and power.

Our single trust and hope are in the Gospel of Jesus Christ, to save us as a heritage of freedom, from destruction, or from a warlike, Roman ambition, worse than destruction. This and this only can clarify the intellect, exalt the aims, chasten the passions, and sanctify the career of a mighty people, bursting away in their untamable energies from all the revered landmarks of the past, and seemingly taking counsel chiefly of their own impassioned youth. But God works by human agencies. And this Gospel, divine as it is in its source, and competent as it is as an illuminator and Mentor, needs to be sent abroad as freely as the flowing waters, and the sweeping breezes, to reach, and elevate, and save the millions of the ignorant, the superstitious, the depraved, and the young, throughout our land.

With these, and similar connected views of the value of Christian politics, we approach the subject of the political character and issues of this conquest, and we would consider it not for one moment as partisans, for such we are not, but as calm and impartial patriots, without reference to parties. Indeed, in the very matter of this war, so far as parties had anything to do with it, and any guilt rests upon its planners and actors, we see both the great parties involved more or less in carrying it on; we shall not stop in this Review to ask, which was more, and which was less. Both parties voted men and money. Both parties fought its battles. Both parties talked of the glory gained by the victories. Both parties have brought home candidates for the highest national offices and honors from its red fields. Both parties have, we believe, to a considerable extent given their sanction to this conflict, and endorsed its effects; while in both parties have been found its earnest denouncers, in its inception, its progress, and its results; witness the words of the great statesman of New England and those of the great statesman of the South; both eminent leaders of their respective parties. We choose then to regard this war as the act of the country, and not the act of any party. As such we review it, criticize it, and condemn it. The nation's mind must have been partially clouded, and the nation's soul must have been temporarily hardened, to declare hostilities and carry out this giant system of evil during two long years. At whatever point, or in whatever person or persons, the evil came to a head, the evil itself must have widely permeated the veins of the whole republic. No single act could have brought on the crisis, had there not been a general war-spirit smouldering deeply in multitudes of hearts, entirely irrespective of all parties, which only needed one breath of the bellows to blow it into a flame.

We think it better to attribute much of such movements in human affairs to the public sentiment that is behind all the forms of law, and that is mightier than the throne itself. We prefer to take much of the guilt of this and like deeds to ourselves, and to remember, that if we have not approved of the precise thing in question, we have probably approved of much which may have been instrumental of leading to such a catastrophe. We have all drank too much of the belligerent spirit.

The demon of war has not yet been exorcised out of the heart of Christendom. We do much to prepare for war. We educate our youth in war-history and war-poetry. We honor the soldier's calling, as a calling. We spend in time of profound peace more for war than we do for peace. We encourage military education, reviews, drills, musters. We manufacture myriads of arms. We put a musket in every house, and a sword in every hand. We stud our ports with grim war-ships, and encamp our militia in every village. And it is not in human nature to be thus always and expressly and enthusiastically preparing for a thing, and never doing the thing itself. Some militia may be necessary as a police, though they often occasion more riots than they suppress. But the boundless preparations everywhere made in all civilized countries for war, unquestionably do much to precipitate international conflicts. Men who have been learning the art of destruction all their days, will occasionally seek and create the opportunities to reduce their art to practice. He who goes armed with a bowie-knife, will be likely sometimes to use it.

We proceed now, after these preliminaries, to consider some of the political evils which have resulted from the event in question.

And in view of these evils, and of others which time may yet develop, we honor the fearless resistance, and the prophetic sagacity, with which the great statesman of South Carolina, in company with others, plead for deliberation, when the nation were about embarking precipitately in the war.

"In the present condition of the world," he said, "war was a tremendous thing. The whole sentiment of the civilized world was turning stronger and stronger against war. And let us not, for the honor of our country, — for the dignity of the republic, be the first to create a state of war. Mortal man cannot see the end of it. When I look and see that we are rushing upon this most tremendous event, I am amazed. I am more than amazed, — I am in a state of wonder and deep alarm."

One of the principal justifications of this warfare against our neighbors was the alleged vindication of the national honor. We had been injured by Mexico, and we must return injury for injury. We must show that we would not be maltreated with impunity. We must demonstrate by the glory of our arms that republican institutions could do as much, as those of a monarchy, to render us formidable in war. Such in brief was the argument. But we propose to suggest, that instead of "covering ourselves with glory," as the military phrase runs, we have contracted a serious reproach among the nations, and lowered instead of raising, the true reputation of the United States, as a republic.

We are far from denying that the words, "national honor" are words of pith and moment. Though often used profanely, they have a sacred significance. They are capable of making the heart beat quicker, and of rousing in the true man a noble thrill of sentiment. True national honor is worth everything. It is the national soul, the pulse of the mighty national heart. Who is willing to live in national disgrace, and to be ashamed when he is abroad among the nations, to have it known that he came from such a place, or that he is the citizen of such a land? Who of any country, though he be an Icelander, or a Kamtschatkan, but takes an honest and an honorable pride in the land that gave him birth? And that land, though it be the frozen north, or the desert south, who does not glory, if he can call it his own, his native land, in its being kept untarnished in fame? Such is the feeling of all men, savage and civilized.

But men misjudge. They do not see what true national honor is. They think it is territory, or wealth, or armies, or success in war or diplomacy, or some other factitious thing. But it is a great error. The noble and honorable nations of antiquity, as they now stand in the eyes of the world, were the just and upright and pacific nations. Their glitter and gold have all perished. But all that they did of the True, and Good, and Just, and Beautiful, now lives in eternal remembrance on the breathing canvas, and the imperishable marble, in song and never-dying history. The gross and sensual, and rich and extended empires of the old world have rotted out of the record of mankind, for they did little worth preserving. While a magnanimous act in the humblest town or city has survived, and is borne on the wings of fame all over the earth. There is a retribution in history.

Much is said of national honor. But what is highly esteemed among men is abomination with God. If we would seek the true honor of our own country, we shall use our influence to carry out the principles and ideas of Free Institutions to their full extent. We shall frown upon all attempts to cast down those glorious principles and ideas to the base and vulgar glory of ages of barbarism. It is no honor to us that we have three millions of slaves. It is no honor to us that we, the stronger republic, and one that can afford to be generous, should make war upon the weaker one. It is no honor to us to grasp the whole continent, when we find it a sufficient work to take care of what we have. But so far as we do what is just, pay our own debts, live in peace with our neighbors, give the poor Indian and African their due, carry forward education and morality, and enterprise in every direction, and at once civilize and Christianize our vast population, we are on the high road to honor, and shall live on the brightest pages of history. So may it be, should be the prayer of every true American.

But the whole war-system of the civilized countries is false and dishonorable. War is for savages, not for citizens, gentlemen, and Christians. Its direct effect, as far as it goes, is to carry back civilization some degrees towards barbarism. It is the animal in man, triumphing over the human. It is an appeal to force, not to right. It is poor policy, as well as bad morality. It generally loses in the end more than it gains. It may gain notoriety, but it destroys true renown. It may conquer new lands, but it wrecks character. It is antagonistical to Christianity, and therefore it must be false and wrong, and in the end evil, and evil continually.

We have not been able to see, thus far, much difference between this and most other wars. It probably had as much cause to excuse its origin, it has been as well conducted, it has had as good a close, as most other wars. We believe it is unjust, that it had no adequate reason to justify it. We believe it is a disgrace, and not an honor, to the American name. We believe that its victories are not glories, and that its results will not be blessings. We know that the conscience of the civilized world, and the sympathy of Christendom, are against us, as they always are against the powerful in their contests with the weak. And it needs no prophet's eye to read, in the future, the impartial condemnation of history. *There* we shall be defeated, without doubt and without help, however successful we may be in blowing up Mexican cities and dispersing Mexican armies.

But this war is only a small part of a great system, — the war-system of nations; and that system is unjust, inglorious, murderous. What we would scourge most severely, if we could wield the pen of a Juvenal or a Pope, would be this whole childish, ridiculous, if it were not much more, this wrong and inhuman method, of settling national disputes. Our Mexican War is as good, and as bad, as the war of France against the Algerines, — that of the Russians against the Circassians, — and that of the English against the Sikhs. And, if we speak of dismemberment, Poland now stands not alone.

What national honor, in fine, could be gained in a contest, which, before it broke out, Mr. Thompson, our Minister to Mexico, said, in his "Recollections,"* would be inadequately expressed by an encounter between "a feeble woman and a strong man armed!"

The political evils of national debt, loss of life, and acts of barbarism, have already been descanted upon at length. We proceed to consider some other mischiefs, that may be classed under the head of "political."

The recent war with Mexico has produced a kind of civil warfare in our own borders. It has been a very embittered topic of debate and division. It has been a firebrand of contention and anger, on the floor of Congress. The press has distilled gall, when the subject has been introduced. And, worse than all, it has created strong sectional alienations, exasperated all the local strifes of the country, and added

* Recollections, p. 245.

new venom to politics. It has brought up the question of slavery, and not brought it up in such a way that we can hope for a happy issue from it.

Words are not, it is true, bullets, and the pen, however sharp, does not prick like the bayonet; but the earnest lover of his country will deprecate the occasions of violent party, and especially sectional conflicts, if they can be avoided without the sacrifice of principle. A quarrelsome nation is but a more extended quarrelsome family. And as, in domestic life, we think it wise to shun petty bickerings, so in national life, great animosities and the causes that fan them up, should be carefully avoided. There will be more or less friction in the social, as in mechanical machinery; but, in both instances, it is well to reduce it as much as possible. "Fraternity" is one of the great words of a true national motto; and no "root of bitterness" should be lightly suffered to spring up and trouble us. The spirit of war is essentially a spirit of discord at home, as well as abroad. It tends to shake, everywhere, the pillars of confidence, good will, and a good understanding between citizens, if they be on opposite sides of party lines.

The Mexican War will be a standing topic of crimination and recrimination, through the present generation, if not during a longer time. It has sown our soil with dragons' teeth, and they will spring up armed men. It has started questions of free territory, slavery, boundaries, pensions, private claims, and new schemes of conquest and annexation, that will embroil the next fifty years, both in our public councils, and among the people and the press. These are no contemptible evils, when we remember that union is the strength of a republic, and peace and love the first duties of the Christian code.

So far especially as the Mexican conquests have banded North and South against each other, and, by widening our domains, weakened the joints of our body politic, they are greatly to be deprecated. In this aspect, they war against the glorious sisterhood of the States, and pave the way for no remote dismemberment. By introducing into the rights and privileges of American citizens a horde of "outside barbarians," the mongrel races of New Mexico and California, they have cheapened the American birthright, and loosened the very corner-stone in our fabric of Federal Freedom. If the spirit, of which this invasion is the first-fruits, be not speedily and effectually discountenanced, the day cannot be far distant when a rupture will take place between the widely-separated States, and clashing interests of different sections of our beloved republic, that will prove incurable. War, in its Anglo-Saxon derivation, means "beware;" and well would it be for us, as a people, if the catastrophe which has befallen us should put us on our guard against evils yet to come, and, above all, the final dissolution of the American Union.

Again; the liberties of mankind, as all history teaches, are so liable to be stolen away from the unwary many by the crafty few, that we can never be too watchful of their unimpaired preservation. The forms, too, of freedom may survive, when the spirit has ebbed away. A republic, like a church, may have a name to live, when it is dead. What, then, needs our perpetual vigilance, as citizens of a free land, is, that the great ideas, out of which our State and national constitutions were born, may be maintained, in their original power, in the minds of the people. There is a meaning in going back to the fathers of the Revolution; for we are then in reality going forward in the prospective career which they marked out, — in that heroic, and, so to say, inspired age of the nation. But, as the love of money, ambition, ease, familiarity with free institutions breeding contempt, corruption in high places, and the power of demagogues, wax stronger, and mould to bad uses large and unsuspecting parties, it is imperatively necessary to quaff anew of the spirit of '76; and, if we do not servilely copy what the sages and heroes of that period did, yet it is wise to consider what, under the influence of such a life-giving, and comparatively disinterested spirit of freedom, as then burned in their bosoms, they would now do, were they in our places.

War is, in itself, a temporary despotism. Slavery is a tremendous evil; but he who hates slavery should just as cordially hate war, for war gave birth to slavery. The captives of war are the victims of slavery. The African slave-trade feeds on war. But, more than that, war enslaves those that are engaged in it. Soldiers are slaves. The inferior officers are all slaves to the superior; and the whole army, or fleet, are subject to the most absolute, and often tyrannical despotism of one man, the commanding general. They have no wills, or consciences, or hearts of their own. If they are ordered to kill the widow's only cow and burn her cottage, they must march up and do it, without flinching. He who undertakes to have a private opinion of his own in an army, will soon find out his mistake, by means of cashiering or the cat-o'-nine-tails. The defender of war is obliged, from the necessity of the case, to defend this absolutism; for otherwise there could be no marching or fighting to any efficient purpose. The better slaves, the better soldiers. The more total, and unquestioning, and mechanical the obedience, the more fit and successful is the army for accomplishing its objects. Can that be a good institution that makes men into machines, that enthrones another's will, however wicked or arbitrary, over the wills, consciences, reason, and every "faculty divine," of thousands and tens of thousands of responsible and immortal beings?

We have already recorded the words of Madison, in which he warns his countrymen to beware of the despotic influence of war. It was timely advice. We would single out, indeed, no one man, or class of men, as aspiring to destroy the liberties of their fatherland. But we cannot avoid seeing that every war furnishes an occasion for a daring march of executive power upon the other functions of government; for the creation of a multitude of offices, dependent upon the gift of one man, or a few men; for the elevation of military talents over those of the civilian; for the increase of a standing army, always a supple tool of arbitrary power; for the erection of military governments over the conquered countries; and for the introduction of officers into every branch of the government, from the highest to the lowest, whose sole or chief distinction is prowess in arms, and who would naturally make military maxims the basis of their official administration. It was when the Pretorian Guards of Rome bore the emperor into office by their despotic will, that the mistress of nations began to decline. And when, in any nation, the glorious gifts of Christian statesmanship, and ripe experience, and large converse among men, and a lifetime of civil services to one's country and the world, are postponed and set aside for "the conquering hero," the Genius of rational, heaven-descended Liberty is already meditating her departure to some more congenial clime.

CHAPTER XVI.

POLITICAL EVILS OF THE WAR ABROAD.

"Freedom is fighting her battles in the world, with sufficient odds against her. Let us not give new chances to her foes." — CHANNING.

THE Mexican War has done incalculable harm to the cause of liberty, throughout our country and the world.

This central idea of our government, institutions, and destiny, has been foully disowned. We had already done great discredit to our good name, by our violations of Indian treaties, our slavery, and our repudiation of State debts. But this attack on weak neighbors, to steal away their lands, is capping the climax of wrong and dishonor. See, says the monarchist, the aristocrat, your boasted government of the people can do as wicked and unjust things, as were ever perpetrated by the kings and kaisers of the old world. It is the same game of ambition, only it is played by different hands. It is the ancient spirit in a new form. The reality is the same, sugar it over with fair names as much as you please. War is war, and tyranny is tyranny, and slavery is slavery, — whether in the United States, or Rome, or England.

The example we have thus set before the world is a most noxious one. The stigma we have brought upon the name of Liberty will not soon be wiped out. We have caused the hearts of pacific lovers of freedom everywhere to sink within them, at the spectacle of a government of the people forgetting the rights and interests of humanity, and waging, on the ground of the old-world notions of retaliation, force, glory, security, and indemnity, a war of invasion, conquest, and terrible barbarity.

But when, to all these considerations of the unfavorable bearing of the Mexican war on the interests of freedom at home and abroad, we add that it was begun, continued, and ended, to subserve the extension of slavery and the slave power, we have revealed its full enormity. That all who were engaged in the contest, as counsellors or actors, on the American side, were actuated by this motive, would be more than any wise man would assert. But we regard ourselves as holding two impregnable and historical positions, when we maintain, that had it not been for the institution of slavery, Texas never would have been conquered and annexed; and that had it not been for the annexation of Texas, and the desire for more Mexican soil, not a drop of human blood would have been shed, nor would such endeared names as "beautiful sight," "true cross," "holy cross," "sacrament," ever have been raised from their innocent obscurity to become the dark and terrible names of battles between two Christian nations. We have already adduced, in the third chapter of this essay, documentary evidence from both the Executive and Legislative Departments of the United States, to substantiate these positions. We need not recapitulate that testimony. Suffice it to say, that since that chapter was written, the most ample declarations have been published by some, who were prominent in the measure of annexation, that they acted either under the influence of a panic got up for the occasion, that Texas was about to throw herself into the arms of some foreign power, or that pledges were given to insure their votes, which were not afterwards fulfilled. We hesitate not to say on these and previous testimonies, that the Texas plot was one of the darkest conspiracies that history anywhere records, against human liberty; and that the plot not only succeeded perfectly, but that it drew after it, as an almost necessary consequence to the same rapacious scheme, a war of conquest, still further to extend this wicked and unnatural, and naturally injurious relation of absolute power on one hand, and helpless, hopeless servitude on the other, over vast regions of God's earth, among unborn millions of his children, and down through too patient years of wrong and suffering. What the result will be for the new territories thus acquired, it would be presumptuous to predict; we can only entertain the strong hope that the Proviso of Freedom, under whatever name of man it may be called, will be extended like the wings of a guardian angel over this immense wilderness of nature. But the feeling and the fear of bringing Mexican land, purged of slavery and the slave-trade, under the dominion of the United States, cannot, in concluding this head of the subject, be better expressed than in the stirring words of a Mexican poet writing at the beginning of the war, and of an American one writing during its progress. This lyric is by Jose Ho Ace de Saltillo.*

"Hearken! from our Northern borders
Sounds Arista's bugle call;
On the banks of Rio Bravo
Bursts the shell and ploughs the ball!

"Ghastly hands in Tenochtitlan
Strike th' old Atzec battle-drum;
Sharp of beak and strong of talon,
Lo! Mexitli's eagles come!

"Coldly sleep our slaughtered brothers;
While above their hasty graves
Sounds the hurrying hoof of rapine,
And the robber-banner waves.

"On they come, the mad invaders,
Like the fire before the wind;
Freedom's harvest-field before them,
Slavery's blackened waste behind!

"From the sellers of God's image,
From the traffickers in man,
Mother gracious, mother holy,
Shield thy dark-browed Mexican!

"Hearken! up the Rio Bravo
Comes the negro-catcher's shout:
Listen! 'tis the Yankee's hammer
Forging human fetters out!

"Let the land we love be wasted,
Black with fire and rough with graves;
Better far for God and Freedom
Die at once than live as slaves!

* "A Mexican of some celebrity." See Montgomery's Life of Gen. Taylor, pp. 316, 317.

"We are few and they are many,
Strong in arms, and wealth, and pride;
But the saints and holy angels,
And man's heart are on our side.

"Hark! from ancient Tenochitlan,
Sounds once more the Atzec drum;
Not for conquest, not for vengeance,
But for Freedom, Faith, and Home!"

In the poem entitled "Yorktown," referring to the compromises of the Constitution, and the perpetuation of slavery in the United States, Whittier breaks forth in these indignant stanzas, —

"Oh! fields still green and fresh in story,
Old days of pride, old names of glory,
Old marvels of the tongue and pen,
Old thoughts which stirred the hearts of men!
Ye spared the wrong; and over all
Behold the avenging shadow fall!
Your world-wide honor stained with shame,
Your Freedom's self a hollow name.

"Where 's now the flag of that old war?
Where flow its stripes? Where burns its star?
Bear witness, Palo Alto's day,
Dark Vale of Palms, red Monterey,
Where Mexic Freedom, young and weak,
Fleshes the Northern eagle's beak:
Symbol of terror and despair,
Of chains and slaves, gó seek it there!

"Laugh, Prussia, 'midst thy iron ranks!
Laugh, Russia, from thy Neva's banks!
Brave sport to see the fledgling born
Of Freedom, by its parents torn!
Safe now your Speilburg's dungeon cell,
Safe drear Siberia's frozen hell:
With Slavery's flag o'er both unrolled,
What of the New World fears the Old?"

But we have gained, still, say the war-advocates, a great renown, and made the nations of the earth, especially poor Mexico, tremblingly afraid of us. This is one of the glories of war, and its avowed merit. But is this a manly, a rational, or a Christian mode of reasoning? Love is as much better than fear among nations as it is among individuals. If we have taught the nations to dread or hate us for our injustice and rapacity, have we probably retarded or advanced the cause of freedom in the world? We have taught them that republics can be as ambitious as monarchies, and can load their people with war-taxes as unsparingly, and squander their lives and happiness as recklessly and as causelessly. We have shown that the eagle has claws as sharp, and a beak as bloody, as the tooth of the lion, or the paw of the bear. Besides, the question is, whether this reputation for military glory is what a nation should chiefly seek? Whether the arts of peace are not a better foundation for honor than the arts of war? And whether those nations or communities,—the mobs of European cities, the cabinets of warlike States, the fierce, and brutal, and bloody men of the age, who have no just sense of the value of human life, and little touch of the spirit of Christ,—whether those are to be our judges, to whom we are to look for approval in our national acts? Are we to kill thousands for the sake of propitiating the military class of Europe, or any other quarter, to the opinion that we are after all as adroit cut-throats as they are themselves? Is such a character the one we should be emulous to gain in the infancy of our republic? Is it not essentially a guilty, blood-stained glory, unbecoming a Christian people, and quite at variance with those smooth and honied professions of liberty and peace which have been upon our lips from the beginning? Injustice never yet gained sincere respect. The truth is, the nations hate and loathe us for this very war. They despise the cowardice that pounced upon a weaker country, and dismembered its territory by force of arms. This war has gained us the good opinion abroad of none whose good opinion is worth possessing.

The political effect of the war on Mexico has been bad. The whole attention of that country has been devoted two years to war. This cannot have been favorable to the working of free institutions. The funds of the nation have been diverted into channels of barren expenditure, yielding no profitable returns. The talent, skill, power, and time of the Mexican people for two years have been turned away from all the works and processes of improvement, to the siege and the battle-field. Her commerce was destroyed, and her agriculture wasted. The manners and morals of large numbers of her people were infected by the pernicious contagion of camp vices and habits. Her national pride and self-respect have received a severe blow, and prepared her to strive with less "might and main" to perfect republican forms of government, or repel future invasions. She has lost between one-third and one-half of her territory. The spirit of revolution, always rampant in her Capital and provinces, has received a new impetus in the generally disordered state of the country. Her military leaders will gather new materials for civil contests in the measures that the war has developed, and new instruments to carry them on in the hordes of disbanded soldiers that are now thrown out of employment, and are ready to join in any scheme of violence and plunder. So wide have been these injurious influences upon the political weal of Mexico, that it has been said by competent authority on the spot, that "the whole male population of Mexico appears to be fast relapsing into a state of brigandage." The system of guerilla warfare must have done much to demoralize the peasantry, and to infuse into the remotest sections of the country the deadly virus of war-habits, vices, cruelty, and abandonment of the regular occupations of industry and honesty.

Not the least of the evils of the war will be an increased bitterness and hostility in Mexico against the United States and against free institutions. This was the result of the Texas difficulties, according to Mr. Thompson, in his Recollections of Mexico. "The feeling of all Mexicans towards us, until the revolution in Texas, was one of unmixed admiration; and it is our high position amongst the nations, and makes our mission all the more responsible, that every people struggling to be free, regard us with the same feelings, — we are indeed the 'looking-glass in which they dress themselves.' As a philanthropist, I have deeply deplored the effects of the annexation of Texas upon the feelings of the people of all classes in Mexico, towards this country, as diminishing their devotion to republican institutions; this should not be so, but it will be."

Much indeed has been said of the political benefits accruing to Mexico from this conquest. But were these benefits commended to us as a people, we should not be long probably in testifying our repugnance to the mission of foreign progagandists. We should altogether prefer to manage our own affairs in our own way; and we should very much question the right of any nation, however wise, or good, or powerful, to rivet their measures upon us by force, slice off hundreds of thousands of square miles of our national territory, kill thousands of our citizens, destroy millions of our property, and ere the seal was hardly cold on the instrument of amity and peace, to plot new schemes of invasion, or allow them to be plotted. So imperfectly can we arrive at a true knowledge of the internal state of affairs in that unhappy, distracted country, that only on the general ground indicated in these brief words do we come to the conclusion, that, though Providence, in its wise chemistry, may elaborate, even out of this war and its miseries, good to the suffering republic, yet we have no commission or license, as a nation, any more than individuals, to "do evil that good may come."

Evil is evil, and sin is sin, and the consequences cannot alter the moral complexion of an act. No doubt, as Nature heals on her beautiful face the scars of the torn battle-plain, wipes away with her tears, shed from heaven, the stains of blood, and even clothes herself with a greener vesture and more blooming flowers than before; so the infinite Providence, in which all worlds and all beings are embosomed, with a like hopefulness and soothing efficacy of time, may work out of the bitter woes of war a greater good than man thought of; but God's goodness, instead of excusing our wickedness, only makes it appear all the more guilty and shocking. Mexico may not fall. The blow she has received may rouse her latent energies of self-improvement. But if the period should ever arrive when the largest republic on earth, next to our own, and the most hopeful and consistent one, is blotted out of the record of nations and becomes the Poland of the West, we shall stand condemned in the eyes of heaven and our own, as the authors of so tremendous a catastrophe.

CHAPTER XVII.

THE NEW TERRITORIES.

"And what, in principle, is war? It is the *duel between nations*, differing in no respect from the duel between individuals, except that the successful combatant is allowed to carry off as spoil the effects of his vanquished antagonist." — Bishop Potter.

The acquisition of the territories of New Mexico and California is regarded by many as a sufficient compensation for all the losses and evils of the war, and a summary answer to all objectors. The ports on the Pacific, the immense extent of country, and above all the astonishing mineral wealth are adduced as reasons to satisfy us that it was well the war was waged; as if these good things were some fair exchange; as if the question had been put to us, what shall it profit the nation, if it gain the whole world, and lose its own soul of faith and freedom; and we had seemed to answer, it shall profit us richly, if we can gain San Francisco, the Pacific port, the Sacramento, river of gold, and a boundless extent of new lands.

There are, however, important drawbacks to the value of our possessions, and to the satisfaction with which an honest man can speak of them.

There is, in the first place, the way in which they were acquired, — by force, by conquest, by might, and not by right. As early as June 24, 1845, Commodore Sloat received secret and confidential orders from the Navy Department, to employ his squadron in the Pacific in warlike operations, seizing and occupying San Francisco, and other Mexican ports, as soon as he had ascertained with certainty the existence of war between Mexico and the United States, Seven ships of war and between 2000 and 3000 men and officers afforded him ample power to carry into execution his orders. Having heard rumors of the battles on the Rio Grande, he seized, July 7, 1846, Monterey, Upper California, without resistance, and issued a proclamation,* in which he annexed the country permanently to the American Union, saying that "henceforward California will be a portion of the United States," and in which he assured the people, that "the same protection would be extended to them as to any other State in the Union;" thus virtually excluding the idea of any changes in the government, which a treaty of peace, or the action of Congress might produce. In the language

* 30th Cong. 2d Session, Ho. of Rep. Ex. Doc. No. 1, p. 1010.

of Commodore Stockton, "the intelligence of the commencement of hostilities between the two nations, although it had passed through Mexico, had reached Commodore Sloat in advance of the Mexican authorities. When he first made his hostile demonstrations, therefore, the enemy, ignorant of the existence of the war, had regarded his acts as an unwarrantable exercise of power by the United States, and the most lively indignation and bitter resentment filled the country." The motives under which the conqueror acted are portrayed in the following extract from a letter to Commander Montgomery, dated Monterey, July 6, 1846,* "since I wrote you last evening, I have determined to hoist the flag of the United States at this place to-morrow, as I *would prefer being sacrificed for doing too much than too little.*" The danger to which he *was* exposed, of being sacrificed for doing too little, was well set forth in a letter from Mr. Bancroft, Secretary of the Navy, which, after chiding him for remaining quiet from June 6th, when he heard of the affairs on the Rio Grande, till July 7th, when he captured Monterey, used this tone; † "but your anxiety not to do wrong has led you into a most unfortunate and unwarranted inactivity." Would it not often be better for our country, and for all countries, if public officers had more of that "anxiety not to do wrong?"

But the part enacted by Fremont in California sufficiently indicated that he was there, and that he took part in the revolutionary and warlike movements, not without high authority implied, though not perhaps distinctly expressed. He left St. Louis in June, 1845, on a topographical and scientific survey of Oregon and California, with a command of sixty-two men and two hundred horses. The Oregon boundary was in dispute, but the California boundary was

* 30th Cong. 1st Session, Senate. Rep. Com. No. 75, p. 73.

† 30th Cong. 1st Session, Senate. Rep. Com. No. 75, p. 71. Also, p. 13.

clearly defined. And no armed party of men from the United States had any more right to be travelling in, and surveying that country, than sixty armed Mexicans to enter Florida and travel through it on a topographical and scientific survey. There was an ulterior motive besides science. It was remarkable too that several months had been devoted to California, which belonged to Mexico, and not a day to Oregon, which did belong to the United States. What Fremont's instructions were when he was sent out, are secrets buried in the archives of the Government. But the facts are indisputable. Fremont *was there*, ready for any movement. He naturally awakened the suspicions of the Californian authorities. Gen. Castro, military commander of California, ordered him to leave the country. But he took an intrenched position and avowed his intention, if attacked, to die in defence of the flag of his country, though he had dishonored that flag by confessedly planting it on the foreign soil of Mexico. He retired however to the north, into Oregon, before the forces of Castro, and was there reached by an officer, Lieut. Gillespie, the bearer of important despatches from the United States through Mexico, which he had committed to memory, that chance might not betray them to the Mexican government. On the 10th of May, 1846, the parties met. The nature of the message will best be told in Fremont's own language: "He brought me a letter of introduction from the Secretary of State, (Mr. Buchanan,) and letters and papers from Senator Benton and his family. The letter from the Secretary imported nothing beyond the introduction, and was directed to me in my private or citizen capacity. The outside envelop of a packet from Senator Benton was directed in the same way, and one of the letters from him, while apparently of mere friendship and family details, contained passages enigmatical and obscure, but which I studied out, and made the meaning to be that I was required by the Government to find out any foreign schemes in relation to the Californias, and to counteract them." * He further says, "the letter from Senator Benton had a decided influence on my next movement." Lieut. Gillespie also testified essentially to the same statement respecting his instructions from the home government. Capt. Owens also declared before the committee on "California claims," that he did not think the revolution against the government would have taken place, or the people been united without the aid and protection of Captain Fremont. They had not confidence enough in their strength to undertake the war without support. Captain Fremont's party was *strong and well armed, and went together like one man.* Another witness, Loker, testified, "then commenced the revolution." †

Turning back from Oregon into "the unsettled parts of the Sacramento," and hearing rumors of warlike movements by Gen. Castro, Fremont put himself, June 10th, at the head of the American settlers at their earnest request, joining them "with his party, and (what they deemed of great moment) his name as an American officer." The first act of this clandestine war was the seizure of some horses of Gen. Castro. The fort of Sonoma was captured, and on July 5th, the Californians declared their independence, and adopted the figure of the grizzly bear as their standard. Soon afterwards, however, Fremont and Stockton united their forces under the flag of the United States, and the republic of California had an even shorter existence than the republic of Texas.

Thus by violence and conquest, hatched, abetted and consummated before it was distinctly known that any declared war existed, was the territory belonging to Mexico torn away, and proclaimed to be an absolute and perpetual possession of the United States. Is it not within the bounds of imagination to conceive, that had the English, instead of the

* 30th Cong. 1st Session, Senate. Ex. Doc. No. 33, pp. 373, 374.

† 30th Cong. 1st Session, Senate. Rep. Com. No. 75, pp. 68, 39.

Mexican, flag been flying over Monterey and San Francisco, these officers would have paused before they pulled it down.

This insolence of power was still further illustrated by the designation which Stockton and other officers gave to those who rose and resisted their violent acts, calling them *rebels* and *insurgents*,* when they were themselves confessedly acting without what are called the rights of war; † Fremont fighting, as he acknowledged, on his own hook, ‡ and Stockton on only *implied* powers from his government.

One word is due to New Mexico, after which other topics relating to the new territories acquired, will be discussed. The conquest of this Mexican province was effected by Gen. Kearney with a command despatched for that purpose. But he overstepped the line of authority, as did the officers in California, by erecting New Mexico into a territory of the United States before peace was made, and by absolving the inhabitants from their allegiance, threatening them with death, if they took up arms, § enacting laws, in some in-

* Cutts' Conquest of California, pp. 129, 130, 133, 157, 161, 163.

† The justification of Mexican cruelties towards the prisoners taken in the Texan war, was that they were rebels, traitors to the government, and therefore deserved to be imprisoned or executed. 28th Cong. 1st Session, Senate, 341, p. 72.

‡ "In June of the year 1846, being then a brevet captain of topographical engineers in the service of the United States, and employed as such in California, he engaged in military operations with the people of the country for the establishment of the independence of California, *before the existence of war between the United States and Mexico was known*, and was successful in said undertaking," etc. 30th Cong. 1st Session, Senate. Rep. Com. No. 75, p. 1. "I informed him, that I had acted solely on my own responsibility, and without any authority from the government to justify hostilities." p. 13.

§ Cutts' Conquest of California, p. 46, 51, 57, 58. Perhaps the best parallel to the ancient anecdote of Alexander and the Pirate is found in the following interview between Gen. Kearney and an Indian warrior: "Just as we were leaving camp to-day, an old Apache chief came in and harangued the general thus: 'You have taken Santa Fé, let us

stances cruel and unnatural, and forcing Mexicans against their will to become Americans. After the conquest, Texas claimed New Mexico as rightfully belonging to her, and endeavored to extend over it her jurisdiction and her system of slavery. What will be the result remains yet to be seen. She is prohibited by the joint resolution of annexation from extending slavery farther north than 36° 30′, but her laws make no such scrupulous limits to the dominions of oppression.

The vast domains acquired from Mexico, partly under pretence of giving them a better government and free institutions, have been more than a year since the treaty of peace was declared, deprived of any but a fluctuating military government, without efficiency or consistency, and the prospect now is that this state of things will exist for some time longer. The determination to reëstablish slavery over lands that have been redeemed and emancipated from its curse, may still farther postpone the erection of suitable territorial governments. Meantime, slaves have been carried into these new regions, the buying and selling of human beings has commenced, and the language of the slave press is, "Here is a vast field opened to the wealth and labor of the South, which if improved, promises a rich harvest. Slave labor can be employed more profitably in mining in California and New Mexico, than it possibly can be in any portion of the United States. Thus an extensive domain will be created for slave labor, the surplus of which is now crushing the Southern states." *

Parts of Tamaulipas, Chihuahua, Coahuila, and the whole

go on and take Chihuahua and Sonora; we will go with you. *You fight for the soil, we fight for plunder; so we will agree perfectly.* These people are bad Christians; let us give them a good thrashing,'" etc. Capt. Johnston's Journal, 30th Cong. 1st Session, Ho. of Rep. Ex. Doc. No. 41, p. 580.

* The *Nashville Union*, 1849.

of New Mexico and Upper California, have all been added by the late war and the treaty succeeding it, to the United States. How much this measure may have done to slake the natural thirst for territory may be considered, when it is kown, that, according to the statistics furnished Congress in 1848 by the War Department, New Mexico contains 77,387 square miles, and California 448,691 square miles; or total 526,078 square miles, or 366,589,920 acres. Besides this boundless surface, that would make more than eleven states as large as New York, Texas has gained additions to her before immense territory, so that she possesses now 325,520 square miles, or 208,322,800 square acres, or a region that would make, in all, more than seven States as large as New York; and if united with New Mexico and California, would constitute a territory carved out of Mexico more than eighteen times as large as the Empire State, or more than one hundred and nine times as large as Massachusetts; a tract of country about as large as England, Ireland, Scotland, France, Spain, Portugal, Italy, and Germany combined!

But vast as these domains of New Mexico and California are, the testimony of many travellers is, that they are not highly valuable either for agricultural, commercial or manufacturing purposes.

Col. Hardin, who was killed at the Battle of Buena Vista, says, "irrigation is necessary to insure all the crops in Mexico." "Nothing strikes an American eye sooner, or more strongly, than the denuded landscape every where presented to his view in Northern Mexico."

Major Gaines, another officer, says, "The country from the Nueces to the Rio Grande is poor, sterile, sandy, and barren, — with not a single tree of any size or value, on our whole route." Yet it was this disputed tract of desert that led to the first conflict of arms. He adds, "I have no hesitation in saying that I would not hazard the life of one valuable and useful man for every foot of land between San Patricio (or the Nueces) and the valley of the Rio Grande. The country is not now and never can be of the slightest value."

We have already quoted Hon. C. J. Ingersoll, as calling it "a stupendous desert."

Ruxton, an English traveller, says of New Mexico, "the general character of the department is extreme aridity of soil, and the consequent deficiency of water, which must ever prevent its being thickly settled. The valley of the Del Norte is fertile, but of limited extent, and other portions of the province are utterly valueless in an agricultural point of view, and their metallic wealth is greatly exaggerated."

Lieut. Peck, of the Corps of Topographical Engineers, says, "the boundaries of the territory (New Mexico) have never been very exactly defined, as a great share of the line lies over desert countries, where very little importance can attach to any exact location." "Many minerals, as iron, copper and lead occur in the mountains; but situated at the distance they are from the markets of the world, they will hardly be wrought."

Mr. Farnham calls the east part of California, "a howling desolation."

Of another portion of California, more to the west, Col. Emory of the U. S. A. says, "the land in the narrow valleys is good, but high, surrounded every where by barren mountains; and where the land is good, the seasons are too dry for men to attempt cultivation without facilities of irrigation." Speaking of all the northern states of Mexico, he says, "in no part of this vast tract can the rains from heaven be relied upon to any extent for the cultivation of the soil. The earth is destitute of trees, and in great part also of any vegetation whatever."

Captain Wilkes, commander of the Exploring Expedition, gives no very sanguine views either of the agricultural or commercial prospects of California, denies the alleged superior excellence of San Francisco, as a great Pacific port, and says, "although I am not disposed to question its extent and safety, yet I think there are many considerations which show that it is not so well adapted for the purposes of trade, or facilities for promoting it, as is generally believed."

The testimony of some of these and other travellers is, that the intellectual and moral aspects of the people are of a kin with the desert character of the soil; that ignorance, licentiousness, idleness, intemperance, and every savage and every civilized vice, have a rank growth among the heterogeneous population. Ruxton represents the whole people as bitterly opposed to the United States, in proof of which fact, so far as New Mexico is concerned, he adduces the insurrection in which Gov. Bent, and his followers were cruelly murdered. We have made a poor bargain to wage an expensive and sanguinary war to attach such a country to our States, and mix such elements of ignorance, vice, and discord with republican blood. Ill especially has been the annexation, when in addition to the war we paid some $20,000,000 for it to Mexico, though as an act, we rejoice that it was done, if the land were to be taken, on the score of its justice.

We may then class this territory among the political evils resulting from the Mexican war. We had more land before than we could settle and till for years to come. We had room enough and to spare. The new territories have introduced new topics of dispute. They will require a large standing army for their protection from the Indians, and others.* They expose our boundaries to perpetual inroads.

* The eleventh article of the Treaty with Mexico obligates the United States to prevent the incursions of the Indians from New Mexico, and California into the adjoining provinces of Mexico, if necessary, by force of arms. But most cruel and devastating wars have been waged in 1848, and 1849, by the Indians both within our own and the limits of Mexico, against the provinces lying on the Rio Grande; and on the other hand the local Mexican authorities, as a desperate measure, have offered Texan troops 50 dollars a head for every Indian killed, as if they were so many wild beasts!

They are not in themselves generally very valuable, except in certain narrow tracts, that minister to the "*auri sacra fames*," the accursed hunger for gold. We have compelled many thousands of people in those regions to come under our government, which is far from practising on the doctrine of civil and religious liberty, and basing government on the consent of the governed. We had established military institutions over these countries, and dissolved the allegiance of the inhabitants to Mexico, and annexed them to the United States, before a treaty of peace, the only proper tribunal, had decided where they should belong. We have inflicted a cureless wound upon the self-respect of Mexico, by dismembering with a violent hand her provinces, and destroying the integrity of the national domains. We have made an implacable enemy where we needed a fast friend. And so far as we have unjustly, by might and not by right, acquired possession of parts of Tamaulipas, Chihuahua, Coahuila, and all of New Mexico and Upper California, we must sooner or later suffer the most condign punishment for the gigantic wrong. As surely as there is a God reigning in heaven, or a Providence taking note of human conduct, the day cannot be far remote, when we shall be overtaken by the penalty of the law we have broken. Yes, our punishment has already begun. The ministers of Infinite Justice are upon us. Every interest of our beloved country, social, pecuniary, political, domestic, and moral has felt the shock of this war. The eagle eye of Liberty has drooped in sadness at the triumphs of oppression. And the Religion, whose interdict is, "Thou shalt not covet any thing that is thy neighbor's," veils her holy face in abhorrence at the apostasy of her professed children.

But finally, it is alleged that the new possessions are rich in the precious metals. Granted. Let every hill be a Potosi, and every stream a Pactolus. Let millions of gold and silver flow into the coffers of our republic from the

El Dorado of the Pacific. But is it a wise prayer to pray that our country should be exposed to such a temptation? that our countrymen should be drawn still deeper into the passion for money? These lands we have seen were as much forced from Mexico against her will, as the robber's booty is extorted from the helpless traveller by arms and threats.

We beat, we threatened, we coaxed Mexico to do what was against her wishes and interests. Can such treasures, thus procured, carry a blessing to their rapacious possessors? Not if life has one lesson left to teach; not if there is any truth in God's word; not if Providence has any oversight over human affairs. Ill-gotten riches, — when as a general rule have they benefitted individuals or nations? Are we not rushing into the love of money, into extravagance and worldliness, and unrepublican and unchristian habits with sufficient rapidity, but we must invoke new powers from the god of gold to add to their momentum? It is quite a sufficient offset, in the judgment of not a few, to all the abominations of this war, that it has resulted in the acquisition of so much more material wealth; as if that were the great good of life, as if that were what we most needed in this country, as if it were not the means of stimulating to greater intensity, the eager desire for gain, and making the dollar more than ever the deity which the multitude worship. Enterprise is spoken of; but had we not already a country resting on two remote oceans? was there any lack of room? Could "the American multiplication table," as it has been called, replenish the land to overflowing in one or two centuries? Must we cast covetous eyes on our neighbors' lands, because we are a progressive people? Read the history of the nations which have most abounded in the precious metals; read the tales of California life thus far developed, and then let the true lover of his country, let the friend of freedom and free institutions, say whether if he were to select any mode of retribution for the stupendous folly and crime of such a war, he could devise any one that under a fascinating disguise carries a Pandora's box of greater evils, than the acquisition of the gold lands of the Sacramento. The wounds of the sword may heal, but to pamper the lust for wealth is to inflict deeper wounds than those of the sword. The scars of the battle-field may be grown over by the unwearied powers of nature, and the bombarded city may again be built, but the deep, eating canker of avarice preys upon the nation's inner life, and frets and poisons and consumes what is most fair and noble and great and good in the character of the chief republic on the globe. The ancient saying may be fulfilled, "He gave them their request, but he sent leanness into their souls." Who that reviews the violent and fraudulent means employed to revolutionize and conquer California, can look with honest complacency on the gold coin stamped with that appellation? Who that understands in any measure what makes a State, what constitutes "the true grandeur of nations," but must lament with an unusual bitterness of sorrow, that, breaking away from the high promise and beautiful charm of our youth, and abjuring the splendid destiny of justice, peace and humanity, we should be content to crawl in the dust to scrape together a little of the perishable pelf of the world; and to care less for obedience to those eternal principles on which the moral universe is built, than for certain plantations stocked with slaves, certain harbors on the Pacific, and certain valleys barren in aught but the fiery gold!*

* "I am a friend to gold currency, but not to gold mining. That is a pursuit which the experience of nations shows to be both impoverishing and demoralizing to a nation. I regret that we have these mines in California; but they are there, and I am for getting rid of them as soon as possible. Make the working as free as possible."

* * * * *

"I care not who digs it up. I want it dug up. I want the fever to

CHAPTER XVIII.

NEW SCHEMES OF INVASION AND ANNEXATION.

"Peace is preëminently our policy. Our road to greatness lies not over the ruins of others, but in the quiet and peaceful development of our immeasurably great internal resources,—in subduing our vast forests, perfecting the means of internal intercourse throughout our widely extended country, and in drawing forth its unbounded agricultural, manufacturing, mineral, and commercial resources. In this ample field, all the industry, ingenuity, enterprize, and energy of our people may find employment for centuries to come; and through its successful cultivation, we may hope to rise, not only to a state of prosperity, but to that of greatness and influence over the destiny of the human race, higher than has ever been attained by arms by the most renowned nations of ancient or modern times. War, so far from accelerating, can but retard our march to greatness."—CALHOUN.

THE alleged benefit of war as ridding society of many of its worst members, and drawing off the vicious and abandoned to supply the decimation of its hospitals and battlefields, is very problematical. For it often returns home more vagabonds and villains, than it enlisted. It demoralizes many who were before pure, and spreads by means of its disbanded troops an immoral influence far and wide in the land. A large class of reckless, adventurous spirits are

be over. I want the mining finished. Let all work that will. Let them ravage the earth—extirpate and exterminate the mines. Then the sober industry will begin which enriches and ennobles a nation. Work as hard as we may we cannot finish soon." Speech of Mr. Benton in the Senate, January 15, 1849.

educated and instigated in times of war to such a pitch of hardened brutality, that they learn by practice to love to fight. They are intoxicated with the excitements of battles, and when peace is declared, they have become so enamored of the profession of the soldier, that they long for some new occasion for wielding the sword ; it matters little what the justice or merits of the cause may be, provided it open a theatre for bravery, promotion and pay.

In accordance with these principles, we find that the soldiers lately embarked in the Mexican Foray, are many of them anxious to go upon another human hunt. Some of them remained in Mexico, and enlisted in the army there. Some of them returned to Vera Cruz, and offered their services to Yucatan in the late contest with the Indians. But still others,—and it has been darkly hinted that thousands are interested in the plan,—propose to renew under the pretext of "a Buffalo Hunt on the Rio Grande," the process of Mexican dismemberment, and erect a new republic out of the provinces between the Siera Madre and that River, at first designed to be independent, but afterwards to fall into the hands of the United States as ripe fruit from the tree. The press has been full of rumors on the subject. Information was requested by Congress from the President of the United States in relation to the expedition ; to which he replied that he had no official information that any citizen or citizens of the United States were planning to revolutionize any part of Mexico.

But however this particular plan may be, it is sufficiently evident to all, that this war has given our countrymen a taste for national aggrandizement, that will ask for more and more. When the wild beast has dipped his tongue in blood, he rages for new prey. The strong passions that have been quickened by this conquest will not soon subside. The Sierra Madre republic may become an exploded idea, but not so the ambition and reckless spirit of adventure and free-booting out of which it sprang. Intimations have been given, in quarters entitled to serious consideration, that Cuba would be a desirable and easy acquisition for the United States.* The present spirit, if long indulged, will become

* The following document, which came out several months after the text was written, proves that the fears expressed there have not been groundless.

PROCLAMATION.—BY THE PRESIDENT OF THE UNITED STATES.

There is reason to believe that an armed expedition is about to be fitted out in the United States with the intention to invade the Island of Cuba, or some of the provinces of Mexico; the best information which the Executive has been able to obtain, points to the Island of Cuba as the object of this expedition. It is the duty of this Government to observe the faith of treaties, and to prevent any aggression by our citizens upon the territories of friendly nations.

I have therefore thought it necessary and proper to issue this proclamation to warn all citizens who shall connect themselves with an enterprise so grossly in violation of our treaty obligations that they will thereby subject themselves to the heavy penalty denounced against them by our acts of Congress, and will forfeit their claim to the protection of their country. No such persons must expect the interference of this Government in any form in their behalf, no matter to what extremities they may be reduced, in consequence of their conduct.

The enterprise to invade the territories of a friendly nation, set on foot and prosecuted within the limits of the United States, is in the highest degree criminal, as tending to endanger the peace and compromise the honor of the nation. And therefore I expect all good citizens, as they regard our national reputation, as they respect our laws, and laws of other nations, as they value the blessing of peace and the welfare of their country, to discourage and prevent, by all lawful means, any such enterprise, and I call upon every officer of this Government, civil or military, to use all efforts in his power to arrest for trial and punish every such offender against the laws providing for the performance of our sacred obligation to friendly powers.

Given under my hand the 11th day of August, in the year of our Lord one thousand eight hundred and forty-nine, and 74th of the independence of the United States.

Z. TAYLOR.

J. M. CLAYTON, Secretary of State.

a perfect lust of conquest, and overrun the continent, if not the world. The fascinating, but false idea of political propagandism may yet wreck our fairest hopes, if it be not seasonably checked by an appeal to right and truth. God grant, in his infinite mercy, not for our sakes only, but for the cause of civil and religious liberty,* and free institutions throughout the world, and the progress of humanity, that these political evils, which we have considered, may so far be counteracted and neutralized by the zeal and fidelity of the friends of peace, and all good men, that we may be spared from disunion, a profligate ambition, and a warlike destiny.†

* Who can fail to recognize the wisdom of the remarks of Mr. Pollock of Pennsylvania in the House of Representatives, Jan. 26, 1847?

"Do gentlemen desire the extension of our civil and religious privileges?—the pure principles of republican institutions? The influence of our example will accomplish this more speedily and certainly than the bayonets of our soldiery, or the thunder of our cannon. You may conquer their teritory, but you cannot *compel* the people to be free; you may overthrow existing governments, but you cannot establish by the sword a system of *self*-government. Self-government imposed by force upon a people would be tyranny to them."—Printed Speech, p. 5.

† A bill was introduced into the Senate of the United States, May 4, 1848, but not passed, to authorize the President "to take temporary military occupation of Yucatan," now the scene of a sanguinary civil war between the Spanish and Indian portion of the inhabitants. A long debate ensued.

Gen. Scott, senior officer in command in the American Army, wrote a letter in 1849, approving of the annexation of Canada in due time to the United States.

CHAPTER XIX.

MILITARY GLORY.

" The drying up a single tear has more
Of honest fame, than shedding seas of gore."
BYRON.

"BUT glory, glory!" shout the defenders of the war. "Much that you say of its evils may be true, but these evils are counterbalanced by a greater good. The war with Mexico has won for our army and country a European renown. None will now ask where are the United States, and what have they done; Monterey and Buena Vista, Vera Cruz and Cerro Gordo have answered that question."

The reply to this claim of glory has already been made in part in chapter seventeenth on the subject of true and false national honor. But the noxious spirit of military ambition among individuals, and the struggle to rise by the arts of war instead of the arts of peace, have been increased by the late events; while many care little what is for the honor and welfare of their country, provided they can win fame and place.

The disposition to laud military heroes, and thus falsify the true and christian scale of intellectual and moral greatness, has received a fresh impulse in the late atrocious war. The great men in these United States, who are they? Are they the poets who are striking the finest chords of the celestial lyre, and awakening, by strains of sublimity that will never die, the tastes and aspirations and immortal energies of men of all generations? Are they the artists who are shaping the marble into beauty, and giving life to the canvas, and thus refining and elevating the soul of the world? Are they the orators who have plead for liberty with angelic tongue, and urged the infinite concerns of religion with a melting persuasion? Are they the princely merchants who have given their tens of thousands of dollars to the cause of education, and the welfare of a hundred ages to come? Are they the retired and humble scholars, who, poor and unnoted by the world, trim the lamp of learning, decipher the meaning of life, unroll the map of antiquity, and extract the wisdom of libraries, and the history of empires gone? No; our great men are not poets, nor philosophers, nor philanthropists, nor artists, nor judges, nor jurists, nor statesmen. Sad day is it for humanity, when the heroes are the destroyers, and hosannas are sung over ruined cities and sinking nations, to those whose weapons are not love and truth, but fire and sword!

Every pains is taken to make the soldiers and officers think that they are the greatest and best of their day. Doubtless they have often acted from an ardent devoted patriotism, and had good intentions, though not the high standard of Christian duty. But we submit, that dinners and speeches, triumphal arches and temples, swords and other costly presents, honors and titles, and all the "pomp and circumstance" with which the troops and their officers are welcomed home from the scene of their terrible work, are calculated to start the germs of a dozen future wars in the breasts of the rising generation, and to make our American youth think that nothing is so glorious as war. Such is the practical lesson. This is our war-education.

This disposition to applaud the men of war, and to raise them to the highest offices in the State, and even to canonize their memories, as if they were also the brightest ornaments of the church, has been conspicuously seen in two celebrated cases, belonging respectively to the two main political parties of the country. Without uttering a word to stir up the embers of strife which are now going out, in the cold ashes of the dead, we are nevertheless clear in the belief that the choice of men from the battle-ground to guide the majestic counsels of a free Christian nation, is in exceedingly poor taste, bad policy, and worse morality. David was not allowed to build the temple, because he was a man of war; those who enter our consecrated temple of liberty ought to have pure hands and clean consciences, and hearts unspotted of their brother's blood, else they are not fit for that place, however well they may be qualified for some other station.

One objection is, that it is to employ men in one profession who have been serving all their lives in another, and very different one. It is not surely a wise man who gets his blacksmith to work on his teeth, or hires his house-carpenter to make a suit of clothes; and yet there is really as little or less incongruity in these respective callings, than there is in appointing military men, who are liable to be despots by the very nature of their command, to manage the civil concerns of a republic. It is to introduce a martial spirit and war maxims into the administration of national affairs. It is to pave the way for future wars, to place camp-schooled and battle-trained Presidents in the White House, who may hoist a flag of defiance against the world, and who will be ready to foster that system of affairs, in whose troubled waters they navigated their course to honor and renown. It is to repudiate still longer, and to hold in abeyance for some centuries the precepts of the Prince of Peace. We want civilians, not swordsmen; Catos, not Cæsars, nor Syllas at the head of Christian America. If our hearts, and our consciences were alive and awake, we should reject the idea with horror of making a military man the great man of the nation, and enthroning him aloft, as our grand representative before the eyes, either of Christendom or heathendom. We virtually should say by such an act, *that* is our highest ideal of what a great and good man is ; *that* is the American man.

It will not be one of the least of the disasters of this Mexican crusade, that it adds new force to a false principle in the working. of our government, and opens still wider to military ambition, not only its peculiar field of distinction, but the nobler walks of civil policy and national statesmanship, where it properly has no part nor lot.* It is time that a policy which is too manifest in its evil effects, through all past history, should be abandoned forever by a government of the people, and a government, therefore, whose great interest is, and always must be, Peace, Peace.

The illustrious Washington, himself a warrior, has testified against war. He says: "How much more delightful to an undebauched mind is the task of making improvements on the earth, than all the vain glory which can be acquired from ravaging it by the most uninterrupted career of conquests. How pitiful in the eye of reason and religion, is that false ambition which desolates the world with fire and sword, compared to the milder virtues of making our fellow-men as happy as their frail condition and perishable natures will permit them to be! It is time for night-errantry and mad heroism to be at an end."

The true patriot, therefore, is he who not only cries,

* "'Tis not in battles that from youth we train
The Governor who must be wise and good,
And temper with the sternness of the brain
Thoughts motherly, and meek as womanhood.
Wisdom doth live with children round her knees:
Books, leisure, perfect freedom and the talk
Man holds with week-day man in the hourly walk
Of the mind's business: these are the degrees
By which true Sway doth mount; this is the stalk
True power doth grow on; and her rights are these."
WORDSWORTH.

peace, peace, but earnestly eschews war. He most honors his native land, and shows himself its best friend and staunchest defender, not who pours oil on the war-flame, and exhorts the young men to fight for their country, "right or wrong," but who advocates peace, by word and deed.

CHAPTER XX.

THE TRUE DESTINY OF OUR COUNTRY.

"Your mission was, to be a model for all governments and for all other less favored nations; to adhere to the most elevated principles of political morality; to apply all your faculties to the gradual improvement of your own institutions and social state; and by your example to exert a moral influence most beneficial to mankind at large. Instead of this, an appeal has been made to your worst passions; to cupidity, to the thirst of unjust aggrandizement by brutal force; to the love of military fame and false glory; and it has even been tried to prevent the noblest feelings of your nature. The attempt is made to make you abandon the lofty position which your fathers occupied, to substitute for it the political morality, and heathen patriotism of the heroes and statesmen of antiquity." — GALLATIN.

ONE of the evils which the success of the Mexican invasion has produced, is to foster the pernicious notion, that we are, in these ambitious movements, following out our destiny.* Men have, in past times, committed the most abom-

* "It is our destiny to occupy that vast region" (Texas). Mr. Calhoun to Mr. King, Aug. 12, 1844. Append. to the Cong. Globe, 28th Cong. 2d Sess. p. 6. When Mr. Adams referred to Gen. 1: 26, 27, 28, as the ground of the American title to Oregon, he was asked by Mr. Kaufman of Texas, if it would not apply equally well to the Rio Grande.

inable deeds under the holiest sanctions and pretexts. The first conquest of Mexico was achieved at an awful cost of human life, under the plea of extending the kingdom of Christ and the church. The second conquest has been perpetrated under the audacious assumption of fulfilling the plans of Providence by extending the so-called "area of freedom," and accomplishing the destiny of the Anglo Saxon race. Many words are not wanted to expose this infatuation, as it has already been handled in an earlier connection of this Review.

There is a genuine Anglo Saxon destiny, of which we can conceive, that would be truly glorious in itself, and beneficial to mankind. But it is a destiny of liberty, not of license. It is a destiny of peace, not of war. It is a destiny of justice and noble ideas, not of invasions and violent annexations. It is a destiny whose emblems and implements are not the bomb and the bowie-knife, but the printing-press and the Bible. It is a destiny of raising up the fallen races, and administering wise and equal laws, wherever our dominion extends, not of trampling under the hoofs of the war-horse the prostrate red man, black man, or "dark browed Mexican." Science, commerce, and Christianity have given England and the United States, the two Anglo Saxon powers, an almost immeasurable influence over the rest of the human family. But God has put this sceptre into their hands for no idle and vain-glorious purpose, but to promote the welfare of mankind. Did the grand vision of a true and providential destiny, the real mission God has sent them to accomplish, dawn upon the minds of our statesmen and orators, our rulers and people, they would sheathe the sword forever. They would "trust not in uncertain riches, but in the living God;" not in carnal, but spiritual weapons. This is the only worthy destiny; the only one that heaven will bless, or futurity honor. It is impious to talk as if any people were fated to be ambitious, and grasping, and a terror to the race, and not a blessing. We might with as much propriety say, that an individual was destined to be a knave, or a ruffian. The Creator has, in one sense, destined all his children to be good and true, to obey his laws, and share in his promises. "He is not willing that any should perish, but that all should come unto repentance." But men have been gifted with the power of choice, and the opportunity of good and of evil, and if they come short of the glory of God, they may be said to have frustrated the divine plan, and not fulfilled their mission and destiny, as immortal beings.

These two nations are capable, if they have grace to seize the memorable opportunity, of leaving a mark upon the history of mankind, "above all Greek, all Roman fame." They can make themselves felt for good, — we yet hope that in a measure they are doing so, — to the remotest isle of the sea, and to the savage tribe, whose name even has not yet been domesticated in a civilized tongue. They have the saving ideas of Science, Freedom, and Christianity, that are able, if diffused, to keep the life-blood flowing, in strong and pure tides through their own hearts, and also to stir the deep sleep of paganism with fresh and waking pulses of regeneration. They have both the *personnel*, and the *materiel*, the ships, tools, arts, studies, truths, men, to do this magnificent work. They and their allies of kindred European races, if faithful to the high vocation, wherewith they are called, and "obedient to the heavenly vision," can, in two centuries, change the aspect of the whole habitable globe, and make the solitary place glad, and the desert blossom like the rose.

But if, abjuring this kingly power of beneficence, and turning away from this sublime mission of realizing the kingdom of Christ on earth, they bow themselves down to the base uses of Mammon and of Mars, they will fling away an opportunity of usefulness, such as has been rarely afforded in any juncture of history. If they consent to track the old bloody round of sordid, guilty ambition, and seek not to bring other tribes and races under the obedience of God, and harmony with his laws, but in subjection to their own tyranny, then it requires no prophet's eye to foresee that they are destined to fall a prey to the same passions, suicidally acting on themselves, which have poured the vials of wrath upon other countries. Their prodigious vices will be whips enough to scourge them. The immense agencies which might have proved the instruments of an incalculable beneficence, will become, when perverted, only the heavier millstones about their necks to pull them down to perdition. Destiny is a fearful word, and when we pronounce it, we remember most vividly the life of that mighty man who called himself the "child of destiny," but whose star, brilliant as it was, rushed headlong in an ill-fated moment from the zenith of its glory into eternal night. Imperial as the nations are, doth not the Lord "sit upon the circle of the earth," and "bring the princes to nothing, and make the judges of the earth as vanity"?

To use an astronomical figure, our national globe has enough centrifugal impulse, but it needs more centripetal tendency. It flies round and round with fearful sweep and speed, but may heaven grant, that it be held to the only true centre of its rotation, God. For a long time past, we have been but too boastful of our career, as if we could run any race out of the circumscription of the Deity, or attain any destiny but perdition, unless we followed his eternal ordinances and achieved his plan, and not our own caprice. Blind and foolish indeed must we be, if with the combined lights of history and Christianity on our path, we see any other or grander destiny for ourselves as a republic than that of righteousness, and freedom, and peace. "Peace hath her victories no less renowned than war." If the Anglo Saxons have any other destiny than that, let them beware before they run upon the thick bosses of those bucklers of the

Almighty, which have already drank up the blood of the proudest victors. God keep us from our own worst passions under a sanctified name!

Besides, the extension of our arms is far from being the extension of our ideas. We are far from believing that our armies have been missionaries of liberty or the cross to our semi-civilized neighbors. The battles they have fought have not been the triumphs of the Prince of Peace. The thousands killed will not be regarded as martyrs to the arts and sciences. The blood of Buena Vista and Cerro Gordo will not prove the seed of a new civilization. Battered cities, and ravaged farms are not the most significant tokens of the march of improvement. For we cannot suppose, that Mexico, after all the infinite evils and sufferings we have heaped upon her, will love us or our institutions any better than she did before. We have, on the contrary, violently arrested all those gentle and irresistible processes of assimilation and amelioration which were in happy progress, and taught her children to curse "the men of Northern tongue." No; the voice of history is clear, that the conquered hate the conquerors, and all that belongs to them, and very reluctantly, if ever, will they adopt their religious belief, social usages, forms of government, arts, and sciences, and methods of advancement, except by stern compulsion. The very idea of fighting a nation into a love of progress, is preposterous. We cannot overlap another country with our improvements, or put upon one civilization the party-colored patch of another. The spear is no instrument to take the place of the pruning-hook, nor the sword to do the work of the ploughshare. The tree of civilization withers and dies, when watered with human blood.

CHAPTER XXI.

THE STATESMAN'S RETRIBUTION.

"If statesmen were more accustomed to calculation, wars would be much less frequent." — FRANKLIN.

ROBERT HALL remarks in his Reflections on War, that, "if statesmen, if Christian statesmen at least, had a proper feeling on this subject, and would open their hearts to the reflections which such scenes must inspire, instead of rushing eagerly to arms, would they not try every expedient, every lenient art consistent with national honor, before they ventured on this desperate remedy, or rather, before they plunged into this gulf of horrors?" None but an affirmative answer can be given to such a question. But the difficulty is, that many statesmen are not Christians, and that they *do not have a proper feeling* on the subject of war. Indeed, as a general rule, it is not warriors that make war in this age, so much as it is statesmen. Warriors know what war is, and they do not involve nations in a conflict so readily oftentimes as those who only know the theory of war: while statesmen, sitting at their ease, in cabinet or congress, by a vote or a slip of the pen, gather vast armies to the field, and give the signal for great nations to dash themselves against each other in mighty conflict. They have little proper feeling of the waste in war of life, treasure, happiness, virtue, liberty.

They know not what they are doing, or if they know, it is a dreamy, misty, distant, and unfelt species of knowledge, that does not press with any motive-power on the springs of action. One day's hard march over the burning plain, one hour of Cerro Gordo, one night's fevered watching in the hospital, the amputation of their little finger, would teach them more what they really do when they set a war in operation, — its wounds, and pains, and horrid deaths, — than the whole experience of their life-time. "I have read," said an actor at Palo Alto, "many *accounts* of battles, but never a *description* of one."

The late sanguinary contest was originated in political causes, as already demonstrated. It was not generals but politicians that filled the magazine, and laid the fatal train. There was a huge mass of combustible war-passions lying latent and ready in the American population, but they are chiefly responsible at the bar of God and man, who wittingly and deliberately touched the explosive spark. Had there been any "proper feeling" in the great body of American statesmen, of the evils and guilt of war, they never would have voted men and money with overwhelming majorities in both houses of Congress to wage a distant and invasive warfare beyond the limits of our own country. Many of those men have already lived to lament the act into which they were betrayed by a sudden temptation, and many others will yet live to see the day when they shall bitterly deplore that deed of darkness, and all its evil consequences to their country and the world. They mistook the age in which they lived, when they feared to be called peace-men. They did not anticipate the glory which would encircle the immortal sixteen, "faithful found among the faithless." If ever an earnest rebuke were deserved by large bodies of men, it is by those who at first weakly yielded to the call for millions of money and thousands of men, and voted year after year, after the odious schemes of conquest and slavery were disclosed, still to uphold such a system of wrong and wretchedness. The inconsistencies of political men and parties are too glaring to be allowed to pass without notice and severe condemnation. Professing freedom, they waged a war to extend slavery. Calling themselves the friends of the people, they sanctioned and supported a war that loaded their country with a heavy war-debt, and sent misery into multitudes of once happy homes. Putting peace forward as their policy, they have been contented with waging, for the short period of its continuance, one of the sharpest, bloodiest, and most injurious of wars. Advocating universal humanity, and the rights of man as men, they have forced our free institutions, as we call them, by stress of arms upon large portions of a foreign land and a foreign people. Such palpable and flagrant violations of right and justice will bring a retribution sooner or later to the authors of the war, and will involve many of the innocent with the guilty. Men of place and power, exalted as their position may be in the sight of men, are amenable to the laws of God. "The statesman's retribution" is no empty phrase, but expresses a most solemn and instructive lesson of history.

For it is well known the actual effect of war is, that instead of raising politicians to honor and authority, it puts them very unceremoniously aside to make way for the elevation to the highest civil offices of those who have fought their way to fame. The revolutionary war furnished one warrior, but more a civilian than a warrior, for the Presidency. The war of 1812 supplied two candidates of opposite parties, who entered the White House under a perfect whirlwind of enthusiasm. The war with Mexico has already given one incumbent to the lofty chair of state, and it has half a score of others in expectancy. Meanwhile, the great statesmen of the country, who have guided by their wisdom and eloquence the national councils, and who have shed an intellectual and historical glory over the pages of the past, and who will live forever on the tongues of men, have been passed by, or if raised to this more than kingly eminence, have occupied it but for the shortest possible period.

"When politicians bring on war," says the *North American Review*, April, 1848, "they must pay the penalty. In republics, if civilians wish to retain their just influence as statesmen, they must preserve peace. War always has given, and always will give, in our own and in every free country, ascendency to military reputation. Snatching the prizes of political ambition from the politician, it will carry the successful general to his seats of power. Some of the politicians who pushed this country into the war of 1812, still live to brood over the fact, that that war raised up military chieftains who clutched from their grasp the presidential crown, which otherwise would have encircled their brows in sure succession. It is a most instructive circumstance in our history, that when James Madison, then at the head of the government, manifested a reluctance to favor a declaration of war with England, a committee of three was despatched from a republican caucus to communicate to him the determination of that party to insist upon the measure. The experienced wisdom of that great statesman was overruled, and constrained by the short-sighted zeal of less wary politicians. Of that caucus Henry Clay and John C. Calhoun were the master spirits, and of that committee they were members. Although quite young men, they had, by their genius and eloquence, even then acquired the greatest degree of popularity that can be attained in the sphere of statesmanship. The whole nation was waiting, with admiring eagerness, to confer upon them, one after the other, its highest honor. They had their way, and war was declared. When the revolutionary series of Presidents was brought to a close, on the retirement of James Munroe, Gen. Jackson, the hero of New Orleans, took from Mr. Clay so many of the electoral votes of the West, and from Mr. Calhoun so many of the votes of the South and Middle States, as to leave them both distanced in the race. The popularity of Jackson yielded only to that of General Harrison, the hero of Tippecanoe; and a fresh crop of military chieftains has just been reared, to destroy, in all probability, the last chance of these veteran aspirants for the great prize. It is not the least of the eminent services they have rendered their country, that, in their baffled ambition, the distinguished statesmen and truly great men whom we have named, teach to all coming times the salutary lesson, that, if politicians will have war, they must step aside forever from the path of honor, and relinquish the posts of power to overshadowing rivals, created by their own suicidal hands. It is not unlikely, that this lesson will be corroborated by the political results of the war in which the country is now involved. Let us hope that it may make a deep and durable impression upon that class of persons whom it so vitally concerns. When the leaders of parties become convinced, that in promoting warlike measures and a military spirit, they are digging their own graves, we confidently rely upon perpetual peace."

The same general rule has held good in regard to a host of other offices. The warrior has ever taken precedence of the statesman, however wise or great. We have preferred men of action to men of thought, and have cared little apparently what their actions were. Nothing shows more distinctly the low and coarse type of modern civilization than this choice of warriors to conduct the affairs of Christian nations. No mistake could be greater than for civilians to encourage the madness of war, and hope in times of turbulence to rise to honor and place. For by every war they foment and wage, they are calling into existence numbers of popular and well-known rivals, who will easily distance them in any race for office. However well educated, large in experience, ripe in civil wisdom, eloquent in council, sagacious in trouble, indefatigable in serving the country, patriotic in sentiment, and really laboring for the true glory of the land and the true good of the human family, the mighty orator, the profound statesman, the far-famed jurist, or the unsullied patriot will be brushed aside from the path to honor of the successful warrior, as if he were a mere fly. The motto at the head of this chapter is significant. When will politicians learn wisdom? When will they pause before they make wars, vainly hoping thus to gain popularity with their countrymen? When will they cease to be instrumental of the bold incongruity of mingling the despotism of war with the working of free institutions, and the professions of a Christian people with the morality, manners, and spirit of the camp? When will they open their eyes to the fact, that so far as they encouraged the spirit of war in their countrymen, they are preparing trouble and ruin for the days to come; that they are going counter at once to the dictates of republicanism and Christianity; that they are reversing the progress of the world, and bringing back the ages of darkness and blood? And when, especially, will they learn that impressive lesson of the past, that statesmen however eminent, legislators however sagacious, diplomatists however successful, and jurists however learned, will stand no chance in the competition for political honors and office with him who has smelt gunpowder? The highest admonitions of patriotism and religion thus combine with the lowest of self-interest to warn them against the folly and the wickedness of seeking to make our country a great military power.

Let them strive to repress and calm the mania for war in our land. Let them direct the energies of a youthful nation into the channels of industry and public improvement. Let them understand that it will be no honor or happiness for us to attempt to live over the warlike past of the old world, and acquire war-debts, war-taxes, and war-customs, that will make the remotest generations groan and curse us for our foolishness. Oh, let the great men of our country understand, that if they would be truly great, and would live in the glad remembrance of their countrymen, they must ally themselves to lofty principles and causes, — Freedom, Peace,

Temperance, Righteousness, Truth, — which will survive the transient excitements of the day, and the little questions of party and place, and bear on the names of their advocates to be loved and reverenced by generations yet unborn. For as the intellectual and moral life of mankind is more developed, and the spiritual aim of the Gospel is more nearly reached, the true benefactors of the race will be more and more associated with this new era of progress, while the names of those who proved false to the high trust of their times, and basely consented to the iniquities which have blasted the life and happiness of successive nations and races in history, will be held in deserved and perpetual execration, as the real traitors to their country and its institutions, who were willing for a mess of pottage to sell the birthright of Freedom, and the Hope of the world.

CHAPTER XXII.

WAR MAXIMS.

"To spoil, to slaughter, and to commit every violence; and then call the manœuvre by a lying name, — government; and when they have spread a general devastation, — call it peace." — Tacitus.

Most men desire to maintain some consistency of character and conduct, and hence, in order to justify the doing of such deeds, as we have recorded, they appeal to certain principles like the following. "Our country, right or wrong;" * or, as paraphrased by a distinguished general, "between my government and a foreign nation, I never ask a question.

* Commodore Decatur.

My government is always right." "Conquer a peace;" "Do evil that good may come." Make war on Mexico that we may extend "the area of freedom," and civilize, and Protestantize her. To all such principles it is enough to reply, that they are good enough as secondary, but not as supreme motives of conduct. Our first and highest relation is to God, and our first duty, therefore, is to ask, "Lord, what would'st thou have us do?" Christ is a greater name than country. He must pronounce upon all social customs and public affairs, and what he condemns, is condemned, and what he approves, is approved by all his faithful followers. We are not allowed to make our country our god, though we are bound to do her good service. The only difference of opinion is, what is good service to her? Is it to encourage and assist her in a wicked and barbarous war, and to fan the war-spirit to greater intensity, or is it to check her going headlong in a heaven-defying career of conquest and usurpation? He does most to keep her fame untarnished, not who fights her unjust battles, but who preserves her truth, and justice, and freedom from becoming obsolete ideas in the working of her institutions. Jesus said, "he that loveth father or mother more than me, is not worthy of me." Even the tenderest social relations were less to be regarded than the spiritual claims of his faith and love; then how much more would he have said the same of the ties of country. They are good, but not the best; they are great, but not the greatest.

This wronging of conscience and sophistication of reason by the maxims of this war are not the least of the ill effects to which it has given birth. How many have adopted the maxim, "our country, right or wrong," cannot be known, but it has had a wide-spread currency and popularity. The ancient doctrine, "the king can do no wrong,"* has been

* *King Henry V. in disguise and three soldiers.*]

K. Henry. "Methinks I would not die any where so contented as in the king's company; his cause being just and his quarrel honorable.

supplanted by another maxim every way as fatal to a Christian manhood. If we are to be ruled by a tyrant, whose behests must be obeyed at whatever sacrifice of individual scruples and remonstrances of conscience, it matters little whether that tyrant be called "king," or "country." A democracy may oppress as well as a monarchy. If we proceed upon the principle, that we are under obligations to do whatever our rulers command, be it an act of pillage or blood, not because it is right, but because they command it, then we are back again, as to all practical intents and purposes, in the age of passive obedience and blind adhesion to authority, slaves, tools, of the make-plots and the mar-plots

Will. "That 's more than we know.

Bates. "Ay, or more than we should seek after; for we know enough, if we are the king's subjects; if his cause be wrong our obedience to the king wipes the crime of it out of us.

Will. "But if the cause be not good, the king himself hath a heavy reckoning to make; when all those legs and arms, and heads chopped off in battle, shall join together at the latter day and cry all, 'We died at such a place;' some swearing, some crying for a surgeon; some, upon their wives being left poor behind them; some upon the debts they owe; some upon their children rawly left. I am afeared there are few die well, that die in battle; for how can they charitably dispose of any thing when blood is their argument? Now if these men do not die well, it will be black matter for the king that led them to it, whom to disobey were against all proportion of subjection.

K. Henry. "Then if they die unprovided, no more is the king guilty of their damnation than he was before guilty for those impieties for which they are now visited. Every subject's duty is the king's; but every subject's soul is his own. Therefore should every soldier in the wars do as every sick man in his bed, wash every moth out of his conscience: and dying so, death is to him an advantage; or not dying, the time was blessedly lost, wherein such preparation was gained: and, in him that escapes, it were not sin to think, that making God so free an offer, he let him outlive that day to see his greatness, and to teach others how they should prepare.

Will. "'T is certain that every man that dies ill, the ill is upon his own head, the king is not to answer for it." — *Shakspeare.*

of the men in power. In foisting such a saying into the mouths of men at this day, and getting it into a newspaper immortality, tyranny has stolen a march upon freedom, and free institutions become but a name "to point a moral, or adorn a tale." The old spirit has revived under a new name. We are to have not the tyrant *One*, but the tyrant *Million*, who may be quite as intolerable, and quite as subversive of that true liberty, which respects the rights of conscience, as the dearest object of life, and the last a moral being would consent to relinquish. If we are to uphold our country in her wrong, as in her right principles and measures, farewell to the prerogatives of an American, the patrimony of freemen. We are then a nation of slaves.

Was it not for these same rights of conscience, that the toil and treasure of the past have been freely lavished? Was it not for this birthright of the soul that our fathers fled their country, lived in exile, crossed the ocean, made the wilderness their home, and companied with wild beasts, and wilder men? What nobler staple runs through the history of the past than this sturdy, lofty independence for conscience' sake? This is the glory that still lingers on many a spot of the old world, and makes holy ground of many a battle-field, tomb, and church, where wise and holy men lifted up the voice of non-conformity to the acts of tyrants, and dared all, and lost all, for the sake of keeping "a conscience void of offence." And shall this new world, in her virgin promise, repudiate the single glorious principle which sheds such splendid renown over the darkest scenes of history? The names of Huguenot, and Covenanter, and Puritan are not lightly thus to be taken in vain.

Instead of this blind and unquestioning devotion to "country, right or wrong," or rather to the existing government of the country, for we believe that a majority of the American people were always hostile to the war, how much more truly noble and Christian it would have been for the officers, who were opposed to the invasion, and many of the leading ones were, to say; "we will defend our country when she is attacked; but our duty can never require of us to go on a warfare of conquest. This is not the purpose of government, and especially of our government, which is to secure the rights, and protect the lives, and liberty, and property of all. We can fight in a defensive, but not in an offensive war; in a defence of freedom, but not in a crusade for slavery. We will rather imitate the example of Lord Effingham in the British army, and Capt. Thrush in the navy, and retire from the service, than wound our consciences, and really wrong our country by encouraging those who hold her destinies in their hand, to plunge into a career of rapine and blood. If this be treason, make the most of it. It is better to rebel against our country than against our God."

If our country be wrong in her *internal* policy, or administration of civil national affairs, does any press or person hesitate a moment to condemn the wrong, and uphold by word and deed, by the potent weapon of a freeman, the ballot-box, the cause of the right? No, never. Why then should so different a rule obtain in international affairs? Are not the questions of war and peace as momentous, as needful to be determined by the principles of right, as the measures of tariffs, internal improvements, or sub-treasury? The same laws bind us as citizens that bind us as men. If we are not at liberty to do wrong as men, we are not at liberty to do so as Americans. If it would be wrong to uphold an evil among ourselves, because it is the voice of the government, which is not always the voice of the people at the time, and which is often far from being the voice of God, shall we advocate the idea of vindicating, even to the death, our country's course, when we openly avow, or strongly suspect, she is in the wrong? Never, never. "For what shall it profit our country, if it gain the whole world at the expense of its soul?"

To "conquer a peace,"* another phrase often used, if it have any ordinary meaning, signifies to destroy a peace, and overthrow it. During two long years of blood, and rapine, and demoralization, did this war subjugate the powers of peace. But at the last the sword settled nothing. Negotiation was more powerful than eighteen-pounders. The pen of the commissioner was mightier than the sword of the conqueror. Two wise men from Mexico and the United States, meeting amicably together, could, upon the basis of the late treaty, have easily secured to the United States, in the way of a business transaction, all the territory she wanted by means of the bonus of $20,000,000 she has now paid, without shedding one drop of human blood. The like has been done before, and it might have been done again.

> "Take away the sword,
> States can be saved without it."

Some other phrases referred to have been considered in other connections of this review, but we turn to another war-maxim.

The coat-of-arms of Great Britain has the motto, with heraldic devices, "*Dieu et mon droit*," "God and my right," flanked by a lion on one side and a unicorn on the other. But where would Great Britain be, if she were treated herself on the principle which she thus holds forth as the highest expression of the spirit of her government? Suppose the nations of the world should insist on the utmost claims of right with her, where would be most of her riches and possessions? What would be the result of carrying out such a doctrine in the world but eternal war? Observe that it is

* Coleridge is said to be the original author of this self-contradictory phrase. Shakspeare better says,

> "A peace is of the nature of a conquest;
> For then both parties nobly are subdued,
> And neither party loser."

not God and right, but *my* right; not yours, but *mine;* that selfish word, *my.* I will have my rights, whether you have yours or not. I will yield nothing, conciliate, compassionate nothing, but exact sternest justice.

So, likewise, we have a much commended saying among us, that we "will ask for nothing which is not right, and will submit to nothing which is wrong." Then we cannot live in this world. For we are often obliged to forego our rights, often obliged to yield to what is wrong in others. What would be our condition as a nation, as individuals, if we were treated one day by God as we propose in this rude and barbarous justice to treat mankind? We should not be at all. We should be non-existent. For we hang upon the skirts of the divine compassion; we live at the momentary merciful will of our God. If he treated us as we deserve, and were strict to mark our iniquities against us, who could stand before him? Could we as a people? could we as individuals? Not one moment. We are not so careful to render to others their dues and their rights, as not often to need their pardon for the wrong; we are not so particular in our conduct towards our Supreme Judge, as not daily and hourly to need his forbearance. We are to claim our right, but not with wrong; we are not, Shylock-like, to practise on a blind and inexorable justice alone. The apostle assures us that sometimes mercy is to rejoice against judgment; at any rate, that he is in imminent danger of having judgment without mercy, who has shown no mercy. It is a fearful declaration, and should make us pause, before we say that we will submit to no wrong; else we commit ourselves to a principle at war with nature, providence, and the whole structure of human society.

In truth, a great proportion of the difficulties in the world arise from this disposition to vindicate our own rights, let whose rights else suffer, and to push matters to the utmost verge of lawful allowance, rather than to pursue a mild and forbearing policy. We are men, mortal, erring, sinful. Who are we, to judge another man's servants? Who are we, to take into our hands the blazing thunderbolts of vengeance? "Dearly beloved, avenge not yourselves, but rather give place to wrath."

We profess to be a Christian nation, and we would feel aggrieved if we were denied this honorable name. And what is the law of our master, and how do we obey it? Is it not mercy, pardon, forbearance, forgiveness, from one end to the other of the Gospels? Did he not enrol it among the beatitudes? "Blessed are the merciful, for they shall obtain mercy." Did he not say with emphatic reiteration, "Bless them that curse you, and pray for them that despitefully use you?" Did he not command us to "forgive our enemies, and to be merciful as our father in heaven is merciful?"

In short, it is right to be merciful, according to Christianity; it is not a weakness, but a duty. It is right sometimes to yield to a wrong, and overlook it, rather than commit a greater wrong by resistance and exaction. It is right sometimes to waive our rights, and generously to suffer ourselves, rather than to make others suffer, though they deserve it. It is not weakness, but strength, not shame, but honor, to forgive, not seven times only, but seventy times seven, if the offender turn and pray to be forgiven.

We cannot better conclude this chapter than by briefly adding, to what has been elsewhere said on the subject of *preparing war by preparing for war*, the late remarks of the Earl of Aberdeen, formerly Secretary of State for Foreign Affairs, in the House of Lords, in England,—"I am disposed to dissent from that maxim which has been so generally received, that, 'if you wish for peace, you must be prepared for war.' It may have applied to the nations of antiquity, and to society in a comparatively barbarous and uncivilized state, when warlike preparations cost but little; but in the state of society in which we now live, when the warlike preparations of great powers are made at enormous expense, I say that so far from their being any security to peace they are directly the contrary, and tend at once to war. For it is natural that men, having adopted means they think efficient to an end, should desire to put their efficiency to the test, and to have some direct result from their labor and expense."

CHAPTER XXIII.

MARTIAL LITERATURE.

" Seven years' fighting sets a whole kingdom back in learning and virtue to which they were creeping, it may be a whole age."—JEREMY BENTHAM.

" The course of education from infancy to manhood, at present pursued, tends to inspire the mind with military ardor and a love of glory. Almost as soon as a boy is born, care is taken to give his mind a military turn."—WILLIAM LADD.

WE have before us a list of forty-eight volumes, which are connected with the late war, and which generally approve highly of its occurrence. They consist of both prose and poetry, history and biography, travels and essays. They are deeply imbued with the martial spirit, and laud to the skies the achievements of the American arms in Mexico.

One of the unhappy consequences of this war is, that it has thus created a literature adverse to morals, refinement and religion. This war-literature has circulated through the newspapers and cheap works over the whole land. The lives of victorious generals, the bloody feats of prowess, the histories of battles and sieges, have formed a good part of the reading of the mass of the people, and especially of many young persons, during the three past years. The sacred power of poetry has been desecrated to laud the cruel deeds of war. The historian has exhausted upon it all his research. The fine arts have been employed to pamper the love of war, and by pictures and panoramas, to set on fire the blood of youth with the intoxicating passion of martial achievements. The country is full of these things. Every village has its "views" of battles, and the siege at Vera Cruz, or the charge at Buena Vista. The eye of youth is taught to sparkle at the sight of a battle-piece, before it knows what war is. The natural effect upon society of such reading, and war-songs, and exhibitions is exceedingly unfavorable to all the leading moral interests of a free country. It places before the individual a false standard of character, and cheats him into the belief that the best end of life is to figure in some important scene, to do some great thing, however wrong or bloody, and to disown the quiet pursuits of peace. It places before the nation a wrong standard, and befools the people with the idea that war, and not peace, is their real interest, that they shall gain some valuable end by invading the domains of their neighbors, and conquering a vast extent of barren and unhealthy territory. The idea of the true destiny of our country in liberty, equality and self-government, has by this miasma of war been corrupted into the false idea of our destiny as consisting in power, military renown, and the vulgar guilt of the savage nations of old, or the unbaptized empires of modern Europe.

The news of war, the descriptions of cities taken, of victories won, of men killed, are of a poisonous moral influence. They paganize a Christian people. They familiarize them with carnage and cruelty. They make them forget the sermon on the mount, and the prayer on the cross. They fill the heads and hearts of the young with perverted notions of right and wrong, and educate them in their day and generation to be men of blood. No nation ever came out of war but with a lowered standard of moral principle, and an increased amount of profligacy, and an augmented number of drunkards, vagabonds, gamblers, and wretched, ruined men.

At the present day, when the people almost universally read, the evil of such a literature is greatly enhanced. It is so cheap that all can buy it. It is so diffused, that it enters every nook and corner of the land. It is so stimulating to the curiosity and passions of half-educated minds, that they find it invested with all the charms of romance. Indeed not less than half a dozen novels of the cheap kind, independently of the histories and biographies above enumerated; have already taken their plots and incidents from the war with Mexico. Nor has this military literature by any means exhausted itself. The advertising columns show that it has new productions in reserve. The seed of future wars has thus been sown broadcast over our country, and wrong impressions have been made upon thousands of young and ductile minds which will never be effaced.

The numerous war-speeches in and out of Congress, the voluminous war-documents issued from the capital of the country, and the public journals spreading before the eyes of millions of readers the "glorious news from Mexico," the "great victory won," all belong to this noxious species of literature. For unless accompanied with proper correctives and remonstrances, they pervert the moral principles of the people, arouse their passion for arms, and withdraw their interest and attention from those humble but praiseworthy pursuits of agriculture, commerce, and manufactures, which cannot compete with the brilliant exploits of sieges and battles, "in pomp and circumstance." "The pestilence that walketh in darkness and the destruction that wasteth at noonday" have been abroad in our land, and gathered from city and country the fearful harvest of death; but better, far better, that an annual cholera should decimate our population, than that the deadly malaria of such a literature should infect the mind and corrupt the heart of America. The evil in one case is death to the body, but in the other it is death to Freedom, death to the progress of Peace, and death to the hopes of the world. Vast and beneficent is the influence of a pure and elevated literature; but when the historians and orators of a nation contribute by their works to foster the spirit of war and the pagan passion of glory, they are calling back the dark ages of blood and oppression again to overshadow the earth. Many a splendid lyric from the poet's burning soul, many a persuasive appeal from the speaker's inmost heart, have gone forth against this war. We are thankful for these indignant remonstrances against evils that could not be arrested. But let us pray, if for one thing more unceasingly than another, that the literature and the fine arts of America may be rescued from following the example of the old world, and that they may consecrate their glorious creations of genius and beauty to the God, not of war, but of Peace. Let them adopt the noble motto of Allston, " No battle-pieces."

CHAPTER XXIV.

WAR AND THE FIRESIDE.

"The tramp of marching hosts disturbs the plough,
The sword, not sickle, reaps the harvest now,
And where the soldier gleans the scant supply,
The helpless peasant but retires to die;
No laws his hut from licensed outrage shield,
And war's least horror is th' ensanguined field.
Fruitful in vain, the matron counts with pride
The blooming youths that grace her honored side;
No son returns to press her widowed hand,
Her fallen blossoms strew a foreign strand."

MRS. BARBAULD.

REGARDING, as we do, the domestic relations of life as the appointment of heaven for the education, and happiness of mankind, and home as the centre of some of the purest and happiest influences known in society, we come now to consider the Mexican war in its bearing on these great interests of the respective countries involved in the conflict. The preceding chapters have already told a part of the tale. But the subject is one of sufficient moment to deserve a separate consideration. "The war and the fireside" need to be brought into direct juxtaposition, that all the wickedness of the one may be revealed in the light and blessedness of the other. When Satan approached the Garden, where dwelt the happy pair, the mighty poet represents him as clothing himself in the most seductive, but most fatal, guise. War puts on its most specious garb of honor, patriotism, and freedom, when it comes to take away the pillars and ornaments of the Christian home, but it allures only to betray, and promises but to disappoint. Its vast multitudes of warring, desperate men, are all sons, many of them fathers, and husbands, most of them brothers. They not only bear the dreadful implements of destruction, and the badges of their respective corps, but they carry in every feature and outline of body some hereditary trace of an endeared parentage, some look of the fireside, some habit of home. These beings are not fiends and devils, though, when they are plunged in the hurricane of the battle-field, they might be so regarded by a spectator from some other planet, unfamiliar with the proceedings of men upon our earth. In that dense array of armed men meet the divergent lines of ten thousand happy firesides ; the cords of love from some far-distant log-cabin, or refined family, are pulling at the hearts of the embattled host, and nothing rises so vividly to memory, while they hang over the giddy risks of life and death before them, as the dear ones that they have left behind, perhaps forever. "War and the fireside"! how contrasted, and yet how connected ! One, the name of every thing most awful in passion, pain, vice, outrage, and death ; the other, the name of all the sweetest joys, hopes, possessions and associations out of heaven.

And when the fight is over, humanity once more reassumes her sway, and returns to the field where thousands lie dead, thousands in the agonies of death, and thousands in the ten-fold agonies of life, disputing with death the possession of her subjects. As the hand of kindness raises this soldier's gory head, what word does he murmur? It is, wife, mother, sister! As the blood gurgles from the shot-hole in the side of that dragoon, and every pulsation grows fainter, what whispered syllables still linger and tremble on the convulsed lips? They are, father, brother, son. O God, we devoutly ejaculate, when we see or think of such scenes, can this be the work of thy human children, and of brothers one of another? Can the tender frames that were once borne in a mother's arms, and nursed at a mother's breast, have made the living breast-work against the cannon's mouth? Can the hand that once grasped a tenderer hand, and vowed the vow "for better for worse, for richer for poorer," now swing the cleaving sword, or urge the piercing bayonet? War has brought all these horrors to pass; and when its dead are buried, and its sick collected in the hospital, then it sends back to the lovely places of domestic happiness the heart-rending intelligence of its dear bought victories, or bloody defeats, and fills a whole land with lamentation and tears. Every mail carries its sorrow to some household. Every newspaper records the bereavement of some fond wife, some aged father, some widowed mother, some orphan children. And into myriads of once happy circles where the messenger of the ill tidings of death never comes, he nevertheless sends the perpetual chill of gloomy fears and forebodings, and keeps every ear on the alert to hear a sinister step, every heart-string quivering with the anguish of hope deferred, or torn by tidings of sickness, or wounds, or captivity.

And then, putting aside all these considerations of the heart, which all that have hearts must feel, how positively does war wage a universal hostility against every physical and economical interest of home. It induces reckless habits, and spendthrift ways. It squanders on the extra finery of the uniform or the equipments, what would fill the larder, or give a book to a child, or a quarter's tuition at school. It raises the taxes already high, and ill borne. It withdraws the prop and best workman of the family to waste his sinews in a remote country. It returns the halt, the lame, the blind, the maimed, the sick, to be nursed and cared for the remainder of their days. It leaves many a widowed and orphan group to the tender mercies of a cold and unfeeling world. And it hands down to succeeding ages the legacy of its debts, taxes, expensive vices, pension list, sinecures, and its immoral histories of violence, blood, and outrage, to sow the seeds of trouble in new bridal homes, and fling a shadow of gloom over the firesides of the third and fourth generations.

The following reflections, after "a famous victory," by one of the most popular editors and writers of the country, are as feeling and beautiful as they are true and melancholy. Why cannot those who make war "think of these things," before they set in operation, by a few strokes of the pen, such an engine of domestic wretchedness and ruin?

"Every battle field," says the *Louisville Journal*, "is the source of inexpressible grief, and woe, and agony. To say nothing of the gory victims that on such fields yield up their latest breath, who shall attempt to portray the agony that must pierce the hearts of their surviving friends? The battle of Buena Vista may be consecrated to fame, and poets may hymn its glories, and attune their harps to sing the praise of its survivors, and to chant mournful requiems over the graves of the gallant dead; but that bloody field will also be consecrated to human woe. Each one of the thousand that were martyred to the fell spirit of war, had his friends, by whom his loss will be mourned. Many fathers there fell, leaving helpless children to struggle with the stormy tides of life, without the protection of the parental arm. Many husbands there died, leaving trusting wives to lament in bitterness of soul their loss. The dearly-beloved sons of hoary-headed sires there sighed their last breath away, to be mourned awhile and soon to be followed to the land of spirits by those to whom their loss is irreparable. When we reflect on the desolation that will be carried to thousands of firesides, — the gloom that will hang like a cloud over numberless homes, lately bright with the hues of happiness, — the tears of orphans, the shrieks of wives, and mothers, and sisters, the groans of fathers, and sons, and brothers, — the wide-spread and lasting grief that will result from the carnage of the field of Buena Vista, what heart can refuse its sympathy with the bereaved, or refrain from cursing the infatuation which renders such scenes of blood necessary?"

"You could tell at a glance," says Capt. Henry, in his "Campaign Sketches," "the wounded of Palo Alto or Resaca de la Palma. The latter were mostly bullet wounds; the amputated limbs told of the cannon's fearful execution in the former. Beside one poor fellow a beautiful girl of seventeen was seated, keeping off the flies. She was his wife. In another corner, a family group, the mother and her children were seated by the wounded father. One bright-eyed little girl quite took my fancy, and my heart bled to think that thus early she should be introduced to so much wretchedness. On one bed was a corpse; on another was one dying, holding in his hand the grape-shot that had passed through his breast. He showed it to us with a sad countenance. I left the hospital shocked with the horrors of war."

"On the field of Resaca de la Palma," says Mr. Thorpe, "there was an affecting scene enacted among the dead soldiers. One of the first that fell mortally wounded was an Irishman, — a remarkably brave fellow. All the night ensuing, his poor wife sat upon the field, the stiffened corpse of her husband resting on her lap, her little child asleep by her side. As the sun rose in the morning, she was discovered, surrounded with the dead, her head upon her husband's breast, absorbed in grief. As the day wore on, the stench of the field became offensive; but still she held her seat by the side of the lifeless clay, and in paroxysms of overwhelming sorrow she was torn from the dead, that it might be consigned to its mother earth."

Speaking of the houses where the wounded were placed at Matamoras, he says; "amidst all their misery and desolation, amidst these places so humbling to pride, so sacrificing to vanity, woman was there, devoted to a husband or a brother; she sat in the dust, fanned away the torturing insects that lived on blood, and revelled in wounds, sanctifying the most menial offices by her spirit and influence, and shedding by her smiles, by her silent attentions, by her teachings of hope in another world, the only bright rays that are seen to glimmer in a Mexican hospital."

Speaking of another battle, he writes, "appalling indeed were the scenes on that field of carnage. Many of the wounded writhed in agony, and others, quiet in their last hour of life, gazed with anxious eyes towards the setting sun; their faces, in the morning glowing with health, were now wan as if with months of consuming disease. All begged but for one drop of water to quench the thirst that consumed their vitals. Along the pathway of the shot that fairly raked through the solid columns of the Tennessee regiment, lay extended the dead in every conceivable position of horror; headless trunks, and limbless bodies cut in twain. The faces of some wore the placid smile of happiness; in others, the life-blood had ebbed away, leaving the expression of defiance and revenge marked upon the inanimate clay. The wounded strove to creep about, or, thrown hurriedly into wagons to be conveyed to the surgeons, were in despair for their condition; for they well knew that war permitted no care for their condition, no thought for their relief, no gentle sympathy for their pain, and before them was wasting disease, perhaps lingering death. Far from home, no assiduous friend, no affectionate sister, no loving mother soothed their anguish. The poor private died unnoticed and unknown, yet by some quiet hearthstone, far from the tumult of cities, tears will be shed for his fall; the stern old father will nerve himself to his loss, by the thought that the sacrifice was made for his country, while the aged mother's heart bleeds with a wound time cannot heal. To such retreats must we go, if we would learn all the suffering that resulted from that scene before the walls of Monterey."

It was in reference to another battle, that Whittier composed the noble poem, entitled, "the Angels of Buena Vista," founded on the following facts.

"A letter writer from Mexico states, that at the terrible fight of Buena Vista, Mexican women were seen hovering near the field of death, for the purpose of giving aid and succor to the wounded. One poor woman was surrounded by the maimed and suffering of both armies, ministering to the wants of Americans as well as Mexicans, with impartial tenderness."

We give a few of the concluding stanzas of this melting, pathetic ballad.

"Look forth once more Ximena!" "Like a cloud before the wind
Rolls the battle down the mountains, leaving blood and death behind;
Ah! they plead in vain for mercy; in the dust the wounded strive;
Hide your faces, holy angels! oh, thou Christ of God, forgive!

"Sink, O night, among thy mountains! let thy cool, gray shadows fall;
Dying brothers, fighting demons — drop thy curtain over all!
Through the quickening winter twilight, wide apart the battle rolled;
In his sheath the sabre rested, and the cannon's lips grew cold.

"But the holy Mexic women still their holy task pursued,
Through that long, dark night of sorrow, worn and faint, and lacking food,
Over weak and suffering brothers with a tender care they hung,
And the dying foeman blessed them in a strange and Northern tongue.

"Not wholly lost, O Father! is this evil world of ours;
Upward through its blood and ashes, spring afresh the Eden flowers;
From its smoking hell of battle, Love and Pity send their prayer,
And still thy white-winged angels hover dimly in our air!"

The personal narratives from trustworthy sources are introduced in this review of the Mexican war, as revealing to us more distinctly than whole pages of general description could do, the indescribable and infinite miseries which alight upon the homes of warring nations. We have much more of the same materials on hand, but these must suffice, and perhaps more than suffice. We have already "supped full of horrors."

War is indiscriminate. It confounds the innocent with the guilty in one fate, or, it may be, spares the bad to involve the righteous man in ruin. It burns the widow's cottage, while it may leave unharmed the tyrant's palace. It kills, perchance, the father's only son, the staff of his old age, and lets the assassin and robber escape with impunity. Fearful, therefore, beyond the power of human thought, is his act who takes the responsibility of involving two nations in its wide-spread havoc. What is it but to assume for the moment the powers of the Omnipotent without his wisdom and mercy? to vault, as it were, into his seat, and let fly the armies of devouring locusts, or lift the lid of the boiling volcano, and inundate cities with floods of fire and lava, or rock the land with earthquakes, and overwhelm multitudes of human beings beneath the ruins of falling temples and dwellings! When will the rulers and legislators of the nations awake to their awful accountableness in being either principals or accessories to bringing on a war?

How shockingly *mal apropos* and incongruous was that sentiment given by some orator on a festive occasion to some companies parading for their departure to the fields of Mexico, — "Washington, our homes, and our country!" For, to omit other considerations, we have seen in this and the last chapter before it, that the warfare against the foreign foe is suicidal; that the sword is two-edged, and cuts us as well as our enemies. The recoil of every blow struck abroad is upon some dear breast at our own fire-side, of father, brother, son, lover, friend. The huzzas of every triumph have been reëchoed by the groans and shrieks of wives, mothers, orphans, bereft, distracted, penniless, friendless. Into how many circles of the wise and good, the prosperous and powerful, has the messenger of heavy tidings come! Into how many lowly homes and cabin doors has the grim image stalked, and youth, and manhood, and age, bowed in speechless agony at his coming! The son of a Clay or a Webster has fallen by the side of the poor and obscure man's son. Tell us not of famine. There is no mutual strife, but the strife of self-sacrifice. Tell us not of cholera. There is no hand wet with a brother's blood, "smelling rank to heaven." But in both instances there is help rendered by the weak and sick to those weaker and sicker than themselves. There is the sharing of the last potato with the famishing. There is danger dared to give but a cup of medicine to the suffering. There is heavenly pity bending with moist eye over the hungry she cannot feed, and over the sick she cannot cure. There is godlike charity, with folded hands and upraised face, invoking that aid from God which man cannot yield.

But it adds immeasurably to the patriotic compunction with which an American should look on this war, when we consider that, terrible as may have been the scenes of bereavement, destitution, and distraction at our own fire-sides, and amid "the pleasant places," the beautiful abodes, of civilized and Christian life, we have been busy actors, as well as stricken sufferers. We have invaded the homes of another nation. We have smitten down young and old, man and woman, rich and poor, sick and well, in the relentless conquest. Verily, we have been guilty in this matter, and our brother's blood cries against us from the ground where it has been spilled. The poor cot, the rich hacienda, the bishop's palace, the church of God, the halls of a republic, have been entered, plundered, bombarded, burnt. Indeed, could a fallen spirit be imagined as hovering over Mexico in the character of its evil genius, and devising an extended system of wrong and suffering, a huge and complicated machine of exquisite, and multiplied, and far-reaching cruelties, one that should do the greatest possible evil with the least possible good; one that should pierce the most hearts, tarnish the most honor, wring forth the most groans, darken the most hearths, and set a-going the most prolific causes of sin and wretchedness in every direction, and to the worst imaginable issues, then we should recognize with a shudder our own country as the evil genius of unhappy Mexico, and war as the infernal engine with which we have worked her nameless and numberless evils. And when, in addition to the essential evil of this instrument of woe, the evil genius be supposed artfully to veil its abominations with the gorgeous drapery of the stars and stripes, and to seduce into its unholy service the flower of youth and the vigor of manhood, to operate at the engine's crushing wheels and dislocating pullies, the picture of that Briarean Inquisition we call WAR would be complete.

CHAPTER XXV.

THE VICES OF THE CAMP.

"We have heard much of the corrupting tendency of some of the rites and customs of the heathen; but what custom of the heathen nations had a greater effect in depraving the human character, than the custom of war." — NOAH WORCESTER.

"War produces the characters necessary for war. The camp is infectious. The few who go there virtuous, if they return at all, generally return vicious, and carry the infection into our peaceful hamlets and the bosom of families." — WILLIAM LADD.

MANY of the battles of the Mexican war were fought wholly or partly on the Sabbath. At Monterey, Sacramento, Cerro Gordo, Chapultepec, and Mexico, more or less of the fighting was done on the Lord's day. While the assemblies of Christians, all over the earth, were met together to hear the word of God, confess their sins, and seek the mercy of heaven through that name which is far "above every name that is named," then, in those hours of sacred rest, devotion, and brotherly love, the death-shots were falling thick and fast, the storm of battle was sweeping with resistless fury over hundreds of the wounded and dying, and many souls cut off unprepared and in the midst of their days, appeared at the bar of a righteous God, to bear witness against the war-system of two professedly Christian nations. Could there be a more shocking *contre-temps* than a desperate, bloody battle, or siege, on the holy day, when God has said, "Thou shalt not do any work," and all the noises of the earth should be hushed, and man should "be still and know that I am God?" The only conceivable case is a fight on Christmas. The battle of Bracito was fought on the generally-received anniversary of that greatest era in the world's history, when angels from heaven sang the birth-anthem of the Saviour of men, "Glory to God in the highest, and on earth peace, good will toward men."

But battles are not the only violations of the law of the Sabbath. Marchings, drills, all kinds of work, preparations for battle, or burying the dead, and all the bustle, din, and dissipation of a camp life, go on comparatively unchecked. In one word, there is no Sabbath to the warrior. He must work, or march, or fight on the day of rest just as much as on any other day, if his commander and circumstances require it. Many of the greatest battles have been fought on that day, though historians have not cared to state the fact. Waterloo and Plattsburg occur to mind now among others. In a very few instances, generals have refused battle on the Sabbath, but the cases are rare. When men commit themselves to this murderous business, they generally shut out God, and the thought of his laws, and their accountableness to him, from their mind, and know no religion, no Sabbath, no mercy. The motto is, kill, kill; plunder, plunder; burn, burn. Suppose two hostile ships meet on the sea on Sunday, what do the chaplains pray for? Is it for love to God and love to man? No! but for death to destroy as many as possible of the other party; for the fire, and powder, and bomb-shells, and sabres, that they do as much execution as possible in marring the image of God, and hurrying mortals before their time to the bar of an eternal Judge. No single extensive cause has worked more efficiently to abolish the Sabbath, and bring it into desecration than war. All history unites in casting this sin at its door, and God will hold war-makers to account as so far Sabbath-breakers.

We need not waste many words on the point that the vices of intemperance, profaneness, and licentiousness have a rank growth in war. The single key of explanation is, that the whole animal nature is called into action. The passions and appetites are supplied with unusual means of excitement. The moral restraints of home and surrounding society are taken off. The refuse of society congregate in the camp, and he must be a moral hero who is not soon laughed out of his virtuous scruples at any vice. The army has in it many good men, as the world goes, but their influence is comparatively overpowered by the daring spirits of wickedness.

Something has been done during the last twenty years to stay the ravages of intemperance, but this war engenders habits of excess, and tends to reopen the flood-gates of desolation. For the recruiting and enlisting rendezvous has not unfrequently been a grog-shop. Rum has been the presiding genius of the mess-room and the camp. Rum has been the spirit of battle. Sutlers and retailers have thronged the encampments, and, in spite of the strictest commands of the officers, they have found way to appropriate the last cent of the poor soldier for a glass of rum. The disbanded soldiers will scatter anew through the length and breadth of the land the prolific seeds of intemperance.

The violent passions and the reckless feelings enraged by war naturally find their vent in the most horrible profaneness. This vice is as congenial to fleets and armies, as birds to the air, or fishes to the sea. It is spoken of in history as a wonderful triumph that Cromwell was able to banish it from his Puritan troops. But most generals have taken no pains, and had no desire to have the third commandment observed by their men; indeed, as an almost universal rule, they have been themselves grossly addicted to this practice, which is neither "brave, polite, nor wise." From the camp, from the man-of-war, more curses than blessings, more oaths than prayers go up before high heaven. If you wish to initiate a young man in a short time into this soul-destroying habit, you could not do better than to send him to the battle-field, where human nature is wrought up to the highest pitch of maddened, defiant, ferocious, blood-thirsty passion (and must be so in order to do the awful work which is to be done there), and pours out volleys of profaneness against heaven while discharging volleys of death at heaven's children. He who wishes to see the doom of a profane and God-insulting people averted from his country, will hold up both hands to vote against war.

Licentiousness is another vice which is diffused by war. The habits of the camp in this particular are too well known to need description. Indeed, multitudes flock to the standard of war because they know that they shall thus find means to gratify their passions. A chaste army would be as novel a thing in the world as a sober one. The camp is the resort of hordes of abandoned females.

When a besieged city is taken, it is sometimes the premium on the bravery of the soldiers to deliver it up to lust and plunder.

Such is the licentiousness of war. The friend of purity will be the friend of peace.

Indeed, when we consider the morals of war, — and the late war, as we have demonstrated in the preceding pages, has been not an exception, but the fulfilment of the general rule, — we would "wreak" our thoughts on some such words as these, O war, what shall we say of thee, thou dark spirit, thou fearful minister of wrath, thou flaming angel of swift destruction? When thou art let loose, there is a shudder in heaven, and the angels veil their faces in horror. The sound of thy trumpet strikes terror to the mother's heart, and makes the sister turn pale with fear and foreboding. Wives shrink from the sound of thy coming, and children flee from the thunder and havoc of thy train as from the whirlwind. Is there purity? Thou dishonorest it. Is there temperance? Thou debauchest it. Is there mercy? Thou turnest it to stone. Is there love? Thou curdlest the milk of human kindness to hatred. Is there prosperity? Thou cuttest off its resources, thou multipliest taxes. Is there home? Thou layest it waste with fire and sword. Is there religion? Thou repealest every law of the decalogue, every precept of Christ. Is there patriotism? Thou puttest in place of the true a vile substitute, current neither among gods nor men. Is there honor? Thou cheatest the world with a base compound, that bears the same relation to true honor that pewter coin does to pure silver. Is there freedom? Thou draggest her a bound captive at thy chariot wheels. Is there commerce? Thou chasest her from the seas. Is there agriculture? Thou tramplest her harvests under the hoofs of thy coursers, and riotest in her plenty. Is there art, practical or ideal? Thou burnest her workshops, thou plunderest her galleries. Is there any good thing on earth, which heaven has given, or which man has made? Thou art the curse and destruction of all. Where thou movest, a garden is before thee, and a desert behind thee. Thou art hell let loose upon the world; and when we see thy banner in the sky, all the good angels of heaven seem to have taken flight, and left us to ourselves and to our own worst passions. Thine attendant spirits are pain, and woe, and despair, and sickness, and licentiousness, and intemperance, and profaneness, and Sabbath-breaking, and murder, and robbery, and cruelty. Thy victories are the defeats of humanity. Thy conquests are the losses of liberty. Thy rejoicings are the wailings of the poor and suffering. Thy glories are the shame of immortals, and the trophies of tigers and hyenas. Thy laurels are red with blood, and thy hosannas are the shrieks of the wounded, the yells of the dying, the sobs of widows, the cries of orphans, and the lamentations of nations.

CHAPTER XXVI.

THE WAR-SPIRIT AND THE GOSPEL OF CHRIST.

"The depravity occasioned by war is not confined to the army. Every species of vice gains ground in a nation during war. And when a war is brought to a close, seldom perhaps does a community return to its former standard of morals." — NOAH WORCESTER.

"What distinguishes war is, not that man is slain, but that he is slain, spoiled, crushed by the cruelty, the injustice, the treachery, the murderous hand of man. The evil is *moral* evil. War is the concentration of all human crimes. Here is its distinguishing, accursed brand. Under its standard gather violence, malignity, rage, fraud, perfidy, rapacity, and lust." -- CHANNING.

WE devote this chapter to what we regard as the chief evils of the Mexican war. The moral and spiritual faculties are at the head of the human constitution, and the interests resulting from them and involving their development and welfare, are the leading interests of human society. Whatever reverses this order, and puts last what should be first, and first what should be last, destroys the true perspective of human life. War, perhaps more than any other single cause, works this stupendous wrong. It discredits and dwarfs the moral man. It supplies undue excitements and gratifications to all the animal passions. It obscures the true end of our existence, and substitutes, in place of the honor and dignity of serving God and man, the gorgeous mockery of military glory.

Had the war now in question been instrumental of the loss of not one dollar or one life, and yet had it laid waste the great moral and religious interests of the United States and Mexico, and left a deep wound upon the cause of Christ, we should assign it a foremost place among the foes of our laws, our liberties, and every social, material, and political interest. For every part of our complicated life is connected with every other part, as joint with joint, and limb with limb in the body. If one suffer, all the others suffer with it. When the moral interests of society are thrown into disorder, the evil extends through every department of thought and action. We have by an enumeration of separate evils demonstrated that, if every other argument failed, the immoralities of this invasion stamp it with the darkest colors of guilt, and cover it with the deepest abhorrence of the feeling heart and the tender conscience. We have examined its leger, and looked into its hospitals, and recited its horrors, but we will now consider its spirit. Space will compel us to be brief, where a volume only could do full justice to the subject.

It is sometimes alleged, that those who fight have no enmity, one towards another, and that it is not that they hate their enemies, or wish them evil ; but they contend at the call of their country, and are just as good friends when they stop firing as any men in the world. Witness, it is said, the kind acts they do each other, and the relief they give to the wounded and dying foeman. So be it. Let all possible palliations relieve the horrid picture of the field of blood. It does us good to think that what is best in man sometimes appears even amid such scenes. But we propose to record some indications of the war-spirit, and to show that where there is such a spirit, the spirit of revenge, hard-heartedness, cruelty, delight in the sufferings of others, or cold-blooded indifference to them, there cannot be the spirit of him, who said, "Love your enemies." And certainly we are not allowed to repeal his laws of love, mutual good will, intercessory prayers for our enemies, and returning them good for evil; no, not even for an hour, though that hour be the period of battle. How then can war and Christianity agree together? If it be possible to love our enemies at the moment we are pouring vollies of grape into their dense ranks, and to pray for them at the time we are meditating a charge with naked bayonets, then we can conceive of a war conducted on Christian principles and sentiments, but not otherwise. "War must be," as Robert Hall says, "a temporary repeal of the principles of virtue." The truth is, that men cannot be brought up to the point of fighting except by the stress of most powerful motives, and those motives in general are drawn from the animal passions. Generals have usually deprecated a strong religious influence in the camp.* Some have gone so far as to declare, the worse man, the better soldier. There is a species of morality in war, but it is of a very abject nature. Far are we from denying that there are many good men engaged in

* The examining committee of the Military Academy at West Point state the significant fact in their report, 1849, that the chapter or section on War in Wayland's Moral Science, a text book in the institution, is not admitted in the course of studies!

the army and navy, but if there are such, it is in spite of the spirit of war, not in obedience to it. The better men, and the more comprehensive Christians they become, the more thoroughly will they abhor their calling, and say, with a British officer of high rank in the army to his associates, "ours is a damnable profession."

The war-spirit of the press has given expression to sentiments during the conflict like the following. We do not give the names of the papers and reviews, because our object is to illustrate a principle, not to attack persons. But we quote from highly-respected and widely-circulated journals.

These are the words of one: "Nothing but a complete subjugation of Mexico seems to answer the present emergency. Foraging on the enemy, and levying contributions were at last agreed upon. The anxiety in every man's countenance to-day is strongly depicted, and the universal cry is, war in earnest—war; not for peace, but for conquest and subjugation,—a real *bona fide* war, which supports itself and seizes on the enemy's treasure. Unless we distress the Mexicans, carry destruction and loss of life to every fireside, and make them feel a rod of iron, they will not respect us."

Another journal speaks thus; "Under these circumstances, and in view of the perfidious conduct of the Mexican Government, our Government is bound by every consideration of honor, duty and justice, to chastise them most effectually, and to beat them into a disposition to ask for peace, and to accept it on such terms as we may be disposed to grant them.

"No more offers of peace, — no more paying for supplies, —no more confidence in the professions and promises of the enemy; but stern, vigorous, relentless war, until our just demands are fully complied with. Such must and will be our policy now."

Another gives utterance to the following; "Our work of

subjugation and conquest must go on rapidly with augmented forces, and, as far as possible, at the expense of Mexico herself. From Mexican contributions, levied and seized, if need be, by the strong hand, our armies must now be subsisted and supported in the field. The policy of forbearance and conciliation, however magnanimously adopted by us, and in however generous an attitude it may have hitherto presented us before the world, is now exhausted. It has met with no response, but new rancor and contumely from our vanquished foe. Henceforth we must seek peace, and compel it, by inflicting upon our enemy all the evils of war."

Another expatiates thus ; "With a nation like Mexico, with whom no accommodation can be hoped for, and as sad experience has shown, no faith in treaties, even when made, can be entertained, there can be no end to the war short of her annihilation as a nation. The matter should be taken in hand, in the spirit of Bonaparte's bulletins, in commencing the Prussian war: "The House of Brandenburgh has ceased to reign in Europe." His vigorous strokes ceased not until that edict was apparently accomplished, and a few weeks sufficed for the purpose. Of the same nature should be our proceedings. "The Spaniards have ceased to rule in Mexico," should be the motto, and corps after corps poured in at all quarters, until it is enacted."

Another speculates after this wise ; "if Santa Anna still holds out, then we must take it for granted that the Mexican people want war to the knife ; and it will be time for our government to resort to the severest measures in order to make the war tell upon the population. It is to be hoped that our army will then forage on the enemy, lay every town and hamlet through which it passes under heavy contribution, and instead of suffering the wealthy citizens to depart and withdraw to the interior, retain them as hostages for keeping the peace."

Still another exhorts to a military colonization ; "Let our

armies begin immediately to radiate from the city of Mexico into all the Mexican States. And then, as a finishing stroke, our Government should give freely of the Mexican domain to as many of our citizens as would emigrate. This would soon fill up the country with armed Americans, who would complete not only the subjugation, but the civilization of Mexico."

"A manifest-destiny" editor holds forth thus; "The glorious sierras and valleys of Mexico are fated to be linked to the mountains and prairies of the United States.* * * Politicians may connive, or quake and tremble as they will; Wilmot Provisos, Abolition, and Disruption of the Union are lost in the tremendous shout of the American people, Mexico must not,—shall not be abandoned! * * Shall we resist Providence, that guides the course of nations? * * A continent for freedom; its boundary the icebergs on the north, the oceans east and west, and Central America, (until we need it,) on the south, and short of that boundary, no human power can stop the irresistible current of the Anglo Saxon race."

But the following atrocious sentences are almost too bad to copy, did they not illustrate a feeling but too prevalent, though sometimes expressed in more refined words.

"We go for giving the Mexicans hell, whether Christ be our guide or not. We go for whipping them thoroughly, any way; and we must do it, or stand disgraced in the eyes of the civilized world. None of your sentimentalism,—none of your "weary, wounded and worn" tales. If we had listened to them in by-gone times, the star-spangled banner would not, as it now does, float in proud triumph over every sea."

One more; "We trust now that we shall hear no more of armistices or suspension of hostilities, at least from our side. War, vigorous, devastating, unrelenting war, is the only resource, and it is to be hoped that the Mexicans will be made to experience it."

A member of Congress said in his official seat; "He trusted it would be a war of conquest; he was not one of those who would have a mild war, who were afraid of striking heavy blows. He would show no mercy till the war was ended. If he would have his own way, one blow should follow another without mercy."

Says a Governor of a State," in my judgment, the motto, to 'conquer a peace,' is now made indispensable—there is no alternative. Then let the nation's power be summoned to a mighty effort, and let it break upon that devoted country, peal after peal, in one unceasing note of thunder. Let the public right arm be made bare, and the sword remain unsheathed until peace is extorted."

Let these suffice to exhibit the war-mania that seized upon a portion of the American press, and politicians. Must not such sentiments demoralize the public mind wherever circulated?

But we proceed to another point. Let us see what is the war-spirit of warriors, and how far it accords with the precepts, spirit, and example of our beloved Redeemer in his sojourn on earth. Here, too, we avoid the invidiousness of giving names for an obvious reason. We attack a system, a custom, not individuals. Our aim is principles, not men. What are the most prominent ideas, which some men attach to such words as *grand, brilliant, splendid, beautiful, glorious,* etc., will appear in these extracts. We copy from official reports chiefly. The italics are ours.

Says Lieut. ——, "Whilst this was being done, I galloped to the top of the hill above Arispa's mills, where a *grand sight* burst upon my view. The whole column (of the enemy) was winding its way along the foot of the mountain and through the ravines, more than half the column being in range of my gun. I galloped back to bring it up, placed it in position and fired rapidly into their crowded ranks, producing considerable confusion, and much execution."

This is the description of another at the terrible siege of Vera Cruz ; "In a few moments the steamers, Spitfire and Vixen, and five gunboats, the whole under command of Captain —— of the navy, ran in close to the lime-kiln, and opened a *beautiful* fire with large Paixhan guns upon the town and castle. Nothing could have been done more *handsomely.*"

"Soon after our batteries opened, Captain —— with Major ——, stepped out to a rather exposed position to witness the effect of our shells. "Major," remarked Captain V., with *enthusiasm,* "as you pass the mortars, please tell the officers that *the shell are doing their duty accurately.*"

Another officer writes as follows ; "The storming of Cerro Gordo was a magnificent spectacle, as well as one of *the most brilliant, if not the most brilliant feat* ever accomplished by American arms. *What a glorious feeling of elation took possession of my soul at that moment!* I cannot describe it. Of the wounded, dead, and dying, we will not speak. I have seen Death robed in all his ghastly terrors, and feel that I am becoming indifferent to the sufferings of my fellows ; my profession demands it."

Of an American Lieutenant, aged 72, a correspondent of the *New York Post* says, "he had left a home of affluence and ease, with the expressed wish to die in the service of his country, and, if need be, on the field of battle. 'They cannot cheat me out of many more years,' said he. When ordered with a battalion, like a forlorn hope, to the trying contest in the mountains, he exclaimed with a *look of joy,* as he drew his sword: 'Now, boys, this looks like doing something.'"

"I remained with him," says the surgeon attendant on the dying Maj. —— "all night. He had but little pain, and at intervals had some sleep. During the night he gave me many incidents of the battle, and spoke with much *pride of the execution of his shot.* He had but one thing to regret, and that was the small number of men at his command." His only regret that he could not kill more Mexicans! "The condition of the brave and esteemed Capt. —— " says an eye-witness, "is melancholy indeed. The whole of his lower jaw, with a part of his tongue and palate, is shot away by a grape-shot. He, however, survives, though entirely incapable of speech. He communicates his thoughts by writing on a slate, and receives the necessary nutriment for the support of life with much difficulty. He does not desire to live, but converses *with cheerfulness and exultation upon the success of our arms*, and concluded an answer to some queries concerning the battle of the 9th, by writing, '*We gave the Mexicans hell!*'"

"When Lieut. ——, during the battle of Buena Vista, was sent by Gen. Taylor," says the *New Orleans Bulletin*, "with a flag to a detached body of 1000 to 1500 Mexicans, that were being cut to pieces by our fire, Col. —— was on the eve of charging them with his dragoons; but as Lieut. —— was passing with his white flag displayed, —— rode out and crossed his path to inquire the object of his mission. 'I am going to tell those fellows to surrender, in order to save their lives.'—'Wait till I have charged them.'—'Impossible; the old man has sent me, and I must go.'—'But, my good fellow,' said —— entreatingly, 'for God's sake just rein up for five minutes, and give us a chance at them.'—'Would do any thing to oblige you, Colonel; but I have the old man's orders, and there is no help for it.' And he gave rein to his horse, while the Colonel returned to the head of his regiment in the worst of all possible humors against the things called flags of truce."

The diabolical passion of fighting for the love of fighting is illustrated by this report of an American General, in the bombardment of a Mexican town, in which 219 were killed, and 300 wounded.

"As we approached, several shots were fired at us, and,

deeming it unsafe to risk a street fight in an unknown town at night, I ordered the artillery to be posted on a hill near the town and overlooking it, and open its fire. — Now ensued one of *the most beautiful sights conceivable.* Every gun was served with the utmost rapidity; and the crash of the walls and the roofs of the houses when struck by our shot and shell, was mingled with the roar of artillery. The bright light of the moon enabled us to direct our shots *to the most thickly populated parts of the town.*"

At another action, in his report says another officer, now promoted to a generalship, "I cannot speak too highly of Capt. K. and his management of his batteries. *His shells and shot fell beautifully upon houses and churches* where the enemy were in great numbers. Whenever his shot took effect, the firing soon ceased."

Such is the spirit of war and warriors,* and such, from the necessity of the case, it ever must be. How totally inconsistent with the spirit of the New Testament! Is it not a hidden art, even in this inventive age, to wage war upon Christian principles and sentiments? Killing men, women, and children can hardly be done on the basis of loving our neighbors, or forgiving our enemies. The single question is, whether Christ be our supreme Master or not. When that is settled, it will be comparatively easy to dispose of the question of war.

* The many controversies and quarrels among the authors and advocates of this war and the officers of the army and navy strikingly illustrate the combustible nature of the materials on which the war-system is built. Perhaps we ask too much of men, who cannot keep the peace among their own countrymen, that they should keep the peace with the rest of mankind. Witness the *quasi* wars of Scott *vs.* Trist, Pillow *vs.* Scott, Scott *vs.* Marcy, Kearney *vs.* Fremont, Fremont *vs.* Mason, Benton *vs.* Kearney, to say nothing of other controversies and duels.

CHAPTER XXVII.

THE SAME SUBJECT CONTINUED.

"War is in itself a mighty evil, an incongruity in a scheme of social harmony, a canker at the heart of improvement, a living lie in a Christian land, a curse at all times." — LONDON TIMES.

IT has already been shown by a detailed examination of separate items, that the late war has been totally inconsistent with the commands and spirit of the Gospel. But we treat now of its general spirit. It has been an appeal to might, and there is no evidence that the success of a battle is any proof of the justice of the cause of the victors. Napoleon once remarked, that he had always taken notice that Providence favored *the heavy battalions!* Victory perches on the banner of might, not always on that of right.

We have seen that even the usual laws of war, and laws of nations, have been rudely broken by the barbarities perpetrated on both sides; how much more then that perfect law of love, revealed by Jesus Christ! If the doctrines of Grotius and Vattel have been set at nought, how much more have those of Paul and John?

The inconsistency of our invasion of Mexico with the Christian faith has been brought into a stronger contrast, from the fact, that at the very moment we were loading down a vessel of war to the very edge with bread-stuffs for the famishing Irish, and despatching them on this mission of mercy, we were sending bomb-ships, laden with the most destructive implements of war, to lay waste the cities of Mexico, and bury men, women, and children in the ruins of their dwellings and churches. It is a serious inquiry for every Christian, whether, while we have thus been aiming fatal blows at the physical life of a sister republic, we may not have placed ourselves in the way of receiving the fruits of spiritual death in ourselves.

We can conceive of no line of antitheses more directly pitched, one against the other, than the qualities called into the most lusty life and growth by such a war, and those recommended and enforced in the instructions of our blessed Lord, and shining with a holy and beautiful light in his character, "as the brightness of the firmament." It is ambition fronting meekness; pride, lowliness of mind; revenge, forgiveness; retaliation, forbearance; cruelty, mercy; wrong, justice; hate, love. "They," said Erasmus, "who defend war, must defend the dispositions which lead to it; and these dispositions are absolutely forbidden by the Gospel."

Mexico was weak, we were strong. Common magnanimity, much more that holy law that bids us "support the weak, and be patient towards all men," condemns the onslaught of war. In private life, our blood boils with indignation to see the feeble beset and maltreated by the robust. Does the magnitude of scale alter the nature of the rule? Speaking of those most immediately responsible for the war, Mr. Gallatin says, in his widely-circulated pamphlet, "there is not one of them, who would not spurn with indignation the most remote hint that, on similar pretences to those alleged for dismembering Mexico, he might be capable of attempting to appropriate to himself his neighbor's farm." But can the law of Christian honesty be so palpably violated in the smaller instance supposed, and does it receive no wound in the larger one?

It has been complained of by the advocates of this war that the pulpit has generally been arrayed against it. The fact is probably true. The great mass of the clergy of every denomination have uttered their condemnation of the war

They have preached and prayed against it. Indeed they have felt that no prayer or song could be made out of the subject, except in distinct and decided opposition to carrying our arms beyond the boundaries of our enormous territory into those of a weak and distracted neighbor. The ecclesiastical bodies of this country, with scarcely an exception in the free States, have come out in votes and resolutions of the most stringent condemnation of the war.* These facts may show how utterly they have deemed it to be opposed to the Gospel of Jesus Christ, and may by some be regarded as an intimation, though by no means a proof, that such was the reality.

But, in marked contrast with the above, we record as exemplifications of the fatal, corrupting influence of the war-miasma, the cases of some even of the ministers of Christ, who entered the army, and who preached and prayed in favor of the war. A private letter from a Lieutenant in the service, says; "We have here among the volunteers a preacher who is a captain, his officers and non-commissioned officers are deacons of his church; and the privates members. He is called the fighting Preacher. He and his company are from ——."

We have already mentioned that a preacher was killed in the ranks in the battle of Buena Vista.

Sermons, which are now before us, were preached both on the Rio Grande, and at the city of Mexico before the troops, justifying the war, talking largely of the "Anglo Saxon destiny," comparing the progress of the American arms with the entrance of the children of Israel into the land of Canaan, and giving the sanctions and benedictions of Christianity to the awful wrongs and barbarities of one of the most cruel, sanguinary, and demoralizing wars on record.

* Advocate of Peace, Nov. and Dec. 1847, pp. 134—137. Feb. 1848, pp. 166, 167. Oct. 1848, pp. 274—276.

But we need not say that this surely is no period of the world for true Christians to justify war, and especially wars of aggrandizement, retaliation, and slavery. When could the Mexican invasion assume a more hideous aspect in the eyes of good men, than at a time when the missionaries of the cross are penetrating to the remotest parts of the earth on their glorious errand of evangelizing the heathen; * and when even Mohammedan powers, the Sultan of Turkey, the Shah of Persia, the Imaum of Muscat, and the Arabian chiefs have either abolished slavery, or very much restricted it; and when there seems to be a universal movement in the world towards a happier age of Freedom, Peace, and Philanthropy. Thus the spirit of the age rebukes and condemns our war. For into that spirit has entered, we believe, some faint portion of "the mind that was in Christ." Surely this of all periods, since the world began, is not the day to exact "the pound of flesh next the heart" with a cruel greediness, nor to resent injuries with a hasty revenge, nor to fight for glory, territory, or oppression. Let us hope that our countrymen will yet come to their senses, and frown upon a spirit and a career so utterly at variance with the holy religion we profess, and check any symptoms of a renewal of wars of invasion, conquest, and slavery.

* A Chinese emperor once said: "Wherever Christians go they whiten the soil with human bones; and I will not have Christianity in my empire."

A Turk at Jerusalem once said to Wolff, the missionary, "Why do you come to us?" The missionary replied, "to bring you peace." "Peace!" replied the Turk, leading him to a window, and pointing to Mount Calvary, "there! upon the very spot where your Lord poured out his blood, the Mohammedan is obliged to interfere to prevent Christians from shedding the blood of each other!"—*Calumet of Peace.*

CHAPTER XXVIII.

THE LESSONS OF THE WAR WITH MEXICO.

"Our sole aim being to promote the cause of permanent peace by turning this war into effectual warnings against resorts to the sword hereafter."—PROPOSALS FOR A REVIEW OF THE WAR BY THE AMERICAN PEACE SOCIETY.

A BRIEF survey of some of the more prominent lessons, taught us by the events of the last two years, is all that can be given now, though the future will no doubt teach us far more upon this subject than the past.

The friends of peace had fondly cherished the hope that *pure republics,* the governments of the many as contradistinguished from monarchies and aristocracies, the governments of the one, or the few, would be *pacific.* War has been charged upon rulers, though it has been confessed it

"Is a game, which, were their subjects wise,
Kings would not play at."

But we are disappointed. We see that republics can wage as fierce, brutal, and unjust wars, as feudal and despotic powers.* The mania of conquest may riot in the veins of a democracy as furiously as in those of a kingdom or empire.

* Witness republican France, waging a cruel war against republican Rome to restore the Pope! The example of our wickedness will find in future history but too many imitators. Such cases need not in the least shake our faith in republicanism; but they should convince us of the necessity, if we would have a true republicanism, of compounding with it large admixtures of sound education, pure religion, and the spirit of universal brotherhood.

In this respect we witness the non-fulfilment of many wise predictions and cherished hopes. The very independence and self-reliance taught by free institutions make the republican the most formidable soldier on earth, when he cuts loose from the scruples of a religious education. The state-rivalry and panting for distinction by the members of different sections of the Union have also blown up the war-passion to a hotter flame, and made the battle-field an arena for the most intense competition.

The Mexican war has accordingly taught us not to trust to political institutions alone, however free and admirable, for the maintenance of pacific relations among mankind. We must strike a higher key. We must appeal to deeper motives. Men may know their rights in a republic, and still be ignorant of their duties. They may know their duties, and not discharge them. They may have a morbid jealousy of tyranny over themselves, and yet play the tyrant over others. We would bring no railing accusation against our own, our native land. Heaven bless it, every acre and rood! But because we love it, and would ever rejoice in its unsullied honor and Christian fame, we deeply, deploringly remonstrate against the spirit of political propagandism. If we have so far lost sight of the nature of free institutions, and the true mission of the United States, as to propose to offer, Mohammed-like, the alternative of freedom in one hand, and the sword in the other, to the other nations of the earth, the sooner our days are numbered and finished, the happier for the peace of the world. We say thus much, not to give "aid or comfort" to any enemy of liberty and the institutions in which liberty is organized, but to "point the moral" of the late war. It is not that we love our country less, but mankind more. It is not that we would be any the less devoted patriots, but that we would sanctify and dignify that character by being the more devoted philanthropists and disciples of Christ.

And, in general, we have been taught by this war how broken a reed we lean upon, when we propose to accomplish the magnificent result of a general, permanent peace *by any temporal expedients,* any carnal weapons, any industrial, social, political, commercial, or selfish arrangements. Satan cannot cast out Satan, nor can even selfishness itself exorcise the demoniac spirit of war. Men will hardly give up the gratification of their lusts, though they could turn a penny by it. Yea, we see that they will, under the instigation of the strong and animal passions, fling every consideration of interest, honest reputation, consistency, and safety to the winds, and embark in a crusade against which their pockets, their love of life, and every apparent interest cry out. But wars and fightings come from a different part of the human constitution than the calculating faculties. A whole boiling cauldron of ambition, excitement, pleasure, revenge, sympathetic ardor, is in the breast of the volunteer. He cannot be controlled except by principles and sentiments mightier than those that have usurped the dominion over his reason and conscience. But "where the spirit of the Lord is, there is liberty;" liberty from those unsanctified lusts and passions of the human heart, out of which all the terrible deeds of war come, as streams of burning lava from the volcano. The motives that are to emancipate even the freest and most refined nations from enacting the appalling tragedy of the battle-field, must descend from a higher plane than the leger, the statute-book, and the laws and interests of conventional life. God must thunder and lighten out of heaven. Jesus must spread out his arms in the agony of the cross, as if to draw all men to their spiritual unity and head. Man's relation to man, as a brother, owning equal rights, and bound by equal duties, must be revealed in its full solemnity and tenderness. Then, and not till then, can we hope to see this foul spirit cast out, from the hearts even of good men, much less out of the sensual mind. We welcome with delight every new tie uniting distant lands in the intercourse of commerce, science, and a material civilization. All hail to the press, the steamboat, the railroad, and the telegraph, as connecting men together more and more, not by links of iron only, but by cords of love. But the causes of war are too inveterate to be cured by any thing short of the miraculous touch of the Son of God. He is the Prince of Peace. He, and he only, can say to a warring world, as he once said to the raging deep, "Peace, be still," and the winds and waves obeyed him. Thanks be accorded to all who are laboring for human improvement in every direction, and by every instrument, for they are co-laborers with the advocates of the uninterrupted brotherhood of nations.

But chiefly as Christianity pervades the mass of mankind in its life-giving spirit and efficacy, will men awake to the unutterable wickedness of war, and learn its horrid arts no more. Civilization itself is no adequate remedy; but civilization, after the Christian type, and uplifted and empowered with Christian ideas, will outgrow war. It has outgrown many barbarous notions and customs, — the ordeal, torture, persecution, superstition, — of earlier ages; and it is only a question of time and faithful effort, when this great embodiment of barbarism shall drop off from the expanding limbs of Freedom, on which it has so long hung as a hideous and monstrous excrescence.

Another lesson from these hostilities is, that what are called *the improvements of warfare* are poor pretexts to justify its continuance. Commend us not to war as a thing which is very susceptible of improvement. The devil cannot be disguised, though he be clothed in a suit of broadcloth, and have a musket and canteen, instead of a bow and arrows. He is still the devil. He was a murderer from the beginning, and he will be a murderer to the end. He will make children orphans, and wives widows, and parents childless. He may use different tools, the bomb instead of the battering-ram, the rifle instead of the cross-bow, and the cannon instead of the scythed chariot; but the devil is the devil yet, and war is war. It cannot be smoothed, civilized, or evangelized. Much assurance indeed was given, that the late contest should be conducted on humane and just principles, so far as such a hellish work could be thus carried on. But the fulfilment of these fine promises must be looked for among the legitimate and illegitimate barbarities perpetrated. If large masses of men are trained to kill in the most dexterous and scientific modes at the behest of their superiors, it cannot be thought very strange if they sometimes do a little murdering on their own private account. If they are led forth to conquest with their passions stimulated to the utmost with the visions of national glory and aggrandizement, it were natural and pardonable, perhaps, that they should pilfer a trifle on their own hook, in view of the splendid example held up perpetually to view. Such has been the fact. Plundering, massacres, cruelties, the killing of the wounded on the field of battle, and even in some cases burning alive at the stake, have been recorded on the highest official authority, as a part of the history of the Mexican war. Two free Christian nations, in the nineteenth century, going to war with one another, and in that war witnessing and perpetrating barbarities that would disgrace New Zealand! Away with the idle pretence, that war can ever be any thing else than barbarous, sanguinary, cruel, and full of all manner of evil! Let not those who uphold it as the true method of settling international disputes, encourage the idea that it ever can be, from the very nature of the case, any thing else but violence, fraud, murder, and a temporary repeal of every commandment of the King of kings. If we are to have war, let us call it war, nor seek to baptize it in any other Christian title or surname. "Woe unto them that call evil good, and good evil; that put darkness for light, and light for darkness; that put bitter for sweet, and sweet for bitter!"

We see another proof in this contest of *the essential injustice of all war.* As a mode of redressing injuries, it is perfectly absurd, for it creates a thousand injuries and wrongs where it redresses one. It runs posterity into debt without their consent, and mortgages the industry and capital of future ages. Instead of punishing the guilty, it often visits the innocent with its heaviest calamities. The battle-field is not entitled in any sense to be regarded as a solemn tribunal of justice. The very notion of a battle is, that men temporarily lay aside all that they had gained by thousands of years of civilizing and Christian processes, resolve themselves into savages, and appeal from right, from reason, from the exercise of all those nobler faculties of our constitution, that had been predominant in peace, to the coarse, rude, and vindictive passions. The greatest of the poets drew it all to the life; —

> "In peace, there's nothing so becomes a man
> As modest stillness and humility;
> But when the blast of war blows in our ears,
> Then imitate the action of the tiger;
> Stiffen the sinews, summon up the blood,
> Disguise fair nature with hard-favored rage;
> Then lend the eye a terrible aspect;
> Let it pry through the portage of the head,
> Like the brass cannon; let the brow o'erwhelm it,
> As fearfully as doth a galled rock
> O'erhang and jutty his confounded base,
> Swilled with the wild and wasteful ocean;
> Now set the teeth, and stretch the nostrils wide;
> Hold hard the breath, and bend up every spirit
> To his full height."

Our actions will, of course, partake of the nature of those passions or feelings which are uppermost at the time we act. If then the deeds of war are performed under the powerful stress of the animal nature, they must of necessity be of like color and character, "earthly, sensual, devilish."

And by what alembic a long career, a campaign, or several campaigns of such actions are to be sublimated into justice, and wrong to be righted, and evils to be cured, and injuries to be placated, is more than we have been yet able to discover. Such temporary returns to the brutal age of the world inflict deep wounds upon a Christian state of society; for they are a virtual renouncement for the time being of the reign of truth and justice, and they cast discredit and discouragement upon all the moral and religious instrumentalities by which society is drawn up from the slough of sensual customs and habits into the light and life of civilization.

The Mexican war was, as we have seen, a signal example of this resorting to *might* instead of right, and employing the strong arm of force to compel the surrender of a part of another country. It was a compound of the crime of the highway-man, who puts his pistol at your head, and cries, "Deliver, or die," and the truckling of the pedlar who trades in small wares, and chuckles over his hard-driven bargain after it is made. Never was there a finer opportunity for what might be called national magnanimity, than for the stronger power in this case to bear and forbear with the weaker one, and aid, not thwart it, in carrying out the experiment of republican institutions.

A score of names, perhaps, in the whole range of history, have been accounted, called *great*. But who are they? How poor are all the results they left on earth compared with his who repressed the ignoble strife of his followers, who should be greatest. They were from below, he was from above. Some good men have attained the title, an Alfred, a Peter, a Charlemagne; but most have been great in crime and blood; an Alexander, a Pompey, a Cæsar, a Herod, a Louis, a Henry, a Frederic, a Charles, a Buonaparte. They were great in many things; great, perhaps, in ability, great in resolution of will, great in means of influence, and striking in their results; but little in the elements of a truly great character; little in honesty, in truth, in love, mean, selfish, crafty, cruel, and implacable. They have been willing to sacrifice any amount of human life or happiness, to secure their end, and be accounted the greatest. But how poor the honor, how blood-stained the glory! How many death-pangs it has taken to refine their thrill of pleasure, how many tears to water their garlands of victory, how much human gore to dye their purple robes of royalty! What curses have loaded their names on earth, what awful memories must haunt them in the world of spirits!

We want no more such great ones. We have had enough of them. We want the truly great, the truly good. And if we would have such from among our youth, we must fill their heads and hearts not with pagan, or Mohammedan, but with Christian ideas and sentiments. We must baptize our children not only into the name of Christ, but also into his spirit. We must show them how much greater in reality Jesus, the well-beloved of the Father, was in washing his disciples' feet, than Xerxes riding forth at the head of his army to lay waste the fairest countries with fire and sword; Jesus dying in ignominy on the cross, than Cæsar making his triumphal procession into Rome with the spoils and captives of vanquished kingdoms.

This strife has repeated, in fresh and distinct tones, this lesson of the perverted standard of judgment created by war. We see how poor a thing is mere animal courage, and martial fame. We see that the most brilliant deeds of the soldier, (*sold*-ier, the man who is sold), are of such a character that, were they done by any other profession, the actors would be convicted and punished as the highest offenders against the peace, and order, and rights of men. What right can man claim thus to invent a system of war-morality, war-honor, war-reputation, which conflicts at every point with the government of the Most High?

The true nature of much that passes current in society as

heroism of the highest kind, when exhibited in war, is so well exposed by a modern writer, Dr. Bushnell, that we need not apologize for repeating his distinction between "bravery" and "courage."*

"No, the true hero is the great, wise man of duty, — he whose soul is armed by truth and supported by the smile of God, — he who meets life's perils with a cautious but tranquil spirit, gathers strength by facing its storms, and dies, if he is called to die, as a Christian victor, at the post of duty. And if we must have heroes, and wars wherein to make them, there is no so brilliant war as a war with wrong, no hero so fit to be sung as he who has gained the bloodless victory of truth and mercy.

"But if bravery be not the same as courage, still it is a very imposing and plausible counterfeit. The man himself is told, after the occasion is past, how heroically he bore himself, and when once his nerves have become tranquillized, he begins even to believe it. And since we cannot stay content in the dull, uninspired world of economy and work, we are as ready to see a hero as he to be one. Nay, we must have our heroes, as I just said, and we are ready to harness ourselves, by the million, to any man who will let us fight him out the name. Thus we find out occasions for war, — wrongs to be redressed, revenges to be taken, such as we may feign inspiration and play the great heart under. We collect armies, and dress up leaders in gold and high colors, meaning, by the brave look, to inspire some notion of a hero beforehand. Then we set the men in phalanxes and squadrons, where the personality itself is taken away, and a vast impersonal person, called an army, a magnanimous and brave monster, is all that remains. The masses of fierce color, the glitter of steel, the dancing plumes, the waving flags, the deep throb of the music lifting every foot, — under

* Phi Beta Oration at Cambridge, 1848, pp. 21, 22.

these the living acres of men, possessed by the one thought of playing brave to-day, are rolled on to battle. Thunder, fire, dust, blood, groans, — what of these? — nobody thinks of these, for nobody dares to think till the day is over, and then the world rejoices to behold a new batch of heroes!

"And this is the Devil's play that we call war."

And, finally, we have been startled by this wild crusade into a new conviction of *the vast latent war-spirit of our country* and of the world, and the necessity of more untiring and devoted labors, and more comprehensive plans to carry the peace enterprize to a triumphant conclusion. We believe in the true mission or destiny of our nation to illustrate the idea of Freedom and a Christian State. But if we disown the glorious career, God is not so poor that he has not other nations and races which he can employ for purposes equally grand and beneficent. We may hug the delusive phantom that we are a species of Israel among other people, but let us not forget that Israel did not escape the fiery furnace of punishment and retribution for all their transgressions and backslidings.

And, as we reflect upon the work to be done to guide this giant republic on a safe and peaceful career, we ask who is sufficient for these things? Oh, for parents of peace, who will make their well-ordered families so many living peace societies! Oh, for Christian teachers, who will early train the tender minds under their care to govern those passions whence wars and fightings come! Oh, for Christian historians, who will write the dark register of crime and cruelty with a melting heart, and a righteous, wholesome indignation, and warn while they instruct! Oh, for statesmen of peace, who will feel that they are amenable to God more than man, to Christ than to country, and that every war is a stab at the very existence of civil society, a reversal of civilization, a suicide of the republic! Oh, for Gospel ministers, who will proclaim the whole counsel of God on this subject, and from the commanding station of the pulpit, with the meek wisdom of their master, win all men to "study the things that make for peace!"

CHAPTER XXIX.

SUBSTITUTES FOR WAR.

"In thirty-one days the natural results of this system of peace and fraternity have been more valuable to the cause of France and of liberty and of Poland herself, than ten battles with torrents of blood."

LAMARTINE.

"For what can war but endless war still breed?"

MILTON.

We have already argued at length on the beginning and ending of the war, as instructive and striking lessons of peace. In continuation and expansion of the same idea, in a little different direction, we would take up the means of preventing war by negotiation, arbitration, congress of nations, or some other method. Surely such an infernal system ought not to go on without the wisest counsels, and the most strenuous efforts of all Christians, patriots, and philanthropists to arrest it. "Shall the sword devour forever?" We believe not. We have full faith, that there is latent abhorrence enough against war in Christendom to sheathe the sword, were it given utterance, and positive, practical application. There is an amount of sleeping indignation and opposition, so to say, in the minds of the Christian men and women in America, were it called forth, organized, and put into execution, to sweep the accursed institution among ourselves into eternal oblivion. But hitherto there have not been sufficient decision and action on the subject. We have tampered and played and compromised with the evil. We have perhaps unconsciously and unintentionally, but actually, nursed the war-passion in the tender minds of our children and youth. Our great institutions of army, navy, militia, arsenals, naval and military schools, have done much to "educate the heart of the people for war." We have gloried in the past wars of our young republic, and promoted their heroes to the most brilliant posts of honor and emolument at home and abroad.

The subject of Peace and War, therefore, comes as surely under the law of cause and effect, as that of any other in the material or moral world. The causes and means of Peace, if properly and faithfully employed, would eventually result in peace, just as the causes and means of War have resulted in war. With a peace-education, a peace-literature, a true, and not a counterfeit "peace-establishment," a peace-administration of the general government, and shall we not say in view of some facts which have been stated in this essay, a peace-religion, the relations of the United States with every other government would be consolidated on a pacific basis, which nothing would be able to shake. And to the furtherance and ultimate carrying out of these peaceful influences on the part of society at large, two or three additional ideas should be incorporated into the permanent law of nations.

1. *Mediation and Arbitration.* These instruments of averting war, settling international questions, or putting an end to hostilities, have been often employed of late, and oftener as the relations of nations to one another have been seen more in a Christian light, and as falling, like the relations of individuals one to another, under all the solemn and binding sanctions of the law of God.

Thus, in the very matter of these difficulties between Mexico and Texas and the United States, we have no less than three instances of the friendly offices of other governments, and in two of them the result was partially or wholly successful, and promoting a good understanding.

In adjusting the claims for Mexican spoliations, 1840—1842, a Prussian umpire was employed to decide between the Mexican and American commissioners.

In 1845, through the intervention of Great Britain and France, Mexico consented to acknowledge the independence of Texas, "provided she would stipulate not to annex herself or become subject to any country whatever." That provision was not however fulfilled.

In 1846, Great Britain offered her mediation both to Mexico and the United States, to effect a treaty of peace, but by both powers it was either declined, or neglected.

But were there a proper spirit prevailing among the high officers of Christian governments, and were they sustained by the good sense and forbearance of the people, it would be held to be no more derogatory for two nations to accept the intervention of a third power to effect a peace, or to prevent war, or to submit their disputes to a friendly arbitration, than it is for individuals to do the same or similar things in their private transactions. Unfortunately however, the sensitivness of national honor is such, that it often refuses, after the duelist's example, to be satisfied with any thing short of human blood. Were the great mass of the population in any civilized country brought to see and understand the miseries, losses, and sins of war, they would sustain their rulers by the omnipotence of public opinion in any honest measures that would avert such an inundation of evils. How much more truly honorable in the sight of God and the nations would it have been, to submit our questions with Mexico to a board of impartial referees, or to accept the mediatorial offices of friendly powers to stay the rivers of blood! He who in private life is bent upon going to law with his neighbor, and rejects the proffers of conciliation, is thought to be governed by sinister motives of revenge, apprehension of the badness of his cause, or of the results of an unbiassed examination. May not a like unfavorable construction be put upon the conduct of the nation that scorns pacific measures, and strides on to its work of blood, deaf to the entreaties, and amicable remonstrances of other powers?

The best method to insure arbitration in all cases of difficulty, is to insert in every treaty an article binding both parties to adopt that mode of adjusting boundaries, claims, and all questions. Mr. Roberts, first President of the Republic of Liberia, stated at the Peace Congress in Brussels, Sept. 1848, that "he had caused to be inserted in treaties, made with many of the African tribes, a clause, binding the parties to refer their difficulties to arbitration, and had thus succeeded in preventing war from breaking out between those savage tribes for ten years. If the measure were practicable among such populations, whose ruling passion was war, what might it not do for peace, if adopted by civilized and Christian nations?'*

There are many reasons why nations should settle their disputes by legal forms, rather than by the uncertain chances of the battle-field. It is done by individuals and in corporations, and in our Union by the several States, and were it done by nations the change from barbarism to law would be completed. Then the chances of justice being fulfilled would be multiplied. The innocent would not be involved with the guilty in the horrid sufferings of war. Vast sums of money would be saved. The unspeakable disgrace and wickedness of nominally Christian nations engaged in cutting one another's throats on some punctilio of claim or ceremony, would be averted. It is to be hoped that every future treaty contracted by the United States and the European nations will contain a specific provision for arbitration, like the following one in the Treaty with Mexico.

* Advocate of Peace, vol. viii., p. 297.

ARTICLE XXI.

"If unhappily any disagreement should hereafter arise between the governments of the two republics, whether with respect to the interpretation of any stipulation in this treaty, or with respect to any other particular concerning the political or commercial relations of the two nations, the said governments in the name of those nations, do promise to each other that they will endeavor, in the most sincere and earnest manner, to settle the difference so arising, and to preserve the state of peace and friendship in which the two countries are now placing themselves ; using, for this end, mutual representations, and pacific negotiations. And if, by these means, they should not be enabled to come to an agreement, a resort shall not, on this account, be had to reprisals, aggression, or hostility of any kind, by the one republic against the other, until the government of that which deems itself aggrieved shall have maturely considered, in the spirit of peace and good neighborship, whether it would not be better that such difference should be settled by the arbitration of commissioners appointed on each side, or by that of a friendly nation. And should such course be proposed by either party, it shall be acceded to by the other, unless deemed by it altogether incompatible with the nature of the difference, or the circumstances of the case."

The next Article in the Treaty is an attempt, as has been said, to bind the parties, if they should again fight, ("which is not to be expected, and which God forbid!") to make war on *Christian principles!*

And let it not be here said, that nations must be left to manage their own concerns for themselves, and that it is the business of no third party to say how they shall settle their quarrels. On the contrary, it does very much concern every nation that every other nation be at peace. It *is* the business, very properly and necessarily the business of every nation, that its neighbors be not embroiled in sanguinary conflicts on shore, spoliations upon one another's commerce on the sea, nor that they should in any way interrupt the great channels of human intercourse, trade, and improvement. There may at particular periods be partial benefits, arising from war among their neighbors, to neutral powers; but in general it is the deranger of commerce, the embroiler of international connections beyond the parties directly involved, the signal to confusion and every evil work through the world. The war-trumpet blows discord into the ear of listening nations. A slight contest between inconsiderable powers has sometimes in history brought on that awful era in human events, called "a general war." Much responsibility rests upon those who first break the peace in the family of nations. And from such considerations it is plainly the interest and duty of neutral nations to use their good offices to restore peace between the belligerents. On every ground, too, of humanity and Christianity, it is imperative that democracies of all governments should cordially welcome the amiable intervention of others to heal their discords; for war is the enemy of the people, the enemy of liberty, the certain subverter of most of the benefits proposed by free institutions. History is full of warnings upon this subject, and if we are not deaf as adders, we shall hearken to the solemn voice that issues from the grave of departed republics.

2. *Congress of Nations.* But mediation or arbitration, valuable as it may be and has been, is not sufficiently systematic and general, to contribute very effectually to extinguish the firebrands of war. We have just had mournful evidence that some more efficacious instrument is demanded for the pacification even of Christian republics and near neighbors.

The most satisfactory plan which has yet been suggested is that of a Congress of Nations; or a Congress and a

Court of Nations, one as the preliminary and legislative body, and the other as the judicial and executive one ; the one to enact rules, and the other to judge cases, and carry its decisions into effect. Many objections have been raised against this, and every other project of perpetual pacification among the nations, but they are in general founded either on a misconception of the plan proposed, or on the old notion, that what has been, must be. If an august body should meet, of the wisest and best men, venerable for age and services, experienced in all matters of a legal, judicial, political, and moral character, elevated far above the aims of a selfish ambition, consulting with a large vision not for any narrow sectional interest of one or a few, but for the welfare of the world, it would be a spectacle in itself to command the universal admiration, homage and obedience of mankind. This object would be as sublime as it would be beneficent, to pacificate a warring world, to staunch the bleeding wounds of kingdoms, to actualize the prophetic and millennial age, and establish in steadfast loyalty the undisputed reign of the Prince of Peace.

The details of such a world-Congress, or Court, one or both, would of course require more discussion than can be given to them in this review. They will be found, however, at length in the Prize Essays on a Congress of nations, published by the American Peace Society, and in a compiled Essay on the same subject by the late distinguished philanthropist, William Ladd. We only insert the subject here in connection with another frightful chapter in our history, that speaks in thunder-tones of the need of such an institution, or some one like it, to avert these wholesale murders. When a new idea is first broken to the mind, there is apt to be some revulsion from it as being novel, extravagant, and aggressive upon our previous views. But the longer it is entertained, if it be true and valuable, the more fully do we become convinced that all truth is harmonious, safe, and profitable; and that precisely what the nations are perishing for, is lack of knowledge; that what the "whole creation groaneth and travaileth" for, is the faithful application of the truths of Christ to the wants of human society, in all public affairs as well as in private conduct and to the individual heart. The word of God is no mere fine theory, but the eternal verity, deeper than the sea, higher than the heavens, of these momentous interests of man living with man, and nation with nation; "neither is there salvation in any other."

But most thoroughly are we persuaded that there is nothing in the plan in question more wild or Quixotic than the institution of civil society itself, especially than the leagues and alliances recorded in history, and the Federal Union of thirty independent States in our own government. What is needed is, that the idea of a great pacific tribunal to settle the disputes of the world, should be broached, familiarized to the people, sent abroad on the wings of the press, hammered by dint of heavy and oft-repeated arguments into the mass of admitted and accredited truths, and then the work is done. We have trained mankind to war, we must now train them to peace. When the spirit of peace is largely developed in the public sentiment of Europe and America, this institution will be born in a day. The tendency of these remarks is to show that the agitation of the subject is what is now most exigent. By books and pamphlets, by the living voice and the inspired pen, this theme must be brought home to the minds and hearts of men, and they must be made to feel that every individual, be he high or low, rich or poor, is vitally concerned in having the great quarrels of kingdoms justly and amicably settled, as he is that justice should be done between man and man, and peace and order prevail in his hamlet or village. For in the earthquake shocks of war a thousand homes are overturned, and the mark of blood is left behind on ten thousand spheres of life once usefully and happily filled by fathers, sons, husbands, brothers. Let us hope, and labor, and pray, that the day may not be far distant when civilized and Christian men will see the madness of war, its bald inconsistency with the theory of a republican government, its hostility to the spirit of the present age, and its nullification of every law, and promise, and prayer of the Lord Jesus Christ.

CHAPTER XXX.

PACIFICATION OF THE WORLD.

"When the drums shall throb no longer,
And the battle-flags be furled
In the Parliament of man,
The Federation of the world." — TENNYSON.

"Neither shall they learn war any more." — ISAIAH.

SINCE war has so many evils, and peace so many blessings, may we not labor with hope for the fulfilment of the prophet's vision? Since the expenditures of military expeditions, the destruction of multitudes of lives, the barbarities, executions, illegalities, personal, domestic, and political evils, the vices of the camp, the creation of a species of martial literature, the introduction of false maxims of conduct, and the counteraction of the Gospel by the war-spirit, chargeable upon our conflict with Mexico, are virtually the same in all wars, may we not hope that the good sense of mankind, and their feelings of human brotherhood, will finally gain such a predominance as to effect the pacification of the whole world? And, especially, is not this expectation encouraged by the well known fact that many other evil customs and habits have disappeared and are disappearing before the more Christian civilization of the present day? What now is witchcraft? An obsolete superstition. Where are torture, and the appeal to fire, or water? Laid away among exploded ideas. Where are the Inquisition and persecution for heresy? Gone beyond all power of recall. Where are privateering, and piracy, and the slave trade? All entered in the "Index Expurgatorius" of international law. Where are slavery, intemperance, and war? Gradually falling under the same ban, and no longer acquiesced in as necessary evils, but recognized as mutable and capable of eradication with the other corrupt usages specified, if efficient and Christian means be applied, with faith and perseverance, for their removal. The day is gone for any man, with the Bible in his hand, and God and heaven above him, to say that war must be eternal. We do not presume to date the year or century of the laying aside by the nations of their cumbrous coats of mail, and the disarmament of their numerous troops and squadrons, and the establishment of those modes of adjusting international difficulties detailed in the last chapter. But we see already symptoms of returning health in the body politic, though joined with some other prognostics less favorable. Cases of mediation, arbitration, and peaceable intervention, are multiplying. Treaties are constructed with more reference to permanency. It has become fashionable even for kings and statesmen, out of deference to a certain rising public sentiment of mankind, to speak well of peace. War has been summoned to answer for itself before the judgment-seat of civilization and of Christianity, and it is found to make but a poor justification. The friends of peace are in earnest and increasing. The solitary protestations of a Penn or Worcester have multiplied into the deep-toned remonstrances of a London, a Brussels, and a Paris World's Convention of Peace. The press and the pulpit are enlisted. The power of association is invoked. "Olive leaves" are flying far and near. While, therefore, the drum-beat still heralds the morning sun round the globe, we will not so far distrust God, or despair of our race, as to believe that, when daily triumphs are achieved over the brute elements of nature; and fire, and water, and steam, and magnetism, and electricity are bowed to the service and control of man, he is never to acquire any better government over those brutal passions of his own nature, whose outbreaks are far more disastrous to life and happiness than the volcano, the earthquake, or the hurricane.

When we consider how little has been done to prevent war, and how much to cultivate its spirit, and to invest its feats with a factitious glory; how literature and the fine arts, and politics, and, sad to confess, even professed Christians have encouraged, applauded, and diffused the passion for arms, we wonder not at the frequency of battles, and the human blood that has stained half the land and sea of the whole earth. Indeed the martial spirit has been so prevalent, mankind have drunk it so greedily as if it were as innocent as water, that we are prone to forget what a thorough education we give our children for war, and how little we do for the pacification of the world.

For when we inquire how this vast underlying passion for war has been educated and ripened in the heart of society, we shall be constrained to answer: It is by the war-songs of childhood, and the studies of the classics. It is by the wooden sword, and the tin drum of boyhood. It is by the trainings and the annual muster. It is by the red uniform and the white plume, and the prancing steed. It is by the cannon's thunder, and the gleam of the bayonet. It is by ballads of Robin Hood, and histories of Napoleon, and "Tales of the Crusaders." It is by the presentation of flags by the hands of the fair, and the huzzas for a victory. It is by the example of the father and the consent of the mother. It is by the fear of cowardice, and the laugh of the scorner. It is by the blood of youth, and the pride of manhood, and stories of revolutionary sires. It is by standing armies, and majestic men-of-war. It is by the maxims of self defence, and the cheapness of human life, and the love of excitement. It is by novels of love, and the "Pirate's Own Book." It is by the jars of home, and the squabbles of party, and the controversies of sects. It is by the misconception of the Bible, and ignorance of God. It is by the bubble of glory, and the emulation of schools, and the graspings of money-making. By one and by all, the heart of the community is educated for war, from the cradle to the coffin. When we sow the seed so copiously, we must not complain that the harvest is abundant.

And if we would inquire, how the heart of the world can be calmed, and enlarged, and inspired with the life-breath of peace; we can only say that such a heart comes from the nurture of home, and the solemnity of the church, and the tomb of the loved and gone. It comes by the closet of prayer, and the communion of nature, and the table of the Lord. It comes by a sister's love and a brother's example, and the memory of "the good old place." It comes in the distilling dew of Christian instruction and the infinite sanctions of death, judgment, and eternity. It comes by the sweetness of Fenelon, and the love of Scougal; by the majesty of Luther, and the humanity of Penn. It comes by the horror of blood, and the courage to be a coward in the wrong. It comes by the testimonies of the wise, and the heroism of the good. It comes by the Beatitudes of the New Testament, and the Lord's Prayer, and Paul's masterpiece of Charity, and John's epistle of Love. It comes by him who was born in a manger and died on a cross, the Son of God, the Prince of Peace, the Saviour of sinners.

By these means the weaker spirit of war may be made to yield to the mightier spirit of peace. "And," in the words of an English divine,* suggestive of some of the foregoing remarks, "it must appear to what most awful obligation and duty we hold all those from whom this heart takes its nature and shape, our king, our princes, our nobles, all who wear the badge of office, or honor; all priests, judges, senators, pleaders, interpreters of law, all instructors of youth, all seminaries of education, all parents, all learned men, all professors of science and art, all teachers of manners. Upon them depends the fashion of the nation's heart. By them it is to be chastised, refined, and purified. By them is the state to lose the character and title of the beast of prey. By them are the iron scales to fall off, and a skin of youth, beauty, freshness, and polish, to come upon it. By them it is to be made so tame and gentle as that a child may lead it."

CHAPTER XXXI.

CONCLUSION.

"I have been apt to think there never has been, nor ever will be, any such thing as a good war, or a bad peace." — FRANKLIN.

"Then, at least shall it be seen, that *there can be no peace that is not honorable, and there can be no war that is not dishonorable.*" — CHARLES SUMNER.

AN able writer of the present day has said, that "the philosophical study of facts may be undertaken for three different purposes; the simple description of the facts; their

* Rev. Dr. Ramsden.

explanation; or prediction, meaning by prediction, the determination of the conditions under which similar facts may be expected again to occur." The Mexican war is now numbered among the things of the past. What has been done, is done; and what has been written, is written. Its consequences, however, will long remain, and will mingle with future events and influences materially to affect our national prospects. A treaty may stop the war, though some symptoms are unfavorable, but it cannot stop the war-results. The question then is, how can this great evil be turned to the best account. After narrating and explaining its events, so as to get a clear idea of its origin, causes, losses of life and treasure, and its social, political, and moral evils, the next step is to state the conditions on which we may predicate the recurrence of similar mischiefs; or draw such lessons of warning and encouragement, as will tend to prevent them. This end the American Peace Society propose to accomplish by publishing a Review of the War, and pointing out clearly and impressively to the citizens of our land, what measures should be taken to save us from plunging again into like calamities. Thus reviewed, and exposed, this darkest of all the passages in our country's history, and most ominous of evil to come, in the judgment of wise statesmen, and sage moralists, may be converted into an unexpected blessing. The wars, consequent upon the French Revolution, aroused the friends of Peace on both sides of the ocean to more positive and combined action in behalf of this cause, and induced the formation of associations to work for the grand object of a universal and perpetual pacification of the world. Much has thus been effected to enlighten both rulers and people, and to impress upon both their solemn duties. Much has been done by the devoted and untiring laborers in this department of Christian philanthropy, over which angels must rejoice, and the King of kings extend his benediction.

But the great work has but just been commenced. We

cannot suppose that so "splendid" a sin as war can at once be stripped of its false and fascinating garb, that the deeply-rooted and long-revered customs of nations can be torn up in a day, martial passions and habits be checked, and a public opinion, and a public conscience and heart too be formed on the subject, of sufficient potency to sheathe the sword forever. But the slowness of progress, the discouragements of efforts, the violent opposition with which a good cause and its advocates meet, do not release us from our duty to that cause, or furnish in reality a solitary reason why we should fold our arms in despair. The cause of Peace only suffers a like fate from opposition, misconstruction and misrepresentation, as the other glorious causes of philanthropy, and as that parent religion of which these causes are the legitimate and hopeful offspring. We may be sure that nothing is lost, that is done in a true spirit and a high aim for the furtherance of human good, and the divine glory. God forbid that we should ever fear that "His ear is heavy that it cannot hear, or His hand shortened, that it cannot save!"

In this faith, the Mexican war is a new weapon, put into the hands of peace, wherewith to win her bloodless victories. It teaches us, were lessons wanting, the folly of all war, its sin against God, and its subversion of His great plan. It teaches us by its gory fields of carnage, and the screaming hells of its hospitals, that a retributive God sits in the heavens, and that those "who take the sword, shall perish by the sword." If rightly interpreted and faithfully laid to heart, it is capable of showing us the emptiness of military glory, the contentious and unchristian spirit which it cherishes among the officers and soldiers of the same side, the torrent of vices that is let loose in the path of armies, and the profuse waste that is made of all that men hold dear, or labor most industriously to attain. It is a lesson at home, a republican, an American lesson. It has been brought nigh to many a heart, alas, and many a home, and burnt as with a red-hot branding-iron upon the memory of thousands, by bereavements and pains, such as God only can know, and eternity measure. And we believe that all the warnings and forebodings of the opponents to the annexation of Texas now stand vindicated in the light of a fearful and guilty history. Their prophecy is now fact. They predicted a war with Mexico, the extension of slavery and the slave-power, and infuriate lust of territory, the hatching of new schemes of war and plunder, and a headlong course of conquest and aggrandizement. We are deep in these evils and their results, or waver on the brink, apparently about to plunge in deeper than ever. If these things be so, then let the predictions and warnings of the friends of peace at this time not fall, Cassandra-like, on cold hearts and insensible consciences. But let every patriot and Christian, every lover of liberty and man, study what he can do to help stay the hour of his country's danger, and, perhaps, ruin. It profits little to sit still and croak, like the ill-boding raven, of ills to come; but we must forth into the field of duty, action, and influence, and by voice and vote, by pen and purse, by example and precept, by a living and by a dying testimony, whether ours be the widow's mite or the rich man's offering, the influence of the high, or the word of the humble, strive, as for life, to arrest the downward tendency of things, recall the promise of our young republic, relight the torch of freedom, shame modern degeneracy with the early doctrines of our history, and set in vivid contrast the heathen nation we are in danger of becoming, with the glory of a true Christian commonwealth.

Let, therefore, these awful lapses in national virtue only serve to arouse to a more comprehensive and resolute course of action the disciples of the Prince of Peace. Let them thank God and take courage, that if they cannot wholly extinguish the wide-spread conflagration of war, they can yet rescue many victims from its fiery passions and its corrupting moral code. Let them bear their testimony against evils, still too powerful to be subdued at once. Let them see the hope and beauty of a brighter to-morrow symbolized in the rainbow that spans the departing thunder-cloud. War is but one section of the kingdom of Satan that is doomed to be overthrown by the kingdom of God. There is as much encouragement in laboring to remove this sin as any other of the gigantic evils that prey upon humanity. Faith, therefore, faith is the word; faith vivified and illuminated by hope; faith made strong, and gentle, and patient by charity; faith in Jesus Christ, our Lord, the spiritual Governor of men, in whose kingdom of liberty, righteousness, and love, all nations, races, colors, clans, and sects, will at last be harmonized, and God shall be all in all.

Yea, despite the late war, despite the belligerent symptoms of the day at home, despite the warlike aspect of Christendom abroad, though all Europe seems to be turned into barracks and camps, and every country to be resounding with the march of armies hastening to the combat, our just and reasonable confidence in the ultimate triumph of the Gospel of peace is not in the least shaken. The last thirty years of comparative pacification have not passed in vain. Darker clouds than now overhang our horizon, have in former times shut out the light of heaven and hope. If in the solid midnight of sin and superstition, when the whole world lay bound at the chariot wheels of a military despotism, Jesus and his apostles knew that a better day was coming, how undying should be our faith amid the breaking of the morning light! For the truth is great, and it will prevail. God is faithful, and his promise will be redeemed. The Gospel is from the Almighty, and it must prevail over man. It is light from heaven, and the darkness of earth must flee before it. Its power is infinite, and its obstacles only finite.

Though for a season then, or for ages its victory may be

delayed, the final result is none the less certain, for it is guaranteed by Him who alone is True. Verily, though the world should again plunge into that gulf of horrors, called a general war; though Christian nations should apostatize, and the churches sink into corruption; though the mighty impulses of philanthropy should fail, and the missionaries of the cross should return home, and renounce the sublime hope of evangelizing the world; though our holy faith should retire from the city and the assembly of men, and hide itself from the gaze of the world, we would yet follow her in fear and darkness to her last holy retreat on earth, to the spot, where a mother was kneeling over her new-born infant, and offering up to the Father of spirits her thanks and supplications, and even there catch a new inspiration of faith and hope for the revival of Christianity. For we should remember the sacred scene, eighteen hundred years ago, when the mother of Bethlehem prayed over the babe in the manger, and blessed her Saviour-child; and angels from heaven sang the anthem of his birth; "Glory to God in the highest, and on earth peace, good will toward men."

APPENDIX.

THE HISTORICAL EVENTS OF THE WAR.

"Lastly, stood War, in glittering arms yclad,
With visage grim, stern look, and blackly hued;
In his right hand a naked sword he had,
That to the hilt was all with blood imbrued;
And in his left (that kings and kingdoms rued)
Famine and fire he held, and therewithal
He razed towers, and threw down towers and all.

"Cities he sacked, and realms (that whilom flowered
In honor, glory, and rule above the rest)
He overwhelmed, and all their fame devoured,
Consumed, destroyed, wasted; and never ceased
Till he their wealth, their name and all oppressed.
His face forehewed with wounds; and by his side
There hung his targe, with gashes deep and wide."

THOMAS SACKVILLE.

ALL honor to the hearty old English Poet, who dared thus, in a warlike age, to unveil the hideous idol men worshipped, under the self-contradictory terms of military glory. He represents the god as no young and knightly cavalier, riding forth, splendidly arrayed, at the sound of martial music, to do the feats of chivalry, and redress the wrongs of the injured. Far truer is his personification. The figure of his brain, moulded in a feeling heart, was that of a grim and ghastly giant, bringing up the rear of the procession of Remorse, Dread, Revenge, Misery, Care, Malady, Famine, and Death; his face dark and stern, and scarred with wounds; his hands filled with the awful besoms of destruction, fire, and hunger, and the sword; his rent and battered shield hanging at his side; and his path marked with burning cities, desolated countries, falling realms, haggard want, and ruin and oblivion. He thus wrote, in the words of Poetry, the solemn truth of History. Would to heaven that all his brethren of the immortal art had been equally faithful!

In recording a brief sketch of the events of the Mexican War, for the purpose of reference, we shall paint no battle-scenes, and utter no eulogies. Enough of them may be found in other quarters, to satisfy the most morbid appetite. The letter-writer, the biographer, the politician, the historian, and the rhymster, have vied with one another, in giving illuminated editions of its fearful tales. The artist has painted the features of its heroes, and the panoramas of its marches and battles. The engraver has traced on wood, and stone, and steel, the deadly charge, the smoke of musketry and artillery, and the dead and dying stretched upon the bloody earth, with the Star-spangled Banner leading on its hosts to victory. Dazzled with the false show, and excited with the intoxication of a momentary triumph, men thus fail to see war as it is, in all its heart-rending realities and its lasting results. It is a mere gorgeous vision, a passing dream of glory to them. They do not look down into its abysses of pains and agonies; its awful Aceldama of groans, and tears, and death. We desire, by no word of ours, to invest these scenes with aught but their own proper character. We would simply narrate coldly, and it may be tamely, the bare facts.

The Mexican War dates virtually, though not actually, from the 3d of March, 1845, when, by a Joint Resolution, which was passed by both branches of Congress — in the House of Representatives, by a vote of 120 to 98; and in the Senate, of 27 to 25 — and which was on that day, the last of his administration, signed by the President, John Tyler, Texas was annexed to the American Union.

The Mexican Minister, Almonte, immediately demanded his passports, and left the country; declaring the act of annexation to be an act of hostility to Mexico. Distinguished statesmen of the United States also took the same view of the subject.

But Mexico was poor, distracted, and revolutionary, and she had no means to vindicate what she regarded as her violated honor. The *act* of war did not follow. She contented herself with protesting.

The United States, however, were not idle. In August, 1845,* Gen. Taylor was despatched, with a regular body of troops, drawn from different posts, — first as an army of "Observation," then of "Occupation," — to the town of Corpus Christi.

* 30th Congress, 1st Session, House of Representatives, Ex. Doc. 60, p. 101.

But on the 13th of January, 1846, Mr. Marcy, Secretary of War of the United States, wrote to Gen. Taylor, as follows: * "I am directed, by the President, to instruct you to advance and occupy, with the troops under your command, positions on or near the east bank of the Rio del Norte, as soon as it can be conveniently done. . . . . . It is not designed, in our present relations with Mexico, that you should treat her as an enemy; but should she assume that character, by a declaration of war, or any open act of hostility towards us, *you will not act merely on the defensive.*" Gen. Taylor obeyed orders. He received the letter early in February, and, on the 11th of March, he commenced his march from Corpus Christi for the Rio Grande, one hundred and fifty miles distant, across a desert, or rolling prairie. On the 20th of the same month he was met, at the river Colorado, by the Mexicans, whose commanding officer, Gen. Mejia, announced, that if the American forces should cross that river, it would be considered as a declaration of war, and actual hostilities would ensue.† But the warning was disregarded, and the troops pursued their way, and arrived on the banks of the Rio Grande without any serious molestation. Repeated remonstrances were made by the authorities, both civil and military, to the American commander, against the occupation of what they regarded as a part of the Mexican province of Tamaulipas. They declared the alternative of his withdrawal to the Nueces or war. But Taylor remained, and erected Fort Brown, on the left bank of the Rio Grande, commanding the city of Matamoras on the other side. Several skirmishes took place between parties of the two nations, in which lives were lost. Fort Brown, and a small force left to keep possession of it, were bombarded, during the absence of the commander-in-chief and his main army, to obtain his military stores, which had been landed at Point Isabel; but the Americans maintained their position, though summoned to surrender.

On his return from Point Isabel, Gen. Taylor was met by the Mexican army, under the command of Gen. Arista, at a point on the prairies, a few miles from the Rio Grande, called *Palo Alto*, which is distinguished, as giving a name to the first battle of the war. The contest occurred on the 8th of May, 1846, commencing at about two o'clock, P. M.; and was sustained during five hours, when the Mexicans were defeated, with great loss in killed and wounded. The

* 30th Congress, 1st Session, House of Representatives, Ex. Doc. 60, pp. 90, 91. Also, for the war-despatches in general, see 30th Congress, 1st Session, House of Representatives, Ex. Doc. 60. Senate, Ex. Doc. 1. 30th Congress, 2d Session, House of Representatives, Ex. Doc. 1.

† 30th Congress, 1st Session, House of Representatives, Ex. Doc. 60, pp. 145, 146.

Americans numbered 2,300, according to the report of their general; while he says "the strength of the enemy is believed to have been about 6,000 men."

On the following day, May 9th, Gen. Taylor advanced two or three miles along the road through the chapparal, towards the Rio Grande, when he found the enemy in position for battle, at a ravine called *Resaca de la Palma.* The action commenced about four o'clock in the afternoon, and lasted one hour and a half; when the Mexicans, under the command of Arista, were entirely routed and pursued to the river, in which multitudes were drowned, in attempting to cross to Matamoras.

The immediate result of these victories was the capture, without resistance, of the city of Matamoras, and the opening of the whole Valley of the Rio Grande to the American arms. The forces of the enemy were dispersed, and, to use the military phrase, *demoralized.* The reverses of Palo Alto and Resaca de la Palma had sent dismay through the country. In the course of the summer Gen. Taylor occupied, without any difficulty, the towns of Reynosa, Camargo, Mier, and Ceralvo, and advanced upon Monterey.

In the meantime, advices had been received at Washington of the critical situation of Gen. Taylor, about the 1st of May; and the President, in a Message to Congress, dated the 11th of that month, used the following language: * "But now, after reiterated menaces, Mexico has passed the boundary of the United States, has invaded our territory, and shed American blood upon American soil. She has proclaimed that hostilities have commenced, and that the two nations are now at war."

"As war exists, and, notwithstanding our efforts to avoid it, exists by the act of Mexico herself, we are called upon, by every consideration of duty and patriotism, to vindicate, with decision, the honor, the rights and the interests of our country."

On the same day, a bill passed the House of Representatives, 174 to 14, and, on the subsequent one, was enacted by the Senate, 42 to 2, declaring, that, "by the acts of the Republic of Mexico, a state of war exists between the United States and that republic;" placing ten millions of dollars at the disposal of the President; and authorizing him to employ the land and naval forces of the United States, and to accept the services of volunteers, to a number not exceeding 50,000, in

* 30th Congress, 1st Session, House of Representatives, Ex. Doc. 60, pp. 8, 9.

prosecuting the war. On the 13th of May, 1846, a Proclamation of War was issued by the highest executive authority.

A warlike enthusiasm ran, like wild-fire, over the Western, South-Western, and Southern sections of the country, and, in many instances, the number of volunteers, said to be 300,000 in all, was far greater than could be mustered into service, according to the general appropriation of the respective States.* The Great Valley resounded with the din of preparation. Fathers and sons enlisted. Some of more than the allotted age of man, seized the musket. More than one of the ministers of the Prince of Peace caught the dangerous contagion. The latent passions of the heart took fire, like tinder, at the cry of war.

In such popular excitements men do not reason, they only feel, and, feeling, act. Thus impelled, they may do the noblest deeds; they may also perpetrate the most wicked crimes, and set in motion the most irretrievable calamities. The call to arms is the occasion, of all others, when human beings seem to lay aside the more manly and Christian attributes of character, and put on those of the beast of prey, or worse. But it is necessary also to admit, that a leaven of well-intentioned, though often mistaken patriotism, mingles with the dark mass of animal and demoniac passions. A wild love of adventure, without reference to the innocence or guilt of the objects to which it is directed, also carries away the settlers in a new state of society, as with a flood. Add some anticipations of booty; some old grudges of Santa Fé, and other border traders; some Texan vengeance, for the massacres of Goliad and the Alamo; some ideas of Anglo-Saxon destiny; some hope of distinction, and desire of bettering perhaps desperate fortunes; and we have glimpses of the more prominent elements that moulded thousands to one purpose, and precipitated them upon a second "conquest of Mexico."

The means, however, of transporting the troops to the theatre of action, were not sufficient to enable the American commander to advance rapidly into the enemy's country. About 9,000 men only were under the command of Gen. Taylor, in the beginning of June; and he assaulted Monterey, the capital of Nuevo Leon, about three hundred and forty miles from Matamoras, with less than 7,000. On the 19th of September, 1846, he appeared before that city, and invested it. Active operations were carried on during Sunday, the 20th, 21st, 22d, and 23d; and on the 24th, the Mexican commander, Gen. Ampudia, surrendered.

* Young's History of Mexico, p. 380.

Santa Anta returned from the West Indies to Vera Cruz,* and on the 15th of September, 1846, he reëntered the capital, from which he had been driven into exile, and was placed at the head of the Mexican armies. He infused new resolution into his countrymen, after all their reverses, and assembled an army of more than 20,000 men, called the "Liberating Army of the North," to oppose Gen. Taylor. He contributed largely, of his own private property, to furnish supplies to his troops, and was engaged for months in equipping, drilling, and organizing the different corps of his forces, at San Luis Potosi.

In the autumn, Gen. Taylor advanced bodies of troops to Saltillo, sixty-five miles from Monterey; while Gen. Wool marched an army of 2,400 over the Rio Grande, at the Presidio del Norte, and occupied Monclova, and subsequently Parras. Gen. Quitman captured the town of Victoria. In fact, the northern frontier of Mexico, upon the Rio Grande, was in the complete possession of the Americans.

But the Mexican commander-in-chief determined to strike a decisive blow against the invaders of his country; and, on the 22d and 23d of February, 1847, he met Gen. Taylor in the valley of Buena Vista, (beautiful sight,) six miles south of Saltillo, with troops, as he stated in his challenge to surrender, amounting to 20,000 men. After a terrible and sanguinary battle, fought two days, the Americans again won a complete victory, at a fearful cost of life.

The Mexicans retreated in great disorder, during the night after the battle, and the late formidable army was wholly disorganized and scattered. The route, by which they retired, was strewed with the dead and dying. Santa Anna returned to the city of Mexico, and Gen. Taylor reöccupied his former positions, and advanced as far as to Encarnacion. No victory could be more decisive in its results.

With the exception of guerilla skirmishes, no other battles were fought by Gen. Taylor except the four successful ones of Palo Alto, Resaca de la Palma, Monterey, and Buena Vista. He urged upon the Mexican Government from time to time the question of peace, but they persisted in declaring that as long as a single invader had his foot upon their soil, they scorned the proposal. "Say to General Taylor," said Santa Anna, when the subject was communicated to him after the

* The following pass gave him admission into Mexico:

"*U. S. Navy Department*, *May* 13, 1846.

"COMMODORE — If Santa Anna endeavors to enter the Mexican ports, you will allow him to pass freely.

"Respectfully yours, GEORGE BANCROFT.

"Commodore David Connor, *Commanding Home Squadron*."

battle of Buena Vista, "that we sustain the most sacred of causes,—the defence of our territory, and the preservation of our nationality and rights; that we are not the aggressors; and that our Government has never offended that of the United States. We can say nothing of peace while the Americans are on this side of the Rio Bravo del Norte, or occupy any part of the Mexican territory, or blockade our ports. We are resolved to perish or vindicate our rights."

After this necessarily brief and imperfect sketch of the operations of what was at first called "the Army of Observation," then "the Army of Occupation," and what finally became, with a significant title, the Army of "Invasion,"* let us turn to view another part of the field of war.

It had been proposed soon after the war broke out, to invade Mexico at three different points, and thus divide and distract her forces. The main army, under Gen. Taylor, was to advance from the Rio Grande towards San Luis Potosi; a second smaller division, called "the Army of the Centre," under Gen. Wool, was to march from Bexar, in Texas, upon Chihuahua, the results of both of which movements have already been given. But a third expedition, to be called "the Army of the West," was to proceed from Missouri, cross the plains, occupy New Mexico, hold its capital, Santa Fé, and after that was achieved, a portion of the same troops was to occupy California.

On the 30th of June, 1846, Gen. Samuel W. Kearney led the Army of the West from Fort Leavenworth, situated on the river Missouri, and after a march of 890 miles, took possession of Santa Fé, without resistance, on the 18th of August, 1846. On the 25th of September, after making provision for a temporary government of New Mexico, he took 300 dragoons, and marched on the route to California. Learning on the way that that territory had been brought under the flag of the United States by Commodore Stockton and Lieut.-Colonel Fremont, after some severe skirmishes with the enemy, he left 200 of his troops in New Mexico, and with the remainder he marched 1,050 miles to San Diego, near the Pacific Ocean. Several conflicts occurred with the enemy, in which a considerable number were killed and wounded on both sides. But victory attended the American arms in most instances, and the territory was hopelessly subdued.

Of the troops left behind in New Mexico, and augmented by reinforcements from the States, one portion was under the command of Col. S. Price, and the remainder under that of Col. A. W. Doniphan.

* See Appendix to Hon. J. H. Crozier's speech, delivered in the House of Representatives, Jan. 21, 1847.

On the 19th of January, 1847, the Mexicans and Indians revolted against Gov. Bent of this territory, and put him and his followers, to the number of fifteen, to death. Col. Price, with a body of 353 men, met the enemy at the town of Canada, on Sunday, Jan. 24, 1847, and dispersed them. A detachment of the same troops, under Capt. Burgwin, engaged and conquered the enemy on Jan. 29th, at the pass of Embudo. On Feb. 3d and 4th, Col. Price besieged a stronghold of the insurgents, called Pueblo de Taos, defended by 600 or 700 men, and took it after a severe contest.

The other section of Gen. Kearney's army, 856 mounted riflemen, under the command of Col. Doniphan, left Santa Fé on the 26th of October, 1846, and traversed New Mexico, Chihuahua, Durango, and New Leon. At Bracito, in New Mexico, on Dec. 25, 1846, on Christmas Day, the Colonel, with about 500 of his troops, met and defeated 1,220 Mexicans. The battle of Sacramento, in Chihuahua, was fought on Sunday, Feb. 28, 1847. After a bloody encounter of three hours and a half, the Mexicans fled.

The following is a short summary of the naval operations carried on in the meantime against Mexico. On the 18th of May, 1846, the American squadron under the flag of Commodore Conner, consisting of five ships of war, blockaded Vera Cruz, and one sloop of war was stationed off Tampico. On the 14th of November, Commodore Conner took possession of the latter port without firing a gun. Previously to this, Commodore Perry ascended the river Tobasco seventy-four miles with several vessels, and on Sunday, Oct. 25th, he anchored opposite the town of the same name, and summoned it to surrender. On the succeeding day the town was severely cannonaded, and nearly demolished.

Several other ports on the eastern coast of Mexico, Tuspan, Alvarado, Panuco, were occupied by the Americans, and many vessels were captured. In fact, the naval power of the enemy was annihilated.

On the Pacific, Commodore Sloat occupied Monterey, the capital of Upper California, on the 7th of July, 1846, and announced by proclamation to the inhabitants that "henceforward California will be a portion of the United States, and promised that all the peaceable inhabitants should enjoy the same rights, privileges, and protection, as the other citizens of the republic." But in the course of the following winter, 1846-7, the Californians rose and offered resistance to their invaders, which was suppressed by Col. Fremont with a handful of soldiers, and by Commodore Stockton with a detachment from his fleet, and subsequently by Gen. Kearney, as before related.

The principal operations of the naval force in the war had thus far been on land, or against ports and towns capable of being reached by vessels at anchor, with the exception of the service of transporting troops from the United States to the scene of action. But a new theatre of greater importance, though of similar character was opened by the siege of Vera Cruz.

Mexico had been repeatedly solicited, after the various successful movements which have been described, to enter into negotiations of peace, but she would hearken to no terms whatever while her soil was covered with hostile forces. Her noble motto was, "The integrity of the national territory." The next step accordingly was, to carry the war more into "the vitals" of the country, and to "conquer a peace" by conquering the capital of the republic. A campaign was therefore entered upon by Gen. Winfield Scott, senior officer of the regular army of the United States, in the early part of 1847. The plan was to capture Vera Cruz, the principal sea-port, make that the base of operations, advance into the interior by the great line of communication, and take the city of Mexico, situated in the heart of the country, about 350 miles from the gulf of the same name.

Vera Cruz and the Castle of San Juan d'Ulloa were invested by land and sea with the American forces under the direction of Gen. Scott and Commodore Perry, in March, 1847; and on Monday the 22nd of that month, after a summons to surrender had been offered and rejected, the batteries were opened upon the city. The inhabitants were in number about 4,000 or 5,000, besides the families of the foreign consuls, who had not taken advantage of the permission granted them by Gen. Scott to retire from the scene of danger. A terrible carnage ensued among the people from the heavy metal and the fatal accuracy of the American gunners. It was computed that 6,700 shot and shell were thrown, weighing 463,600 pounds, in four days. On the 26th, Gen. Landero, commanding officer of the place, made overtures for a capitulation. The awful desolation that reigned over the devoted city counselled submission. The terms of capitulation were signed on the 27th, executed on the 29th, and possession given of both the town and the almost impregnable castle.

The next principal engagement took place on the heights of Cerro Gordo, fifty miles from Vera Cruz, on Saturday and Sunday, April 17th and 18th, between Gen. Scott and Gen. Santa Anna, in which the latter was entirely defeated, and narrowly escaped being taken prisoner as he fled from the field.

On the 15th of May, the city of Puebla, eighty miles from Perote, on the route to Mexico, was taken without opposition. During the summer, reinforcements of men and arms were accumulated by Gen. Scott at Puebla, at which place, leaving a competent garrison, he began his march toward the capital, the 17th of August, 1847, a distance of from 100 to 120 miles.

On the 19th and 20th of August, the successive actions of Contreras, San Antonio, and Churubusco, were fought in the Valley of Mexico, and in the immediate neighborhood of the capital. In all these battles the usual rule held good, and the victory was won by the Americans.

After these engagements an armistice was agreed upon, and negotiations for peace were entered into by N. P. Trist, Commissioner on the part of the Executive of the United States, and Commissioners on the part of Mexico. But they were ineffectual, and the law of force was again resorted to instead of the law of reason. The *ultimatum* of boundaries was understood to be the rock on which this new attempt at peace was wrecked.

The armistice was thrown up, and the battle of El Molino del Rey, or King's Mill, was fought on Sept. 8, 1847.

On Sunday, Monday, and Tuesday, Sept. 12th, 13th, and 14th, the strong fortress of Chapultepec, outside of the city, was cannonaded, stormed, and carried, the defences at the gates assaulted and captured, and early on the morning of the 14th, the city surrendered to Gen. Scott. The operations consisted of a succession of assaults and engagements from point to point, and from one battery to another, until, by the skill and the fierce bravery of the American troops, the object of their ambition was attained, and they entered "the halls of Montezuma." But victory was bought at a costly sacrifice. A scattering fire by *leperos*, — criminals set free from prison, and disbanded soldiers, from the streets and houses, was kept up on the troops after the city was surrendered, in which many lives were lost, but which was finally suppressed by severe measures. The destruction of limb and life during these fatal days on the part of the Mexicans never was precisely known, but it must have been immense. The accuracy of the American aim, both of infantry and artillery, always told upon the crowded masses of the enemy with terrible effect.

Meanwhile, there were other engagements which form a part of the historical survey of the war. Major Lally, conducting about 1,000 men from Vera Cruz to Jalapa, was beset at different points in his march by numerous guerilla forces, on Aug. 10th, 12th, Sunday 15th, and 19th, but reached his destination, and retook possession of Jalapa, which had been vacated by Gen. Scott in his advance to the capital. The Mexican loss in killed and wounded was very great.

A garrison had been left at Puebla, with 1,800 sick in the hospitals, under the command of Col. Childs. A close investment and assault were maintained by the Mexicans during twenty-eight days, from Sept. 13th until the American troops were relieved by the arrival of Gen. Lane with 2,000 troops from Vera Cruz. Santa Anna, flying from the conquerors of the capital, conducted operations with large reinforcements during the latter part of the siege, but was unable to force capitulation.

On Oct. 9th, Gen Lane had an engagement with Gen. Santa Anna at Huamantla.

The town of Alixco, a resort of guerillas, was bombarded and taken by Gen. Lane on Oct. 19th.

On the 16th of March, 1848, Gen. Price fought a battle in the town of Santa Cruz de Rozales, belonging to the province of Chihuahua, and about sixty miles south of the capital of the same name, against Gen. Angel Trias, defeated him, and took him and his troops prisoners.

Other inconsiderable affairs with bands of the Mexicans occurred in various quarters of the country, but not of sufficient moment to be recorded in this dark calendar of misery and death. In another connection a statement has been made of the mortality of the war.

During the autumn of 1847, Gen. Scott was largely reinforced by troops from other garrisons in Mexico, and by regulars and volunteers from home, until his army exceeded 20,000 men. He retained possession of the capital until negotiations of peace were concluded between N. P. Trist, late Commissioner on the side of the United States, but not at that time authorized to act in that capacity, and Commissioners on the part of Mexico. The treaty of Guadalupe Hidalgo was finally signed by the parties, Feb. 2, 1848, and ratified with amendments by the American Senate, and signed by the President, March 10th. It was then returned to the Congress, and finally accepted by that body on May 25th, and ratified at Queretaro, by Ambrose H. Sevier and Nathan Clifford, Commissioners on the part of the United States, and Luis de la Rosa, Minister of Relations of the Mexican Republic, on the part of that Government. During the month of June, the capital and country of Mexico were generally evacuated by the American troops, and the blockade of the Mexican ports raised.

In concluding this imperfect historical sketch, it is only necessary to state that the facts have been mainly derived from the official documents relating to the war, published under the authority of the Congress of the United States. The inferences and uses to be drawn from these facts have occupied preceding pages of this review. But we can only pause here a moment to remark, how awful is the simplest record of war! How much of all that is most horrible in pain, and sickness, and loss of character, and ruin of "body, mind, or estate," is comprehended under the bald and dry statistics of marchings, fightings, sieges, and conquests! If all this operation be glory, then, in the name of heaven and humanity, we ask what is shame? If this be a work for which we should applaud, honor, and reward the actors, then for what deeds, in the range of possibility, should we condemn and execrate them?

> "First, Envy, eldest born of hell, imbrued
> Her hands in blood, and taught the sons of men
> To make a death which nature never made,
> And God abhorred. * * *
> One murder made a villain,
> Millions a hero. Princes assumed a right
> To kill; did numbers sanctify the crime?"*

* Bishop Porteus's Poem on "Death."

www.ingramcontent.com/pod-product-compliance
Lightning Source LLC
LaVergne TN
LVHW020241110826
845151LV00003B/993